TRILBY

L du Maurier

TRILBY

George du Maurier

DOVER PUBLICATIONS, INC.
New York

Published in Canada by General Publishing Company, Ltd., 30 Lesmill Road, Don Mills, Toronto, Ontario.
Published in the United Kingdom by Constable and Company, Ltd., 3 The Lanchesters, 162–164 Fulham Palace Road, London W6 9ER.

Bibliographical Note

This Dover edition, first published in 1994, is an unabridged republication of the original text as published in 1895 by Harper & Brothers Publishers, New York. The illustrations are reprinted from a copy of the special first edition of 600 copies, where they were originally in red.

Library of Congress Cataloging-in-Publication Data

Du Maurier, George, 1834–1896.
    Trilby / George du Maurier.
       p.   cm.
    ISBN 0-486-28319-4 (pbk.)
    1. Paris (France)—Social life and customs—19th century—Fiction.
2. Artists' models—France—Paris—Fiction. 3. Singers—France—Paris—Fiction. 4. Hypnotism—Fiction. I. Title.
PR4634.T7 1994
823'.8—dc20
                                                  94-29799
                                                      CIP

Manufactured in the United States of America
Dover Publications, Inc., 31 East 2nd Street, Mineola, N.Y. 11501

"Hélas! Je sais un chant d'amour,
Triste et gai, tour à tour!"

ILLUSTRATIONS

PAGE

GEORGE DU MAURIER ....*Frontispiece*

"IT WAS TRILBY!" xiii

TAFFY, ALIAS TALBOT WYNNE 3

"THE LAIRD OF COCKPEN" 4

"THE THIRD HE WAS 'LITTLE BILLEE'" 5

"IT DID ONE GOOD TO LOOK AT HIM" 6

AMONG THE OLD MASTERS 9

"WISTFUL AND SWEET" 12

THE "ROSEMONDE" OF SCHUBERT 17

TRILBY'S LEFT FOOT 21

THE FLEXIBLE FLAGEOLET 23

THE BRIDGE OF ARTS 27

"THREE MUSKETEERS OF THE BRUSH" 29

TAFFY MAKES THE SALAD 31

"THE GLORY THAT WAS GREECE" 33

TRILBY'S FOREBEARS 40

TAIL-PIECE 43

"AS BAD AS THEY MAKE 'EM" 46

"A VOICE HE DIDN'T UNDERSTAND" 48

"AND SO, NO MORE" 50

"'TWO ENGLANDERS IN ONE DAY'" 53

"'HIMMEL! THE ROOF OF YOUR MOUTH'" 56

"'ÇA FERA UNE FAMEUSE CRAPULE DE MOINS!'" 59

"'AV YOU SEEN MY FAHZERE'S OLE SHOES?'" 63

TAFFY À L'ECHELLE! 65

"THE FOX AND THE CROW" 68

THE LATIN QUARTER 71

CUISINE BOURGEOISE EN BOHÈME 73

"THE SOFT EYES" 76

ILYSSUS 78

"'VOILÀ L'ESPAYCE DE HOM KER JER SWEE!'" 81

TIT FOR TAT 87

THE HAPPY LIFE 90

"'LET ME GO, TAFFY . . .'" 91

"'QU'EST CE QU'IL A DONC, CE LITREBILI?'" 93

REPENTANCE 95

CONFESSION 99

"ALL AS IT USED TO BE" 102

"TWIN GRAY STARS" 103

"AN INCUBUS" 106

THE CAPITALIST AND THE SWELL 110

THE TWO APPRENTICES 113

"'I WILL NOT! I WILL NOT!'" 116

DODOR IN HIS GLORY 118

HÔTEL DE LA ROCHEMARTEL 120

CHRISTMAS EVE 125

"'ALLONS GLYCÈRE! ROUGIS MON VERRE . . .'" 127

SOUVENIR 131

"MY SISTER DEAR" 135

A DUCAL FRENCH FIGHTING-COCK 137

"'ANSWER ME, TRILBY!'" 139

A CARY*HAT*IDE 140

"'LES GLOUGLOUX DU VIN À QUAT' SOUS . . .'" 141

"'IS SHE *A LADY*, MR. WYNNE?'" 144

"'*FOND* OF HIM? AREN'T *YOU*?'" 149

"SO LIKE LITTLE BILLEE" 152

"'I MUST TAKE THE BULL BY THE HORNS'" 154

"'TRILBY! WHERE IS SHE?'" 158

LA SŒUR DE LITREBILI 159

"HE FELL A-WEEPING, QUITE DESPERATELY" 162

"THE SWEET MELODIC PHRASE" 164

"SORROWFULLY, ARM IN ARM" 167

DEMORALIZATION 175

FRED WALKER 177

PLATONIC LOVE 179

"DARLINGS, OLD OR YOUNG" 183

	PAGE
"THE MOON-DIAL"	184
THE CHAIRMAN	187
A HAPPY DINNER	190
"A-SMOKIN' THEIR POIPES AND CIGYARS"	193
"BONJOUR, SUZON!"	198
A HUMAN NIGHTINGALE	200
CUP-AND-BALL	204
SWEET ALICE	208
"MAY HEAVEN GO WITH HER!"	210
"'SO MUCH FOR ALICE, TRAY'"	214
"'YOU'RE A *THIEF*, SIR!'"	223
"AN ATMOSPHERE OF BANK-NOTES AND GOLD"	228
"A LITTLE PICTURE OF THE THAMES"	231
"AH! THE BEAUTIFUL INTERMENT, MESSIEURS!'"	234
"PAUVRE TRILBY"	236
"'JE PRONG!'"	239
"'OON PAIR DE GONG BLONG'"	243
GECKO	246
"AU CLAIR DE LA LUNE"	249
"OUVRE-MOI TA PORTE POUR L'AMOUR DE DIEU!"	250
"MALBROUCK S'EN VA-T'EN GUERRE"	254
"AUX NOUVELLES QUE J'APPORTE, VOS BEAUX YEUX VONT PLEURER!"	256
UN IMPROMPTU DE CHOPIN	259
"AND THE REMEMBRANCE OF THEM—HAND IN HAND"	263
"'I BELIEVE YOU, MY BOY!'"	266
"MAMAN DUCHESSE"	272
THE CUT DIRECT	275
"PETIT ENFANT, J'AIMAIS D'UN AMOUR TENDRE . . ."	278
"'VITE! VITE! UN COMMISSAIRE DE POLICE!'"	282
"I SUPPOSE YOU DO ALL THIS KIND OF THING FOR MERE AMUSEMENT, MR. WYNNE?"	285
THE FIRST VIOLIN LOSES HIS TEMPER	290
"HAST THOU FOUND ME, O MINE ENEMY?"	292
"'OH, DON'T YOU REMEMBER SWEET ALICE, BEN BOLT?'"	294
"THE LAST THEY SAW OF SVENGALI"	297
"'THREE NICE CLEAN ENGLISHMEN'"	301
"PŒNA PEDE CLAUDO"	303
"THE OLD STUDIO"	305

PAGE

"'ET MAINTENANT DORS, MA MIGNONNE!'" 308

"TAFFY WAS ALLOWED TO SEE GECKO" 312

A FAIR BLANCHISSEUSE DE FIN 313

A THRONE IN BOHEMIA 318

"'OH, MY POOR GIRL! MY POOR GIRL!'" 320

"'AH, POOR MAMMA! SHE WAS EVER SO MUCH PRETTIER THAN THAT!'" ...324

"'TO SING LIKE THAT IS *TO PRAY!*'" 329

"'THE REMEMBRANCE OF THAT PALM SUNDAY!'" 331

FOR GECKO 335

"OUT OF THE MYSTERIOUS EAST" 337

"'SVENGALI! . . .SVENGALI! . . .SVENGALI! . . .'" 339

"TOUT VIENT À POINT, POUR QUI SAIT ATTENDRE!" 342

"I, PETE COELESTES . . ." 344

"PETITS BONHEURS DE CONTREBANDE" 348

ENTER GECKO 351

"'WE TOOK HER VOICE NOTE BY NOTE'" 354

THE NIGHTINGALE'S FIRST SONG 358

"'ICH HABE *GELIEBT UND GELEBET!*'" 360

TAIL-PIECE 362

"IT WAS TRILBY!"   (Page 247)

TRILBY

PART FIRST

" Mimi Pinson est une blonde,
  Une blonde que l'on connait;
Elle n'a qu'une robe au monde,
  Landérirette ! et qu'un bonnet ! "

IT was a fine, sunny, showery day in April.

The big studio window was open at the top, and let in a pleasant breeze from the north-west. Things were beginning to look shipshape at last. The big piano, a semi-grand by Broadwood, had arrived from England by " the Little Quickness " (*la Petite Vitesse*, as the goods trains are called in France), and lay, freshly tuned, alongside the eastern wall; on the wall opposite was a panoply of foils, masks, and boxing-gloves.

A trapeze, a knotted rope, and two parallel cords, supporting each a ring, depended from a huge beam in the ceiling. The walls were of the usual dull red, relieved by plaster casts of arms and legs and hands and feet; and Dante's mask, and Michael Angelo's alto-rilievo of Leda and the swan, and a centaur and Lapith from the Elgin Marbles—on none of these had the dust as yet had time to settle.

There were also studies in oil from the nude; copies of Titian, Rembrandt, Velasquez, Rubens, Tintoret, Leonardo da Vinci—none of the school of Botticelli, Mantegna, and Co.—a firm whose merits had not as yet been revealed to the many.

Along the walls, at a great height, ran a broad shelf, on which were other casts in plaster, terra-cotta, imitation bronze : a little Theseus, a little Venus of Milo, a little discobolus; a little flayed man threatening high heaven (an act that seemed almost pardonable under the circumstances !); a lion and a boar by Barye; an anatomical figure of a horse, with only one leg left and no ears; a horse's head from the pediment of the Parthenon, earless also; and the bust of Clytie, with her beautiful low brow, her sweet wan gaze, and the ineffable forward shrug of her dear shoulders that makes her bosom as a nest, a rest, a pillow, a refuge—the likeness of a thing to be loved and desired for ever, and sought for and wrought for and fought for by generation after generation of the sons of men.

Near the stove hung a gridiron, a frying-pan, a toasting-fork, and a pair of bellows. In an adjoining glazed corner cupboard were plates and glasses; black-handled knives, pewter spoons, and three-pronged steel forks; a salad-bowl, vinegar cruets, an oil-flask, two mustard-pots (English and French), and such like things—all scrupulously clean. On the floor, which had been stained and waxed at considerable cost, lay two cheetah-skins and a large Persian praying-rug. One half of it, however (under the trapeze and at the end farthest from the window, beyond the model-throne), was covered with coarse matting, that one might fence or box without slipping down and splitting one's self in two, or fall without breaking any bones.

Two other windows of the usual French size and pattern, with shutters to them and heavy curtains of baize, opened east and west, to let in dawn or sunset, as the case might be, or haply keep them out. And there were alcoves, recesses, irregularities, odd little nooks and corners, to be filled up as time wore on with endless personal nick-nacks, bibelots, private properties and acquisitions—things that make a place genial, homelike, and good to remember, and sweet to muse upon (with fond regret) in after years.

And an immense divan spread itself in width and length and delightful thickness just beneath the big north window, the business window—a divan so immense that three well-fed, well-contented Englishmen could all lie lazily smoking their pipes on it at once without being in each other's way, and very often did !

At present one of these Englishmen—a Yorkshireman, by the way, called Taffy (and also the Man of Blood, be-cause he was supposed to be distantly related to a baronet)—was more energetically engaged. Bare-armed, and in his shirt and trousers, he was twirling a pair of Indian clubs round his head. His face was flushed, and he was perspiring freely and looked fierce. He was a very big young man, fair, with kind but choleric blue eyes, and the muscles of his brawny arm were strong as iron bands.

For three years he had borne Her Majesty's commission, and had been through the Crimean campaign without a scratch. He would have been one of the famous six hundred in the famous charge at Balaklava but for a sprained ankle (caught playing leapfrog in the trenches), which kept him in hospital on that momentous day. So that he lost his chance of glory or the grave, and this humiliating misadventure had sickened him of soldiering for life, and he never quite got over

it. Then, feeling within himself an irresistible vocation for art, he had sold out; and here he was in Paris, hard at work, as we see.

He was good-looking, with straight features; but I regret to say that, besides his heavy plunger's moustache, he wore an immense pair of drooping auburn whiskers, of the kind that used to be called Piccadilly weepers, and were afterwards affected by Mr. Sothern in Lord Dundreary. It was a fashion to do so then for such of our gilded youth as could afford the time (and the hair); the bigger and fairer the whiskers, the

TAFFY, ALIAS TALBOT WYNNE

more beautiful was thought the youth ! It seems incredible in these days, when even Her Majesty's Household Brigade go about with smooth cheeks and lips, like priests or play-actors.

> " What's become of all the gold
> Used to hang and brush their bosoms . . .? "

Another inmate of this blissful abode—Sandy, the Laird of Cockpen, as he was called—sat in similarly simple attire at his easel, painting at a lifelike little picture of a Spanish toreador serenading a lady of high degree (in broad daylight). He had never been to Spain, but he had a complete toreador's kit—a bargain which he had picked up for a mere song in the Boulevard du Temple—and he had hired

the guitar. His pipe was in his mouth—reversed; for it
had gone out, and the ashes were spilled all over his trousers
where holes were often burned in this way.

Quite gratuitously, and with a pleasing Scotch accent,
he began to declaim :

> " A street there is in Paris famous
> For which no rhyme our language yields;
> Roo Nerve day Petty Shong its name is—
> The New Street of the Little Fields. . . ."

And then, in his keen appreciation of the immortal
stanza, he chuckled audibly, with a face so blithe and merry
and well pleased that it
did one good to look at
him.

He also had entered life
by another door. His
parents (good, pious people
in Dundee) had intended
that he should be a
solicitor, as his father and
grandfather had been be-
fore him. And here he was
in Paris famous, painting
toreadors, and spouting the
" Ballad of the Bouilla-

" THE LAIRD OF COCKPEN "   baisse," as he would often
do out of sheer lightness
of heart—much oftener, indeed, than he would say his
prayers.

Kneeling on the divan, with his elbow on the window-sill,
was a third and much younger youth. The third he was
" Little Billee." He had pulled down the green baize
blind, and was looking over the roofs and chimney-pots of
Paris and all about with all his eyes, munching the while
a roll and a savoury saveloy, in which there was evidence of
much garlic. He ate with great relish, for he was very
hungry; he had been all the morning at Carrel's studio,
drawing from the life.

Little Billee was small and slender, about twenty or
twenty-one, and had a straight white forehead veined with

blue, large dark blue eyes, delicate, regular features, and coal-black hair. He was also very graceful and well built, with very small hands and feet, and much better dressed than his friends, who went out of their way to outdo the denizens of the Quartier Latin in careless eccentricity of garb, and succeeded. And in his winning and handsome face there was just a faint suggestion of some possible very remote Jewish ancestor—just a tinge of that strong, sturdy, irrepressible, indomitable, indelible blood which is of such priceless value in diluted homœopathic doses, like the dry white Spanish wine called montijo, which is not meant to be taken pure ; but without a judicious admixture of which no sherry can go round the world and keep its flavour intact; or like the famous bulldog strain, which is not beautiful in itself, and yet just for lacking a little of the same no grey-hound can ever hope to be a champion. So, at least, I have been told by wine-merchants and dog-fanciers—the most veracious persons that can be. Fortunately for the world, and especially for ourselves, most of us have in our veins at least a minim of that precious fluid, whether we know it or show it or not. *Tant pis pour les autres !*

" THE THIRD HE WAS ' LITTLE BILLEE ' "

As Little Billee munched he also gazed at the busy place below—the Place St. Anatole des Arts—at the old houses opposite, some of which were being pulled down, no doubt lest they should fall of their own sweet will. In the gaps between he would see discoloured, old, cracked, dingy walls, with mysterious windows and rusty iron balconies of great antiquity—sights that set him dreaming dreams of mediæval French love and wickedness and crime, bygone mysteries of Paris !

One gap went right through the block, and gave him a glimpse of the river, the " Cité," and the ominous old Morgue ; a little to the right rose the gray towers of Notre Dame de Paris into the checkered April sky. Indeed, the top of nearly all Paris lay before him, with a little stretch of the imagination on his part; and he gazed with a sense of novelty, an interest and a pleasure for which he could not have found any expression in mere language.

Paris ! Paris !! Paris !!!

The very name had always been one to conjure with, whether he thought of it as a mere sound on the lips and in

the ear, or as a magical written or printed word for the eye. And here was the thing itself at last, and he, he himself, *ipsissimus*, in the very heart of it, to live there and learn there as long as he liked, and make himself the great artist he longed to be.

Then, his meal finished, he lit a pipe, and flung himself on the divan and sighed deeply, out of the over-full contentment of his heart.

He felt he had never known happi-

"IT DID ONE GOOD TO LOOK AT HIM"

ness like this, never even dreamed its possibility. And yet his life had been a happy one. He was young and tender, was Little Billee; he had never been to any school, and was innocent of the world and its wicked ways; innocent of French especially, and the ways of Paris and its Latin Quarter. He had been brought up and educated at home, had spent his boyhood in London with his mother and sister, who now lived in Devonshire on somewhat straitened means. His father, who was dead, had been a clerk in the Treasury.

He and his two friends, Taffy and the Laird, had taken
this studio together. The Laird slept there, in a small bedroom off the studio. Taffy had a bedroom at the Hôtel de
Seine, in the street of that name. Little Billee lodged at
the Hôtel Corneille, in the Place de l'Odéon.

He looked at his two friends, and wondered if any one,
living or dead, had ever had such a glorious pair of chums
as these.

Whatever they did, whatever they said, was simply
perfect in his eyes; they were his guides and philosophers
as well as his chums. On the other hand, Taffy and the
Laird were as fond of the boy as they could be.

His absolute belief in all they said and did touched them
none the less that they were conscious of its being somewhat
in excess of their deserts. His almost girlish purity of
mind amused and charmed them, and they did all they
could to preserve it, even in the Quartier Latin, where
purity is apt to go bad if it be kept too long.

They loved him for his affectionate disposition, his lively
and caressing ways; and they admired him far more than
he ever knew, for they recognised in him a quickness, a
keenness, a delicacy of perception, in matters of form and
colour, a mysterious facility and felicity of execution, a
sense of all that was sweet and beautiful in nature, and a
ready power of expressing it, that had not been vouchsafed
to them in any such generous profusion, and which, as they
ungrudgingly admitted to themselves and each other,
amounted to true genius.

And when one within the immediate circle of our intimates
is gifted in this abnormal fashion, we either hate or love
him for it, in proportion to the greatness of his gift; according to the way we are built.

So Taffy and the Laird loved Little Billee—loved him
very much indeed. Not but what Little Billee had his
faults. For instance, he didn't interest himself very warmly
in other people's pictures. He didn't seem to care for the
Laird's guitar-playing toreador, nor for his serenaded lady
—at all events, he never said anything about them, either
in praise or blame. He looked at Taffy's realisms (for
Taffy was a realist) in silence, and nothing tries true friendship so much as silence of this kind.

But, then, to make up for it, when they all three went
to the Louvre, he didn't seem to trouble much about Titian
either, or Rembrandt, or Velasquez, Rubens, Veronese, or
Leonardo. He looked at the people who looked at the
pictures, instead of at the pictures themselves; especially
at the people who copied them, the sometimes charming
young lady painters—and these seemed to him even more
charming than they really were—and he looked a great
deal out of the Louvre windows, where there was much to
be seen : more Paris, for instance—Paris, of which he
could never have enough.

But when, surfeited with classical beauty, they all three
went and dined together, and Taffy and the Laird said
beautiful things about the old masters, and quarrelled about
them, he listened with deference and rapt attention and
reverentially agreed with all they said; and afterwards
made the most delightfully funny little pen-and-ink
sketches of them, saying all these beautiful things (which
he sent to his mother and sister at home); so lifelike, so
real, that you could almost hear the beautiful things they
said; so beautifully drawn that you felt the old masters
couldn't have drawn them better themselves; and so
irresistibly droll that you felt that the old masters could
not have drawn them at all—any more than Milton could
have described the quarrel between Sairey Gamp and
Betsy Prig; no one, in short, but Little Billee.

Little Billee took up the " Ballad of the Bouillabaisse "
where the Laird had left it off, and speculated on the future
of himself and his friends, when he should have got to forty
years—an almost impossibly remote future.

These speculations were interrupted by a loud knock at
the door, and two men came in.

First, a tall bony individual of any age between thirty
and forty-five, of Jewish aspect, well-featured but sinister.
He was very shabby and dirty, and wore a red *béret* and
a large velveteen cloak, with a big metal clasp at the collar.
His thick, heavy, languid, lustreless black hair fell down
behind his ears on to his shoulders, in that musician-like
way that is so offensive to the normal Englishman. He
had bold, brilliant black eyes, with long heavy lids, a thin,
sallow face, and a beard of burnt-up black, which grew

AMONG THE OLD MASTERS

almost from his under eyelids; and over it his moustache, a shade lighter, fell in two long spiral twists. He went by the name of Svengali, and spoke fluent French with a German accent and humorous German twists and idioms, and his voice was very thin and mean and harsh, and often broke into a disagreeable falsetto.

His companion was a little swarthy young man—a gypsy, possibly—much pitted with the smallpox, and also very shabby. He had large, soft, affectionate brown eyes, like a King Charles spaniel. He had small, nervous, veiny hands, with nails bitten down to the quick, and carried a fiddle and a fiddlestick under his arm, without a case, as though he had been playing in the street.

" Ponchour, mes enfants," said Svengali. " Che vous amène mon ami Checko, qui choue du fiolon gomme un anche ! "

Little Billee, who adored all " sweet musicianers," jumped up and made Gecko as warmly welcome as he could in his early French.

" Ha ! le biâno ! " exclaimed Svengali, flinging his red *béret* on it, and his cloak on the ground. " Ch'espère qu'il est pon, et pien t'accord ! "

And sitting down on the music-stool, he ran up and down the scales with that easy power, that smooth even crispness of touch, which reveal the master.

Then he fell to playing Chopin's impromptu in A flat, so beautifully that Little Billee's heart went nigh to bursting with suppressed emotion and delight. He had never heard any music of Chopin's before, nothing but British provincial home-made music—melodies with variations, " Annie Laurie," " The Last Rose of Summer," " The Blue Bells of Scotland "; innocent little motherly and sisterly tinklings, invented to set the company at their ease on festive evenings, and make all-round conversation possible for shy people, who fear the unaccompanied sound of their own voices, and whose genial chatter always leaves off directly the music ceases.

He never forgot that impromptu, which he was destined to hear again one day in strange circumstances.

Then Svengali and Gecko made music together, divinely. Little fragmentary things, sometimes consisting of but a

few bars, but these bars of *such* beauty and meaning!
Scraps, snatches, short melodies, meant to fetch, to charm
immediately, or to melt or sadden or madden just for a
moment, and that knew just when to leave off—czardas,
gypsy dances, Hungarian love-plaints, things little known
out of eastern Europe in the fifties of this century, till the
Laird and Taffy were almost as wild in their enthusiasm as
Little Billee—a silent enthusiasm too deep for speech. And
when these two great artists left off to smoke, the three
Britishers were too much moved even for that, and there
was a stillness. . . .

Suddenly there came a loud knuckle-rapping at the outer
door, and a portentous voice of great volume, and that
might almost have belonged to any sex (even an angel's),
uttered the British milkman's yodel, "Milk below!" and
before any one could say "Entrez," a strange figure
appeared, framed by the gloom of the little antechamber.

It was the figure of a very tall and fully-developed young
female, clad in the gray overcoat of a French infantry
soldier, continued netherwards by a short striped petticoat,
beneath which were visible her bare white ankles and insteps, and slim, straight, rosy heels, clean cut and smooth
as the back of a razor; her toes lost themselves in a huge
pair of male slippers, which made her drag her feet as she
walked.

She bore herself with easy, unembarrassed grace, like a
person whose nerves and muscles are well in tune, whose
spirits are high, who has lived much in the atmosphere of
French studios, and feels at home in it.

This strange medley of garments was surmounted by a
small bare head with short, thick, wavy brown hair, and a
very healthy young face, which could scarcely be called
quite beautiful at first sight, since the eyes were too wide
apart, the mouth too large, the chin too massive, the complexion a mass of freckles. Besides, you can never tell how
beautiful (or how ugly) a face may be till you have tried
to draw it.

But a small portion of her neck, down by the collar-bone,
which just showed itself between the unbuttoned lapels of
her military coat collar, was of a delicate privet-like whiteness that is never to be found on any French neck, and very

"WISTFUL AND SWEET"

few English ones. Also, she had a very fine brow, broad and low, with thick level eyebrows much darker than her hair, a broad, bony, high bridge to her short nose, and her full, broad cheeks were beautifully modelled. She would have made a singularly handsome boy.

As the creature looked round at the assembled company and flashed her big white teeth at them in an all-embracing smile of uncommon width and quite irresistible sweetness, simplicity, and friendly trust, one saw at a glance that she was out of the common clever, simple, humorous, honest, brave, and kind, and accustomed to be genially welcomed wherever she went. Then suddenly closing the door behind her, dropping her smile, and looking wistful and sweet, with her head on one side and her arms akimbo, " Ye're all English, now, aren't ye ? " she exclaimed. " I heard the music, and thought I'd just come in for a bit, and pass the time of day : you don't mind ? Trilby, that's my name— Trilby O'Ferrall."

She said this in English, with an accent half Scotch and certain French intonations, and in a voice so rich and deep and full as almost to suggest an incipient *tenore robusto ;* and one felt instinctively that it was a real pity she wasn't a boy, she would have made such a jolly one.

" We're delighted, on the contrary," said Little Billee, and advanced a chair for her.

But she said, "Oh, don't mind me ; go on with the music," and sat herself down cross-legged on the model-throne near the piano.

As they still looked at her, curious and half embarrassed, she pulled a paper parcel containing food out of one of the coat-pockets, and exclaimed :

"I'll just take a bite, if you don't object; I'm a model, you know, and it's just rung twelve—'the rest.' I'm posing for Durien the sculptor, on the next floor. I pose to him for the altogether."

" The altogether ? " asked Little Billee.

" Yes—*l'ensemble,* you know—head, hands, and feet— everything—especially feet. That's my foot," she said, kicking off her big slipper and stretching out the limb. " It's the handsomest foot in all Paris. There's only one in all Paris to match it, and here it is," and she laughed heartily (like a merry peal of bells), and stuck out the other.

And in truth they were astonishingly beautiful feet, such as one only sees in pictures and statues—a true inspiration of shape and colour, all made up of delicate lengths and subtly-modulated curves and noble straightnesses and happy little dimpled arrangements in innocent young pink and white.

So that Little Billee, who had the quick, prehensile, æsthetic eye, and knew by the grace of Heaven what the shapes and sizes and colours of almost every bit of man, woman, or child should be (and so seldom are), was quite bewildered to find that a real, bare, live human foot could be such a charming object to look at, and felt that such a base or pedestal lent quite an antique and Olympian dignity to a figure that seemed just then rather grotesque in its mixed attire of military overcoat and female petticoat, and nothing else !

Poor Trilby !

The shape of those lovely slender feet (that were neither large nor small), facsimiled in dusty pale plaster of Paris, survives on the shelves and walls of many a studio throughout the world, and many a sculptor yet unborn has yet to marvel at their strange perfection, in studious despair.

For when Dame Nature takes it into her head to do her very best, and bestow her minutest attention on a mere detail, as happens now and then—once in a blue moon, perhaps—she makes it uphill work for poor human art to keep pace with her.

It is a wondrous thing, the human foot—like the human hand ; even more so, perhaps ; but, unlike the hand, with which we are so familiar, it is seldom a thing of beauty in civilised adults who go about in leather boots or shoes.

So that it is hidden away in disgrace, a thing to be thrust out of sight and forgotten. It can sometimes be very ugly indeed—the ugliest thing there is, even in the fairest and highest and most gifted of her sex ; and then it is of an ugliness to chill and kill romance, and scatter love's young dream, and almost break the heart.

And all for the sake of a high heel and a ridiculously-pointed toe—mean things, at the best !

Conversely, when Mother Nature has taken extra pains in the building of it, and proper care or happy chance has kept it free of lamentable deformations, indurations, and discolorations—all those grewsome boot-begotten abominations which have made it so generally unpopular—the sudden sight of it, uncovered, comes as a very rare and singularly pleasing surprise to the eye that has learned how to see !

Nothing else that Mother Nature has to show, not even the human face divine, has more subtle power to suggest high physical distinction, happy evolution, and supreme development; the lordship of man over beast, the lordship of man over man, the lordship of woman over all !

En voilà de l'éloquence—à propos de bottes !

Trilby had respected Mother Nature's special gift to herself—had never worn a leather boot or shoe, had always taken as much care of her feet as many a fine lady takes of her hands. It was her one coquetry, the only real vanity she had.

Gecko, his fiddle in one hand and his bow in the other, stared at her in open-mouthed admiration and delight, as she ate her sandwich of soldier's bread and *fromage à la crème* quite unconcerned.

When she had finished she licked the tips of her fingers clean of cheese, and produced a small tobacco-pouch from another military pocket, made herself a cigarette, and lit it and smoked it, inhaling the smoke in large whiffs, filling her lungs with it, and sending it back through her nostrils, with a look of great beatitude.

Svengali played Schubert's " Rosemonde," and flashed a pair of languishing black eyes at her with intent to kill.

But she didn't even look his way. She looked at Little Billee, at big Taffy, at the Laird, at the casts and studies, at the sky, the chimney-pots over the way, the towers of Notre Dame, just visible from where she sat.

Only when he finished she exclaimed: " Maïe, aïe ! c'est rudement bien tapé, c'te musique-là ! Seulement, c'est pas gai, vous savez ! Comment q'ça s'appelle? "

" It is called the ' Rosemonde ' of Schubert, matemoiselle," replied Svengali. (I will translate)."

" And what's that—Rosemonde? " said she.

"Rosemonde was a princess of Cyprus, matemoiselle, and Cyprus is an island."

"Ah, and Schubert, then—where's that?"

"Schubert is not an island, matemoiselle. Schubert was a compatriot of mine, and made music, and played the piano, just like me."

"Ah, Schubert was a *monsieur*, then. Don't know him; never heard his name."

"That is a pity, matemoiselle. He had some talent. You like this better, perhaps," and he strummed,

> "Messieurs les étudiants,
> S'en vont à la chaumière
> Pour y danser le cancan,"

striking wrong notes, and banging out a bass in a different key—a hideously grotesque performance.

"Yes, I like that better. It's gayer, you know. Is that also composed by a compatriot of yours?" asked the lady.

"Heaven forbid, matemoiselle."

And the laugh was against Svengali.

But the real fun of it all (if there was any) lay in the fact that she was perfectly sincere.

"Are you fond of music?" asked Little Billee.

"Oh, ain't I just!" she replied. "My father sang like a bird. He was a gentleman and a scholar, my father was. His name was Patrick Michael O'Ferrall, Fellow of Trinity, Cambridge. He used to sing 'Ben Bolt.' Do you know 'Ben Bolt'?"

"Oh yes, I know it well," said Little Billee. "It's a very pretty song."

"I can sing it," said Miss O'Ferrall. "Shall I?"

"Oh, certainly, if you will be so kind."

Miss O'Ferrall threw away the end of her cigarette, put her hands on her knees as she sat cross-legged on the model-throne, and sticking her elbows well out, she looked up to the ceiling with a tender, sentimental smile, and sang the touching song,

> "Oh, don't you remember sweet Alice, Ben Bolt?
> Sweet Alice, with hair so brown?" etc., etc.

As some things are too sad and too deep for tears, so some things are too grotesque and too funny for laughter.

THE "ROSEMONDE" OF SCHUBERT

Of such a kind was Miss O'Ferrall's performance of " Ben
Bolt."

From that capacious mouth and through that high-
bridged bony nose there rolled a volume of breathy sound,
not loud, but so immense that it seemed to come from all
round, to be reverberated from every surface in the studio.
She followed more or less the shape of the tune, going up
when it rose and down when it fell, but with such immense
intervals between the notes as were never dreamed of in
any mortal melody. It was as though she could never
once have deviated into tune, never once have hit upon a
true note, even by a fluke—in fact, as though she were
absolutely tone-deaf, and without ear, although she stuck
to the time correctly enough.

She finished her song amid an embarrassing silence. The
audience didn't quite know whether it were meant for fun
or seriously. One wondered if she were not paying out
Svengali for his impertinent performance of " Messieurs les
étudiants." If so, it was a capital piece of impromptu tit-
for-tat admirably acted, and a very ugly gleam yellowed the
tawny black of Svengali's big eyes. He was so fond of
making fun of others that he particularly resented being
made fun of himself—couldn't endure that any one should
ever have the laugh of *him*.

At length Little Billee said : " Thank you so much.
It's a capital song."

" Yes," said Miss O'Ferrall. " It's the only song I
know, unfortunately. My father used to sing it, just like
that, when he felt jolly after hot rum-and-water. It used
to make people cry ; he used to cry over it himself. *I*
never do. Some people think I can't sing a bit. All I can
say is that I've often had to sing it six or seven times
running in *lots* of studios. I vary it, you know—not the
words, but the tune. You must remember that I've only
taken to it lately. Do you know Litolff ? Well, he's a
great composer, and he came to Durien's the other day,
and I sang ' Ben Bolt,' and what do you think he said ?
Why, he said Madame Alboni couldn't go nearly so high
or so low as I did, and that her voice wasn't half so big.
He gave me his word of honour. He said I breathed
as natural and straight as a baby and all I want is to

get my voice a little more under control. That's what *he*
said."

" Qu'est-ce qu'elle dit ? " asked Svengali. And she said
it all over again to him in French—quite French French—
of the most colloquial kind. Her accent was not that of
the Comédie Française, nor yet that of the Faubourg St.
Germain, nor yet that of the shop, or the pavement.
It was quaint and expressive—" funny without being
vulgar."

" Barpleu ! he was right, Litolff," said Svengali. " I
assure you, matemoiselle, that I have never heard a voice
that can equal yours ; you have a talent quite exceptional."

She blushed with pleasure, and the others thought him
a " beastly cad " for poking fun at the poor girl in such a
way. And they thought Monsieur Litolff another.

She then got up and shook the crumbs off her coat, and
slipped her feet into Durien's slippers, saying, in English :
" Well, I've got to go back. Life ain't all beer and skittles,
and more's the pity ; but what's the odds, so long as you're
happy ? "

On her way out she stopped before Taffy's picture—a
chiffonnier with his lantern, bending over a dust-heap.
For Taffy was, or 'thought himself, a passionate realist in
those days. He has changed, and now paints nothing but
King Arthurs and Guineveres and Lancelots and Elaines,
and floating Ladies of Shalott.

" That chiffonnier's basket isn't hitched high enough,"
she remarked. " How could he tap his pick against the
rim and make the rag fall into it if it's hitched only half-
way up his back ? And he's got the wrong sabots, and the
wrong lantern ; it's *all* wrong."

" Dear me ! " said Taffy, turning very red ; " you seem
to know a lot about it. It's a pity you don't paint,
yourself."

" Ah ! now you're cross ! " said Miss O'Ferrall. " Oh,
maïe aïe ! "

She went to the door and paused, looking round benignly.
" What nice teeth you've all three got ! That's because
your Englishmen, I suppose, and clean them twice a day.
I do too. Trilby O'Ferrall, that's my name, 48 Rue des
Pousse-Cailloux !—pose pour l'ensemble, quand ça l'amuse !

va-t-en ville, et fait tout ce qui concerne son état ! Don't forget. Thanks all, and good-bye."

" En v'là une orichinale," said Svengali.

" I think she's lovely," said Little Billee, the young and tender. " Oh heavens, what angel's feet ! It makes me sick to think she sits for the figure. I'm sure she's quite a lady."

And in five minutes or so, with the point of an old compass, he scratched in white on the dark red wall a three-quarter profile outline of Trilby's left foot, which was perhaps the more perfect poem of the two.

Slight as it was, this little piece of impromptu etching, in its sense of beauty, in its quick seizing of a peculiar individuality, its subtle rendering of a strongly-received impression, was already the work of a master. It was Trilby's foot and nobody else's, nor could have been, and nobody else but Little Billee could have drawn it in just that inspired way.

" Qu'est-ce que c'est, ' Ben Bolt ' ? " inquired Gecko.

Upon which Little Billee was made by Taffy to sit down to the piano and sing it. He sang it very nicely with his pleasant little throaty English baritone.

It was solely in order that Little Billee should have opportunities of practising this graceful accomplishment of his, for his own and his friends' delectation, that the piano had been sent over from London, at great cost to Taffy and the Laird. It had belonged to Taffy's mother, who was dead.

Before he had finished the second verse, Svengali exclaimed : " Mais c'est tout-à-fait chentil ! Allons, Gecko, chouez-nous ça ! "

And he put his big hands on the piano, over Little Billee's, pushed him off the music-stool with his great gaunt body, and, sitting on it himself, he played a masterly prelude. It was impressive to hear the complicated rich-ness and volume of the sounds he evoked after Little Billee's gentle " tink-a-tink."

And Gecko, cuddling lovingly his violin and closing his upturned eyes, played that simple melody as it had prob-ably never been played before—such passion, such pathos, such a tone !—and they turned it and twisted it, and went

TRILBY'S LEFT FOOT

from one key to another, playing into each other's hands,
Svengali taking the lead; and fugued and canoned and
counterpointed and battledored and shuttlecocked it, high
and low, soft and loud, in minor, in pizzicato, and in sordino
—adagio, andante, allegretto, scherzo—and exhausted all
its possibilities of beauty; till their susceptible audience of
three was all but crazed with delight and wonder; and the
masterful Ben Bolt, and his over-tender Alice, and his too
submissive friend, and his old schoolmaster so kind and so
true, and his long-dead schoolmates, and the rustic porch
and the mill, and the slab of granite so gray,

> " And the dear little nook
> By the clear running brook,"

were all magnified into a strange, almost holy poetic
dignity and splendour quite undreamed of by whoever
wrote the words and music of that unsophisticated little
song, which has touched so many simple British hearts
that don't know any better—and among them, once, that
of the present scribe—long, long ago !

" Sacrepleu ! il choue pien, le Checko, hein ? " said
Svengali, when they had brought this wonderful double
improvisation to a climax and a close.   " C'est mon élèfe !
che le fais chanter sur son fiolon, c'est comme si c'était
moi qui chantais ! ach ! si ch'afais pour teux sous de voix,
che serais le bremier chanteur du monte !   I cannot sing ! "
he continued. (I will translate him into English, without
attempting to translate his accent, which is a mere matter
of judiciously transposing p's and b's, and t's and d's, and
f's and v's, and g's and k's, and turning the soft French j
into sch, and a pretty language into an ugly one.)

" I cannot sing myself, I cannot play the violin, but I
can teach—hein, Gecko? And I have a pupil—hein,
Gecko?—la betite Honorine; "   and here he leered all
round with a leer that was not engaging.   " The world
shall hear of la betite Honorine some day—hein, Gecko?
Listen all—this is how I teach la betite Honorine !   Gecko,
play me a little accompaniment in pizzicato."

And he pulled out of his pocket a kind of little flexible
flageolet (of his own invention, it seems), which he screwed
together and put to his lips, and on this humble instru-

THE FLEXIBLE FLAGEOLET

ment he played "Ben Bolt," while Gecko accompanied him, using his fiddle as a guitar, his adoring eyes fixed in reverence on his master.

And it would be impossible to render in any words the deftness, the distinction, the grace, power, pathos, and passion with which this truly phenomenal artist executed the poor old twopenny tune on his elastic penny whistle —for it was little more—such thrilling, vibrating, piercing tenderness, now loud and full, a shrill scream of anguish, now soft as a whisper, a mere melodic breath, more human almost than the human voice itself, a perfection unattainable even by Gecko, a master, on an instrument which is the acknowledged king of all !

So that the tear, which had been so close to the brink of Little Billee's eye while Gecko was playing, now rose and trembled under his eyelid and spilled itself down his nose; and he had to dissemble and surreptitiously mop it up with his little finger as he leaned his chin on his hand, and cough a little husky, unnatural cough—*pour se donner une contenance !*

He had never heard such music as this, never dreamed such music was possible. He was conscious, while it lasted, that he saw deeper into the beauty, the sadness of things, the very heart of them, and their pathetic evanescence, as with a new, inner eye—even into eternity itself, beyond the veil—a vague cosmic vision that faded when the music was over, but left an unfading reminiscence of its having been, and a passionate desire to express the like some day through the plastic medium of his own beautiful art.

When Svengali ended, he leered again on his dumbstruck audience, and said : " That is how I teach la betite Honorine to sing; that is how I teach Gecko to play; that is how I teach ' *il bel canto* ' ! It was lost, the *bel canto*—but I found it, in a dream—I, and nobody else—I—Svengali—I —I—*I !* But that is enough of music; let us play at something else—let us play at this ! " he cried, jumping up and seizing a foil and bending it against the wall. . . .

" Come along, Little Pillee, and I will show you something more you don't know. . . ."

So Little Billee took off coat and waistcoat, donned mask and glove and fencing-shoes, and they had an " assault of arms," as it is nobly called in French, and in which poor Little Billee came off very badly. The German Pole fenced wildly, but well.

Then it was the Laird's turn, and he came off badly too; so then Taffy took up the foil, and redeemed the honour of Great Britain, as became a British hussar and a Man of Blood. For Taffy, by long and assiduous practice in the best school in Paris (and also by virtue of his native aptitudes), was a match for any *maître d'armes* in the whole French army, and Svengali got " what for."

And when it was time to give up play and settle down to work, others dropped in—French, English, Swiss, German, American, Greek; curtains were drawn and shutters opened; the studio was flooded with light—and the afternoon was healthily spent in athletic and gymnastic exercises till dinner-time.

But Little Billee, who had had enough of fencing and gymnastics for the day, amused himself by filling up with black and white and red-chalk strokes the outline of Trilby's foot on the wall, lest he should forget his fresh vision of it, which was still to him as the thing itself—an absolute reality, born of a mere glance, a mere chance—a happy caprice !

Durien came in and looked over his shoulder, and exclaimed : " Tiens ! le pied de Trilby ! vous avez fait ça d'après nature ? "

" Nong ! "

" De mémoire, alors ? "

" Wee ! "

" Je vous en fais mon compliment ! Vous avez eu la main heureuse. Je voudrais bien avoir fait ça, moi ! C'est un petit chef-d'œuvre que vous avez fait là—tout bonnement, mon cher ! Mais vous élaborez trop. De grâce, n'y touchez plus ! "

And Little Billee was pleased, and touched it no more; for Durien was a great sculptor and sincerity itself.

And then—well, I happen to forget what sort of day this particular day turned into at about six of the clock.

If it was decently fine, the most of them went off to dine at the Restaurant de la Couronne, kept by the Père

Trin (in the Rue de Monsieur), who gave you of his best
to eat and drink for twenty sols Parisis, or one franc in the
coin of the empire. Good distending soups, omelets that
were only too savoury, lentils, red and white beans, meat
so dressed and sauced and seasoned that you didn't
know whether it was beef or mutton—flesh, fowl, or good
red herring—or even bad, for that matter—nor very greatly
cared.

And just the same lettuce, radishes, and cheese of Gruyère
or Brie as you got at the Trois Frères Provençaux (but not
the same butter !). And to wash it all down, generous
wine in wooden *brocs*—that stained a lovely æsthetic blue
everything it was spilled over.

And you hobnobbed with models, male and female,
students of law and medicine, painters and sculptors,
workmen and *blanchisseuses* and grisettes, and found them
very good company, and most improving to your French, if
your French was of the usual British kind, and even to
some of your manners, if these were very British indeed.
And the evening was innocently wound up with billiards,
cards, or dominoes at the Café du Luxembourg opposite;
or at the Théâtre du Luxembourg, in the Rue de Madame,
to see funny farces with screamingly droll Englishmen
in them; or, still better, at the Jardin Bullier (la Closerie
des Lilas), to see the students dance the cancan, or try
and dance it yourself, which is not so easy as it seems;
or, best of all, at the Théâtre de l'Odéon, to see some piece
of the classical *répertoire*.

Or, if it were not only fine, but a Saturday afternoon
into the bargain, the Laird would put on a necktie and a
few other necessary things, and the three friends would
walk arm-in-arm to Taffy's hotel in the Rue de Seine,
and wait outside till he had made himself as presentable
as the Laird, which did not take very long. And then
(Little Billee was always presentable) they would, arm-in-
arm, the huge Taffy in the middle, descend the Rue de
Seine and cross a bridge to the Cité, and have a look in at
the Morgue. Then back again to the quays on the *rive
gauche* by the Pont Neuf, to wend their way westward;
now on one side to look at the print and picture shops and
the *magasins* of bric-à-brac, and haply sometimes buy

thereof, now on the other to finger and cheapen the second-hand books for sale on the parapet, and even pick up one or two utterly unwanted bargains, never to be read or opened again.

When they reached the Pont des Arts they would cross it, stopping in the middle to look up the river towards the old Cité and Notre Dame, eastward, and dream unutterable things, and try to utter them. Then, turning westward, they would gaze at the glowing sky and all it glowed

THE BRIDGE OF ARTS

upon—the corner of the Tuileries and the Louvre, the many bridges, the Chamber of Deputies, the golden river narrowing its perspective and broadening its bed as it went flowing and winding on its way between Passy and Grenelle to St. Cloud, to Rouen, to the Havre, to England perhaps—where *they* didn't want to be just then; and they would try and express themselves to the effect that life was uncommonly well worth living in that particular city at that particular time of the day and year and century, at that particular epoch of their own mortal and uncertain lives.

Then, still arm-in-arm, and chatting gaily across the courtyard of the Louvre, through gilded gates well guarded by reckless imperial Zouaves, up the arcaded Rue de Rivoli as far as the Rue Castiglione, where they would stare with greedy eyes at the window of the great corner pastry-cook, and marvel at the beautiful assortment of bonbons, *pralines*, *dragées*, *marrons glacés*—saccharine, crystalline substances of all kinds and colours, as charming to look at as an illumination; precious stones, delicately-frosted sweets, pearls and diamonds so arranged as to melt in the mouth; especially, at this particular time of the year, the monstrous Easter-egg, of enchanting hue, enshrined like costly jewels in caskets of satin and gold; and the Laird, who was well read in his English classics and liked to show it, would opine that " they managed these things better in France."

Then across the street by a great gate into the Allée des Feuillants, and up to the Place de la Concorde—to gaze, but quite without base envy, at the smart people coming back from the Bois de Boulogne. For even in Paris " carriage people " have a way of looking bored, of taking their pleasure sadly, of having nothing to say to each other, as though the vibration of so many wheels all rolling home the same way every afternoon had hypnotised them into silence, idiocy, and melancholia.

And our three musketeers of the brush would speculate on the vanity of wealth and rank and fashion; on the satiety that follows in the wake of self-indulgence and overtakes it; on the weariness of the pleasures that become a toil—as if they knew all about it, had found it all out for themselves, and nobody else had ever found it out before !

Then they found out something else—namely, that the sting of healthy appetite was becoming intolerable; so they would betake themselves to an English eating-house in the Rue de la Madeleine (on the left-hand side near the top), where they would renovate their strength and their patriotism on British beef and beer, and household bread, and bracing, biting, stinging yellow mustard, and heroic horseradish, and noble apple-pie, and Cheshire cheese; and get through as much of these in an hour or so as they could for talking, talking, talking; such happy talk ! as full of sanguine hope and enthusiasm, of cocksure commendation or condemnation of all painters, dead or alive, of modest but firm belief in themselves and each other, as a Paris Easter-egg is full of sweets and pleasantness (for the young).

"THREE MUSKETEERS OF THE BRUSH"

And then a stroll on the crowded, well-lighted boulevards, and a bock at the café there, at a little three-legged marble table right out on the genial asphalt side pavement, still talking nineteen to the dozen.

Then home by dark, old, silent streets and some deserted bridge to their beloved Latin Quarter, the Morgue gleaming cold and still and fatal in the pale lamplight, and Notre Dame pricking up its watchful twin towers, which have looked down for so many centuries on so many happy, sanguine, expansive youths walking arm-in-arm by twos and threes, and for ever talking, talking, talking. . . .

The Laird and Little Billee would see Taffy safe to the door of his *hôtel garni* in the Rue de Seine, where they would find much to say to each other before they said good-night—so much that Taffy and Little Billee would see the Laird safe to *his* door, in the Place St. Anatole des Arts. And then a discussion would arise between Taffy and the Laird on the immortality of the soul, let us say, or the exact meaning of the word "gentleman," or the relative merits of Dickens and Thackeray, or some such recondite and quite unhackneyed theme, and Taffy and the Laird would escort Little Billee to *his* door, in the Place de l'Odéon, and he would re-escort them both back again, and so on till any hour you please.

Or again, if it rained, and Paris through the studio window loomed lead-coloured, with its shiny slate roofs under skies that were ashen and sober, and the wild west wind made woeful music among the chimney-pots, and little gray waves ran up the river the wrong way, and the Morgue looked chill and dark and wet, and almost uninviting (even to three healthy-minded young Britons), they would resolve to dine and spend a happy evening at home.

Little Billee, taking with him three francs (or even four), would dive into back streets and buy a yard or so of crusty new bread, well burned on the flat side, a fillet of beef, a litre of wine, potatoes and onions, butter, a little cylindrical cheese called "bondon de Neufchâtel," tender curly lettuce, with chervil, parsley, spring onions, and other fine herbs, and a pod of garlic, which would be rubbed on a crust of bread to flavour things with.

Taffy would lay the cloth English-wise, and also make the salad, for which, like everybody else I ever met, he had a special receipt of his own (putting in the oil first and the vinegar after); and indeed his salads were quite as good as everybody else's.

The Laird, bending over the stove, would cook the onions and beef into a savoury Scotch mess so cunningly that you could not taste the beef for the onions—nor always the onions for the garlic.

And they would dine far better than at le Père Trin's, far better than at the English Restaurant in the Rue de la Madeleine—better than anywhere else on earth !

And after dinner, what coffee, roasted and ground on the spot, what pipes and cigarettes of *caporal*, by the light of the three shaded lamps, while the rain beat against the big north window, and the wind went howling round the quaint old mediæval tower at the corner of the Rue Vieille des Trois Mauvais Ladres (the old street of the three bad lepers), and the damp logs hissed and crackled in the stove !

What jolly talk into the small hours ! Thackeray and

TAFFY MAKES THE SALAD

Dickens again, and Tennyson and Byron (who was " not deed yet " in those days); and Titian and Velasquez, and young Millais and Holman Hunt (just out); and Monsieur Ingres and Monsieur Delacroix, and Balzac and Stendhal and George Sand; and the good Dumas ! and Edgar Allan Poe ; and the glory that was Greece and the grandeur that was Rome. ﹡ ﹡ ﹡

Good, honest, innocent, artless prattle—not of the wisest, perhaps, nor redolent of the very highest culture (which, by the way, can mar as well as make), nor leading to any very practical result; but quite pathetically sweet from the sincerity and fervour of its convictions, a profound belief in their importance, and a proud trust in their life-long immutability.

Oh, happy days and happy nights, sacred to art and friendship ! oh, happy times of careless impecuniosity, and youth and hope and health and strength and freedom—with all Paris for a playground, and its dear old unregenerate Latin Quarter for a workshop, and a home !

And, up to then, no kill-joy complications of love !

No, decidedly no ! Little Billee had never known such happiness as this—never even dreamed of its possibility.

A day or two after this, our opening day, but in the afternoon, when the fencing and boxing had begun and the trapeze was in full swing, Trilby's " Milk below ! " was sounded at the door, and she appeared—clothed this time and in her right mind, as it seemed : a tall, straight, flat-backed, square-shouldered, deep-chested, full-bosomed young grisette, in a snowy frilled cap, a neat black gown and white apron, pretty faded, well-darned brown stockings, and well-worn, soft, gray, square-toed slippers of list, without heels and originally shapeless ; but which her feet, uncompromising and inexorable as boot-trees, had ennobled into everlasting classic shapeliness, and stamped with an unforgettable individuality, as does a beautiful hand its well-worn glove—a fact Little Billee was not slow to perceive, with a curious conscious thrill that was only half æsthetic.

Then he looked into her freckled face, and met the kind and tender mirthfulness of her gaze and the plucky frankness of her fine wide smile with a thrill that was not æsthetic at all (nor the reverse), but all of the heart. And in one of his quick flashes of intuitive insight he divined far down beneath the shining surface of those eyes (which seemed for a moment to reflect only a little image of himself against the sky beyond the big north window) a well of sweetness ; and floating somewhere in the midst of it the

"THE GLORY THAT WAS GREECE"

very heart of compassion, generosity, and warm sisterly
love; and under that—alas ! at the bottom of all—a thin
slimy layer of sorrow and shame. And just as long as it
takes for a tear to rise and gather and choke itself back
again, this sudden revelation shook his nervous little
frame with a pang of pity and the knightly wish to help.
But he had no time to indulge in such soft emotions.
Trilby was met on her entrance by friendly greetings on
all sides.

"Tiens ! c'est la grande Trilby !" exclaimed Jules
Guinot through his fencing-mask. "Comment ! t'es déjà
debout après hier soir ? Avons-nous assez rigolé chez
Mathieu, hein ? Crénom d'un nom, quelle noce ! V'là
une crémaillère qui peut se vanter d'être diantrement bien
pendue, j'espère ! Et la petite santé, c' matin ? "

"Hé, hé ! mon vieux," answered Trilby. "Ça bou-
lotte, apparemment ! Et toi ? et Victorine ? Comment
qu'a s' porte à c't'heure ? Elle avait un fier coup d'chas-
selas ! c'est-y jobard, hein ? de s' fich 'paf comme ça
d'vant l' monde ! Tiens, v'là, Gontran ! ça marche-t-y,
Gontran, Zouzou d' mon cœur ? "

"Comme sur des roulettes, ma biche !" said Gontran,
alias l'Zouzou—a corporal in the Zouaves. "Mais tu
t'es donc mise chiffonnière, à présent ? T'as fait banque-
route ? "

(For Trilby had a chiffonnier's basket strapped on her
back, and carried a pick and lantern.)

"Mais-z-oui, mon bon !" she said. "Dame ! pas d'
veine hier soir ! t'as bien vu ! Dans la dêche jusqu'aux
omoplates, mon pauv' caporal-sous-off ! nom d'un canon
—faut bien vivre, s' pas ? "

Little Billee's heart-sluices had closed during this inter-
change of courtesies. He felt it to be of a very slangy
kind, because he couldn't understand a word of it, and he
hated slang. All he could make out was the free use of the
tu and the toi, and he knew enough French to know that
this implied a great familiarity, which he misunderstood.

So that Jules Guinot's polite inquiries whether Trilby
were none the worse after Mathieu's house-warming
(which was so jolly), Trilby's kind solicitude about the
health of Victorine, who had very foolishly taken a drop

too much on that occasion, Trilby's mock regrets that her own bad luck at cards had made it necessary that she should retrieve her fallen fortunes by rag-picking—all these innocent, playful little amenities (which I have tried to write down just as they were spoken) were couched in a language that was as Greek to him—and he felt out of it, jealous and indignant.

"Good-afternoon to you, Mr. Taffy," said Trilby, in English. "I've brought you these objects of art and virtu to make the peace with you. They're the real thing, you know. I borrowed 'em from le père Martin, chiffonnier en gros et en détail, grand officier de la Légion d'Honneur, membre de l'Institut et cetera, treize bis Rue du Puits d'Amour, rez-de-chaussée au fond de la cour à gauche, vis-à-vis le mont-de-piété! He's one of my intimate friends, and——"

"You don't mean to say you're the intimate friend of a *rag-picker* ?" exclaimed the good Taffy.

"Oh yes! Pourquoi pas? I never brag; besides, there ain't any beastly pride about le père Martin," said Trilby, with a wink. "You'd soon find that out if *you* were an intimate friend of his. This is how it's put on. Do you see? If *you'*ll put it on I'll fasten it for you, and show you how to hold the lantern and handle the pick. You may come to it yourself some day, you know. Il ne faut jurer de rien! Père Martin will pose for you in person, if you like. He's generally disengaged in the afternoon. He's poor but honest, you know, and very nice and clean; quite the gentleman. He likes artists, especially English —they pay. His wife sells bric-à-brac and old masters: Rembrandts from two francs fifty upwards. They've got a little grandson—a love of a child. I'm his godmother. You know French, I suppose?"

"Oh yes," said Taffy, much abashed. "I'm very much obliged to you—very much indeed—a—I—a——"

"Y a pas d' quoi!" said Trilby, divesting herself of her basket and putting it, with the pick and lantern, in a corner. "Et maintenant, le temps d'absorber une fine de fin sec [a cigarette] et je m' la brise [I'm off]. On m'attend à l'Ambassade d'Autriche. Et puis zut! Allez toujours, mes enfants. En avant la boxe!"

She sat herself down cross-legged on the model-throne, and made herself a cigarette, and watched the fencing and boxing. Little Billee brought her a chair, which she refused; so he sat down on it himself by her side, and talked to her, just as he would have talked to any young lady at home—about the weather, about Verdi's new opera (which she had never heard), the impressiveness of Notre Dame, and Victor Hugo's beautiful romance (which she had never read), the mysterious charm of Leonardo da Vinci's Lisa Gioconda's smile (which she had never seen)— by all of which she was no doubt rather tickled and a little embarrassed, perhaps also a little touched.

Taffy brought her a cup of coffee, and conversed with her in polite formal French very well and carefully pronounced; and the Laird tried to do likewise. *His* French was of that honest English kind that breaks up the stiffness of even an English party; and his jolly manners were such as to put an end to all shyness and constraint, and make self-consciousness impossible.

Others dropped in from neighbouring studios—the usual cosmopolite crew. It was a perpetual come-and-go in this particular studio between four and six in the afternoon.

There were ladies too, *en cheveux*, in caps and bonnets, some of whom knew Trilby, and thee'd and thou'd with familiar and friendly affection, while others mademoiselle'd her with distant politeness, and were mademoiselle'd and madame'd back again. "Absolument comme à l'Ambassade d'Autriche," as Trilby observed to the Laird, with a British wink that was by no means ambassadorial.

Then Svengali came and made some of his grandest music, which was as completely thrown away on Trilby as fireworks on a blind beggar, for all she held her tongue so piously.

Fencing and boxing and trapezing seemed to be more in her line; and indeed, to a tone-deaf person, Taffy lunging his full spread with a foil, in all the splendour of his long, lithe, youthful strength, was a far gainlier sight than Svengali at the keyboard flashing his languid bold eyes with a sickly smile from one listener to another, as if to say: "N'est-ce pas que che suis peau? N'est-ce

pas que ch'ai tu chénie? N'est-ce pas que che suis
suplime, enfin? "

Then enter Durien the sculptor, who had been presented
with a *baignoire* at the Porte St. Martin to see *La Dame
aux Camélias*, and he invited Trilby and another lady to
dine with him *au cabaret* and share his box.

So Trilby didn't go to the Austrian embassy after all,
as the Laird observed to Little Billee, with such a good
imitation of her wink that Little Billee was bound to laugh.

But Little Billee was not inclined for fun; a dulness, a
sense of disenchantment, had come over him; as he
expressed it to himself, with pathetic self-pity :

> " A feeling of sadness and longing
> That is not akin to pain,
> And resembles sorrow only
> As the mist resembles the rain."

And the sadness, if he had known, was that all beautiful
young women with kind sweet faces and noble figures and
goddess-like extremities should not be good and pure as
they were beautiful; and the longing was a longing that
Trilby could be turned into a young lady—say the vicar's
daughter in a little Devonshire village—his sister's friend
and co-teacher at the Sunday school, a simple, pure, and
pious maiden of gentle birth.

For he adored piety in women, although he was not
pious by any means. His inarticulate intuitive perceptions were not of form and colour secrets only, but strove
to pierce the veil of deeper mysteries in impetuous and
dogmatic boyish scorn of all received interpretations.
For he flattered himself that he possessed the philosophical
and scientific mind, and piqued himself on thinking clearly,
and was intolerant of human inconsistency.

That small reserve portion of his ever-active brain
which should have lain fallow while the rest of it was at
work or play, perpetually plagued itself about the mysteries
of life and death, and was for ever propounding unanswer-
able arguments against the Christian belief, through a kind
of inverted sympathy with the believer. Fortunately for
his friends, Little Billee was both shy and discreet, and
very tender of other people's feelings; so he kept all his
immature juvenile agnosticism to himself.

To atone for such ungainly strong-mindedness in one
so young and tender, he was the slave of many little
traditional observances which have no very solid founda-
tion in either science or philosophy. For instance, he
wouldn't walk under a ladder for worlds, nor sit down
thirteen to dinner, nor have his hair cut on a Friday, and
was quite upset if he happened to see the new moon
through glass. And he believed in lucky and unlucky
numbers, and dearly loved the sights and scents and
sounds of high mass in some dim old French cathedral, and
found them secretly comforting.

Let us hope that he sometimes laughed at himself, if
only in his sleeve !

And with all his keenness of insight into life he had a
well-brought-up, middle-class young Englishman's belief
in the infallible efficacy of gentle birth—for gentle he
considered his own and Taffy's and the Laird's, and that
of most of the good people he had lived among in England
—all people, in short, whose two parents and four grand-
parents had received a liberal education and belonged to
the professional class. And with this belief he combined
(or thought he did) a proper democratic scorn for bloated
dukes and lords, and even poor inoffensive baronets, and
all the landed gentry—everybody who was born an inch
higher up than himself.

It is a fairly good middle-class social creed, if you can
only stick to it through life in despite of life's experience.
It fosters independence and self-respect, and not a few
stodgy practical virtues as well. At all events, it keeps
you out of bad company, which is to be found both above
and below. *In medio tutissimus ibis !*

And all this melancholy preoccupation, on Little
Billee's part, from the momentary gleam and dazzle of a
pair of over-perfect feet in an over-æsthetic eye, too much
enamoured of mere form !

Reversing the usual process, he had idealised from the
base upward !

Many of us, older and wiser than Little Billee, have
seen in lovely female shapes the outer garment of a lovely
female soul. The instinct which guides us to do this is,
perhaps, a right one, more often than not. But more

often than not, also, lovely female shapes are terrible
complicators of the difficulties and dangers of this earthly
life, especially for their owner, and more especially if she
be a humble daughter of the people, poor and ignorant,
of a yielding nature, too quick to love and trust. This
is all so true as to be trite—so trite as to be a common
platitude !

A modern teller of tales, most widely (and most justly)
popular, tells us of Californian heroes and heroines who,
like Lord Byron's Corsair, were linked with one virtue and
a thousand crimes. And so dexterously does he weave
his story that the Young Person may read it and learn
nothing but good.

My poor heroine was the converse of these engaging
criminals ; she had all the virtues but one ; but the virtue
she lacked (the very one of all that plays the title-rôle,
and gives its generic name to all the rest of that goodly
company) was of such a kind that I have found it impossible
so to tell her history as to make it quite fit and proper
reading for the ubiquitous young person so dear to us all.

Most deeply to my regret. For I had fondly hoped it
might one day be said of me that whatever my other
literary shortcomings might be, I at least had never
penned a line which a pure-minded young British mother
might not read aloud to her little blue-eyed babe as it lies
sucking its little bottle in its little bassinette.

Fate has willed it otherwise.

Would indeed that I could duly express poor Trilby's
one shortcoming in some not too familiar medium—in
Latin or Greek, let us say—lest the Young Person (in this
ubiquitousness of hers, for which Heaven be praised)
should happen to pry into these pages when her mother
is looking another way.

Latin and Greek are languages the Young Person should
not be taught to understand—seeing that they are highly
improper languages, deservedly dead—in which pagan
bards who should have known better have sung the filthy
loves of their gods and goddesses.

But at least I am scholar enough to enter one little Latin
plea on Trilby's behalf—the shortest, best, and most
beautiful plea I can think of. It was once used in extenua-

tion and condonation of the frailties of another poor weak woman, presumably beautiful, and a far worse offender than Trilby, but who, like Trilby, repented of her ways, and was most justly forgiven—

"Quia multum amavit ! "

TRILBY'S FOREBEARS

Whether it be an aggravation of her misdeeds or an extenuating circumstance, no pressure of want, no temptations of greed or vanity, had ever been factors in urging Trilby on her downward career after her first false step in that direction— the result of ignorance, bad advice (from her mother, of all people in the world), and base betrayal. She might have lived in guilty splendour had she chosen, but her wants were few. She had no vanity, and her tastes were of the simplest, and she earned enough to gratify them all, and to spare.

So she followed love for love's sake only, now and then, as she would have followed art if she had been a man— capriciously, desultorily, more in a frolicsome spirit of

camaraderie than anything else. Like an amateur, in
short—a distinguished amateur who is too proud to sell
his pictures, but willingly gives one away now and then
to some highly-valued and much-admiring friend.
Sheer gaiety of heart and genial good-fellowship, the
difficulty of saying nay to earnest pleading. She was
bonne camarade et bonne fille before everything. Though
her heart was not large enough to harbour more than one
light love at a time (even in that Latin Quarter of genially
capacious hearts), it had room for many warm friendships;
and she was the warmest, most helpful, and most com-
passionate of friends, far more serious and faithful in
friendship than in love.

Indeed, she might almost be said to possess a virginal
heart, so little did she know of love's heartaches and
raptures and torments and clingings and jealousies.

With her it was lightly come and lightly go, and never
come back again; as one or two, or perhaps three, picturesque Bohemians of the brush or chisel had found, at some
cost to their vanity and self-esteem; perhaps even to a
deeper feeling—who knows?

Trilby's father, as she had said, had been a gentleman,
the son of a famous Dublin physician and friend of George
the Fourth's. He had been a Fellow of his college, and
had entered holy orders. He also had all the virtues but
one; he was a drunkard, and began to drink quite early
in life. He soon left the Church and became a classical
tutor, and failed through this besetting sin of his, and fell
into disgrace.

Then he went to Paris, and picked up a few English
pupils there, and lost them, and earned a precarious
livelihood from hand to mouth, anyhow, and sank from
bad to worse.

And when his worst was about reached, he married the
famous tartaned and tam-o'-shantered barmaid at the
Montagnards Écossais, in the Rue du Paradis Poissonnière
(a very fishy paradise indeed); she was a most beautiful
Highland lassie of low degree, and she managed to support
him, or helped him to support himself, for ten or fifteen
years. Trilby was born to them, and was dragged up in
some way—*à la grâce de Dieu !*

Patrick O'Ferrall soon taught his wife to drown all care and responsibility in his own simple way, and opportunities for doing so were never lacking to her.

Then he died, and left a posthumous child—born ten months after his death, alas! and whose birth cost its mother her life.

Then Trilby became a *blanchisseuse de fin*, and in two or three years came to grief through her trust in a friend of her mother's. Then she became a model besides, and was able to support her little brother, whom she dearly loved.

At the time this story begins, this small waif and stray was *en pension* with le père Martin, the rag-picker, and his wife, the dealer in bric-à-brac and inexpensive old masters. They were very good people, and had grown fond of the child, who was beautiful to look at, and full of pretty tricks and pluck and cleverness—a popular favourite in the Rue du Puits d'Amour and its humble neighbourhood.

Trilby, for some freak, always chose to speak of him as her godson, and as the grandchild of le père et la mère Martin, so that these good people had almost grown to believe he really belonged to them.

And almost every one else believed that he was the child of Trilby (in spite of her youth), and she was so fond of him that she didn't mind in the least.

He might have had a worse home.

La mère Martin was pious, or pretended to be; le père Martin was the reverse. But they were equally good for their kind, and though coarse and ignorant and unscrupulous in many ways (as was natural enough), they were gifted in a very full measure with the saving graces of love and charity, especially he. And if people are to be judged by their works, this worthy pair are no doubt both equally well compensated by now for the trials and struggles of their sordid earthly life.

So much for Trilby's parentage.

And as she sat and wept at Madame Doche's impersonation of *La Dame aux Camélias* (with her hand in Durien's) she vaguely remembered, as in a waking dream, now the noble presence of Taffy as he towered cool and erect, foil

in hand, gallantly waiting for his adversary to breathe,
now the beautiful sensitive face of Little Billee and his
deferential courtesy.

And during the *entr'actes* her heart went out in friendship to the jolly Scotch Laird of Cockpen, who came out
now and then with such terrible French oaths and abomin-
able expletives (and in the presence of ladies, too !), without
the slightest notion of what they meant.

For the Laird had a quick ear, and a craving to be
colloquial and idiomatic before everything else, and made
many awkward and embarrassing mistakes.

It would be with him as though a polite Frenchman
should say to a fair daughter of Albion, " D——my eyes,
mees, your tea is getting —— cold; let me tell that good
old —— of a Jules to bring you another cup."

And so forth, till time and experience taught him
better. It is perhaps well for him that his first experi-
ments in conversational French were made in the uncon-
ventional circle of the Place St. Anatole des Arts.

PART SECOND

NOBODY knew exactly how Svengali lived, and very few knew where (or why). He occupied a roomy dilapidated garret, *au sixième*, in the Rue Tire-Liard, with a truckle-bed and a pianoforte for furniture, and very little else.

He was poor, for in spite of his talent he had not yet made his mark in Paris. His manners may have been accountable for this. He would either fawn or bully, and could be grossly impertinent. He had a kind of cynical humour, which was more offensive than amusing, and always laughed at the wrong thing, at the wrong time, in the wrong place. And his laughter was always derisive and full of malice. And his egotism and conceit were not to be borne; and then he was both tawdry and dirty in his person; more greasily, mattedly unkempt than even a really successful pianist has any right to be even in the best society.

He was not a nice man, and there was no pathos in his poverty—a poverty that was not honourable, and need not have existed at all; for he was constantly receiving supplies from his own people in Austria—his old father and mother, his sisters, his cousins, and his aunts, hardworking, frugal folk of whom he was the pride and the darling.

He had but one virtue—his love of his art; or, rather, his love of himself as a master of his art—*the* master; for he despised, or affected to despise, all other musicians, living or dead—even those whose work he interpreted so divinely, and pitied them for not hearing Svengali give utterance to their music, which of course they could not utter themselves.

" Ils safent tous un peu toucher du biâno, mais pas grand'chose ! "

44

He had been the best pianist of his time at the Conservatory in Leipsic; and, indeed, there was perhaps some excuse for this overweening conceit, since he was able to lend a quite peculiar individual charm of his own to any music he played, except the highest and best of all, in which he conspicuously failed.

He had to draw the line just above Chopin, where he reached his highest level. It will not do to lend your own quite peculiar individual charm to Handel and Bach and Beethoven; and Chopin is not bad as a *pis-aller*.

He had ardently wished to sing, and had studied hard to that end in Germany, in Italy, in France, with the forlorn hope of evolving from some inner recess a voice to sing with. But nature had been singularly harsh to him in this one respect—inexorable. He was absolutely without voice, beyond the harsh, hoarse, weak raven's croak he used to speak with, and no method availed to make one for him. But he grew to understand the human voice as perhaps no one has understood it—before or since.

So in his head he went for ever singing, singing, singing, as probably no human nightingale has ever yet been able to sing out loud for the glory and delight of his fellow-mortals; making unheard heavenly melody of the cheapest, trivialest tunes—tunes of the café concert, tunes of the nursery, the shop-parlour, the guard-room, the schoolroom, the pothouse, the slum. There was nothing so humble, so base even, but what his magic could transform it into the rarest beauty without altering a note. This seems impossible, I know. But if it didn't, where would the magic come in?

Whatever of heart or conscience—pity, love, tenderness, manliness, courage, reverence, charity—endowed him at his birth had been swallowed up by this one faculty, and nothing of them was left for the common uses of life. He poured them all into his little flexible flageolet.

Svengali playing Chopin on the pianoforte, even (or especially) Svengali playing " Ben Bolt " on that penny whistle of his, was as one of the heavenly host.

Svengali walking up and down the earth seeking whom he might cheat, betray, exploit, borrow money from, make brutal fun of, bully if he dared, cringe to if he must—man, woman, child, or dog—was about as bad as they make 'em.

To earn a few pence when he couldn't borrow them he played accompaniments at café concerts, and even then he gave offence; for in his contempt for the singer he would play too loud, and embroider his accompaniments with brilliant improvisations of his own, and lift his hands on high and bring them down with a bang in the sentimental parts, and shake his dirty mane and shrug his shoulders, and smile and leer at the audience, and do all he could to attract their attention to himself. He also gave a few music lessons (not at ladies' schools, let us hope),

" AS BAD AS THEY MAKE 'EM "

for which he was not well paid, presumably, since he was always without a sou, always borrowing money, that he never paid back, and exhausting the pockets and the patience of one acquaintance after another.

He had but two friends. There was Gecko, who lived in a little garret close by in the Impasse des Ramoneurs, and who was second violin in the orchestra of the Gymnase, and shared his humble earnings with his master, to whom, indeed, he owed his great talent, not yet revealed to the world.

Svengali's other friend and pupil was (or rather had been) the mysterious Honorine, of whose conquest he was much given to boast, hinting that she was *une jeune femme du monde*. This was not the case. Mademoiselle Honorine Cahen (better known in the Quartier Latin as Mimi la Salope) was a dirty, drabby little dolly-mop of a Jewess, a model for the figure—a very humble person indeed, socially.

She was, however, of a very lively disposition, and had a charming voice, and a natural gift of singing so sweetly that you forgot her accent, which was that of the *tout ce qu'il y a de plus canaille*.

She used to sit at Carrel's, and during the pose she

would sing. When Little Billee first heard her he was so
fascinated that "it made him sick to think she sat for
the figure"—an effect, by the way, that was always
produced upon him by all specially attractive figure
models of the gentler sex, for he had a reverence for
woman. And before everything else, he had for the
singing woman an absolute worship. He was especially
thrall to the contralto—the deep low voice that breaks
and changes in the middle and soars all at once into a
magnified angelic boy treble. It pierced through his ears
to his heart, and stirred his very vitals.

He had once heard Madame Alboni, and it had been an
epoch in his life; he would have been an easy prey to the
sirens! Even beauty paled before the lovely female
voice singing in the middle of the note—the nightingale
killed the bird of paradise.

I need hardly say that poor Mimi la Salope had not the
voice of Madame Alboni, nor the art; but it was a beautiful voice of its little kind, always in the very middle of the
note, and her artless art had its quick seduction.

She sang little songs of Béranger's—"Grand'mère,
parlez-nous de lui!" or "T'en souviens-tu? disait un
capitaine——" or "Enfants, c'est moi qui suis Lisette!"
and such like pretty things, that almost brought the tears
to Little Billee's easily-moistened eyes.

But soon she would sing little songs that were not by
Béranger—little songs with slang words Little Billee
hadn't French enough to understand; but from the kind
of laughter with which the points were received by the
"rapins" in Carrel's studio he guessed these little songs
were vile, though the touching little voice was as that of
the seraphim still; and he knew the pang of disenchantment and vicarious shame.

Svengali had heard her sing at the Brasserie des Por-
cherons in the Rue du Crapaud volant, and had volunteered
to teach her; and she went to see him in his garret, and
he played to her, and leered and ogled, and flashed his
bold, black, beady Jew's eyes into hers, and she straightway mentally prostrated herself in reverence and adoration
before this dazzling specimen of her race.

So that her sordid mercenary little gutter-draggled

"A VOICE HE DIDN'T UNDERSTAND"

soul was filled with the sight and the sound of him, as of a lordly, godlike, shawm-playing, cymbal-banging hero and prophet of the Lord God of Israel—David and Saul in one !

And then he set himself to teach her—kindly and patiently at first, calling her sweet little pet names—his " Rose of Sharon," his " pearl of Pabylon," his " cazelle-eyed liddle Cherusalem skylark "—and promised her that she should be the queen of the nightingales.

But before he could teach her anything he had to unteach her all she knew; her breathing, the production of her voice, its emission—everything was wrong. She worked indefatigably to please him, and soon succeeded in forgetting all the pretty little sympathetic tricks of voice and phrasing Mother Nature had taught her.

But though she had an exquisite ear she had no real musical intelligence—no intelligence of any kind except about sous and centimes; she was as stupid as a little downy owl, and her voice was just a light native warble, a throstle's pipe, all in the head and nose and throat (a voice he *didn't* understand, for once), a thing of mere youth and health and bloom and high spirits—like her beauty, such as it was—*beauté du diable, beauté damnée.*

She did her very best, and practised all she could in this new way, and sang herself hoarse : she scarcely ate or slept for practising. He grew harsh and impatient and coldly severe, and of course she loved him all the more; and the more she loved him the more nervous she got and the worse she sang. Her voice cracked; her ear became demoralised; her attempts to vocalise grew almost as distressing as Trilby's. So that he lost his temper completely, and called her terrible names, and pinched and punched her with his big bony hands till she wept worse than Niobe, and borrowed money of her—five-franc pieces, even francs and demifrancs—which he never paid her back ; and browbeat and bullied and bully-ragged her till she went quite mad for love of him, and would have jumped out of his sixth-floor window to give him a moment's pleasure !

He did not ask her to do this—it never occurred to him, and would have given him no pleasure to speak of. But one fine Sabbath morning (a Saturday, of course) he took

her by the shoulders and chucked her, neck and crop, out
of his garret, with the threat that if she ever dared to show
her face there again he would denounce her to the police—
an awful threat to the likes of poor Mimi la Salope !

"For where did all those five-franc pieces come from
—*hein ?*—with which she had tried to pay for all the
singing lessons that had been thrown away upon her?
Not from merely sitting to
painters—*hein ?* "

Thus the little gazelle-eyed
Jerusalem skylark went back
to her native streets again—
a mere mud-lark of the Paris
slums—her wings clipped, her
spirit quenched and broken,
and with no more singing left
in her than a common or
garden sparrow—not so much !
And so, no more of " la
betite Honorine ! "

The morning after this adventure Svengali woke up in
his garret with a tremendous
longing to spend a happy day ;
for it was a Sunday, and a very
fine one.

He made a long arm and

"AND SO, NO MORE"   reached his waistcoat and
trousers off the floor, and
emptied the contents of their pockets on to his tattered
blanket; no silver, no gold, only a few sous and two-sou
pieces, just enough to pay for a meagre *premier déjeuner !*

He had cleared out Gecko the day before, and spent the
proceeds (ten francs, at least) in one night's riotous living
—pleasures in which Gecko had had no share ; and he
could think of no one to borrow money from but Little
Billee, Taffy, and the Laird, whom he had neglected and
left untapped for days.

So he slipped into his clothes, and looked at himself in
what remained of a little zinc mirror, and found that his

forehead left little to be desired, but that his eyes and
temples were decidedly grimy. Wherefore, he poured a
little water out of a little jug into a little basin, and twist-
ing the corner of his pocket-handkerchief round his dirty
forefinger, he delicately dipped it, and removed the
offending stains. His fingers, he thought, would do very
well for another day or two as they were; he ran them
through his matted black mane, pushed it behind his ears,
and gave it the twist he liked (and that was so much disliked by his English friends). Then he put on his *béret*
and his velveteen cloak, and went forth into the sunny
streets, with a sense of the fragrance and freedom and
pleasantness of Sunday morning in Paris in the month of
May.

He found Little Billee sitting in a zinc hip-bath, busy
with soap and sponge; and was so tickled and interested
by the sight that he quite forgot for the moment what he
had come for.

" Himmel ! Why the devil are you doing that ? " he
asked, in his German-Hebrew-French.

" Doing *what ?* " asked Little Billee, in his French of
Stratford-atte-Bowe.

" Sitting in water and playing with a cake of soap and
a sponge ! "

" Why, to try and get myself *clean,* I suppose ! "

" Ach ! And how the devil did you get yourself *dirty,*
then ? "

To this Little Billee found no immediate answer, and
went on with his ablutions after the hissing, splashing,
energetic fashion of Englishmen; and Svengali laughed
loud and long at the spectacle of a little Englishman
trying to get himself clean—*tâchant de se nettoyer !*

When such cleanliness had been attained as was possible
under the circumstances, Svengali begged for the loan of
two hundred francs, and Little Billee gave him a five-franc
piece.

Content with this, *faute de mieux,* the German asked
him when he would be trying to get himself clean again,
as he would much like to come and see him do it.

" Demang mattang, à votre sairveece ! " said Little
Billee, with a courteous bow.

"*What!! Monday too!!* Gott in Himmel! you try to get yourself clean *every day?*"

And he laughed himself out of the room, out of the house, out of the Place de l'Odéon—all the way to the Rue de Seine, where dwelt the " Man of Blood," whom he meant to propitiate with the story of that original, Little Billee, trying to get himself clean—that he might borrow another five-franc piece, or perhaps two.

As the reader will no doubt anticipate, he found Taffy in his bath also, and fell to laughing with such convulsive laughter, such twistings, screwings, and doublings of himself up, such pointings of his dirty forefinger at the huge naked Briton, that Taffy was offended, and all but lost his temper.

" What the devil are you cackling at, sacred head of pig that you are? Do you want to be pitched out of that window into the Rue de Seine? You filthy black Hebrew sweep! Just you wait a bit; *I'll* wash your head for you!"

And Taffy jumped out of his bath, such a towering figure of righteous Herculean wrath that Svengali was appalled, and fled.

" Donnerwetter!" he exclaimed as he tumbled down the narrow staircase of the Hôtel de Seine; " what for a thick head! what for a pigdog! what for a rotten, brutal, *verfluchter kerl* of an Englander!"

Then he paused for thought.

" Now will I go to that Scottish Englander, in the Place St. Anatole des Arts, for that other five-franc piece. But first will I wait a little while till he has perhaps finished trying to get himself clean."

So he breakfasted at the crémerie Souchet, in the Rue Clopin-Clopant, and, feeling quite safe again, he laughed and laughed till his very sides were sore.

Two Englanders in one day—as naked as your hand!— a big one and a little one, trying to get themselves clean!

He rather flattered himself he had scored off those two Englanders.

After all, he was right perhaps, from his point of view; you can get as dirty in a week as in a lifetime, so what's the use of taking such a lot of trouble? Besides, so long as you are clean enough to suit your kind, to be any cleaner would be priggish and pedantic, and get you disliked.

"'TWO ENGLANDERS IN ONE DAY'"

Just as Svengali was about to knock at the Laird's door, Trilby came downstairs from Durien's, very unlike herself. Her eyes were red with weeping, and there were great black rings round them; she was pale under her freckles.

"Fous afez du chacrin, matemoiselle?" asked he.

She told him that she had neuralgia in her eyes, a thing she was subject to; that the pain was maddening, and generally lasted twenty-four hours.

" Perhaps I can cure you ; come in here with me."
The Laird's ablutions (if he had indulged in any that
morning) were evidently over for the day. He was
breakfasting on a roll and butter, and coffee of his own
brewing. He was deeply distressed at the sight of poor
Trilby's sufferings, and offered whisky and coffee and
gingernuts, which she would not touch.

Svengali told her to sit down on the divan, and sat
opposite to her, and bade her look him well in the white
of the eyes.

" Recartez-moi pien tans le planc tes yeux."

Then he made little passes and counterpasses on her
forehead and temples and down her cheek and neck. Soon
her eyes closed and her face grew placid. After a while, a
quarter of an hour perhaps, he asked her if she suffered still.

" Oh ! presque plus du tout, monsieur—c'est le ciel."

In a few minutes more he asked the Laird if he knew
German.

" Just enough to understand," said the Laird (who had
spent a year in Düsseldorf), and Svengali said to him in
German : " See, she sleeps not, but she shall not open her
eyes. Ask her."

" Are you asleep, Miss Trilby ? " asked the Laird.
" No."

" Then open your eyes and look at me."

She strained to open her eyes, but could not, and said so.
Then Svengali said, again in German, " She shall not
open her mouth. Ask her."

" Why couldn't you open your eyes, Miss Trilby ? "

She strained to open her mouth and speak, but in vain.

" She shall not rise from the divan. Ask her."

But Trilby was spellbound, and could not move.

" I will now set her free," said Svengali.

And, lo ! she got up and waved her arms, and cried
" Vive la Prusse ! me v'là guérie ! " and in her gratitude
she kissed Svengali's hand; and he leered, and showed
his big brown teeth and the yellow whites at the top of
his big black eyes, and drew his breath with a hiss.

" Now I'll go to Durien's and sit. How can I thank
you, monsieur ? You have taken all my pain away."

" Yes, matemoiselle. I have got it myself; it is in my

elbows. But I love it, because it comes from you.
Every time you have pain you shall come to me, 12 Rue
Tire-Liard, au sixième au-dessus de l'entresol, and I will
cure you and take your pain myself——"

" Oh, you are too good ! " and in her high spirits she
turned round on her heel and uttered her portentous war-
cry, " Milk below ! " The very rafters rang with it, and
the piano gave out a solemn response.

" What is that you say, matemoiselle ? "

" Oh, it's what the milkmen say in England."

" It is a wonderful cry, matemoiselle—*wunderschön !*
It comes straight through the heart; it has its roots in
the stomach, and blossoms into music on the lips like the
voice of Madame Alboni—voce sulle labbre ! It is good
production—c'est un cri du cœur ! "

Trilby blushed with pride and pleasure.

" Yes, matemoiselle ! I know only one person in the
whole world who can produce the voice so well as you !
I give you my word of honour."

" Who is it, monsieur—yourself ? "

" Ach, no, matemoiselle; I have not that privilege. I
have unfortunately no voice to produce. . . . It is a
waiter at the Café de la Rotonde, in the Palais Royal;
when you call for coffee, he says ' Boum ! ' in basso
profondo. Tiefstimme—F moll below the line—it is
phenomenal ! It is like a cannon—a cannon also has very
good production, matemoiselle. They pay him for it a
thousand francs a year, because he brings many customers
to the Café de la Rotonde, where the coffee isn't very good,
although it costs three sous a cup dearer than at the Café
Larsouille in the Rue Flamberge-au-Vent. When he dies
they will search all France for another, and then all
Germany, where the good big waiters come from—and the
cannons—but they will not find him, and the Café de la
Rotonde will be bankrupt—unless you will consent to take
his place. Will you permit that I shall look into your
mouth, matemoiselle ? "

She opened her mouth wide, and he looked into it.

" Himmel ! the roof of your mouth is like the dome of
the Panthéon; there is room in it for ' toutes les gloires
de la France,' and a little to spare ! The entrance to your

"'HIMMEL! THE ROOF OF YOUR MOUTH'"

throat is like the middle porch of St. Sulpice when the doors are open for the faithful on All Saints' Day; and not one tooth is missing—thirty-two British teeth as white as milk and as big as knuckle-bones ! and your little tongue is scooped out like the leaf of a pink peony, and the bridge of your nose is like the belly of a Stradivarius—what a sounding-board ! and inside your beautiful big chest the lungs are made of leather ! and your breath, it embalms— like the breath of a beautiful white heifer fed on the buttercups and daisies of the Vaterland ! and you have a quick, soft, susceptible heart, a heart of gold, matemoiselle —all that sees itself in your face !

" ' Votre cœur est un luth suspendu !
Aussitôt qu'on le touche, il résonne. ; ; .'

What a pity you have not also the musical organisation ! "

" Oh, but I *have*, monsieur; you heard me sing ' Ben Bolt,' didn't you? What makes you say that? "

Svengali was confused for a moment. Then he said : " When I play the ' Rosemonde ' of Schubert, matemoiselle, you look another way and smoke a cigarette. . . . You look at the big Taffy, at the Little Billee, at the pictures on the walls, or out of window, at the sky, the chimney-pots of Notre Dame de Paris; you do not look at Svengali !—Svengali, who looks at you with all his eyes, and plays you the ' Rosemonde ' of Schubert ! "

" Oh, maïe aïe ! " exclaimed Trilby; " you *do* use lovely language ! "

" But never mind, matemoiselle; when your pain arrives, then shall you come once more to Svengali, and he shall take it away from you, and keep it himself for a soufenir of you when you are gone. And when you have it no more, he shall play you the ' Rosemonde ' of Schubert, all alone for you; and then ' Messieurs les étutiants, montez à la chaumière ! ' . . . because it is gayer ! *And you shall see nothing, hear nothing, think of nothing but Svengali, Svengali, Svengali !* "

Here he felt his peroration to be so happy and effective that he thought it well to go at once and make a good exit. So he bent over Trilby's shapely freckled hand and kissed it, and bowed himself out of the room, without even borrowing his five-franc piece.

" He's a rum 'un, ain't he ? " said Trilby. " He reminds
me of a big hungry spider, and makes me feel like a fly !
But he's cured my pain ! he's cured my pain ! Ah ! you
don't know what my pain is when it comes ! "

" I wouldn't have much to do with him, all the same ! "
said the Laird. " I'd sooner have any pain than have it
cured in that unnatural way, and by such a man as that !
He's a bad fellow, Svengali—I'm sure of it ! He mes-
merised you ; that's what it is—mesmerism ! I've often
heard of it, but never seen it done before. They get you
into their power, and just make you do any blessed thing
they please—lie, murder, steal—anything ! and kill
yourself into the bargain when they've done with you !
It's just too terrible to think of ! "

So spake the Laird, earnestly, solemnly, surprised out of
his usual self, and most painfully impressed—and his own
impressiveness grew upon him and impressed him still
more. He loomed quite prophetic.

Cold shivers went down Trilby's back as she listened.
She had a singularly impressionable nature, as was shown
by her quick and ready susceptibility to Svengali's hyp-
notic influence. And all that day, as she posed for
Durien (to whom she did not mention her adventure), she
was haunted by the memory of Svengali's big eyes and the
touch of his soft, dirty finger-tips on her face ; and her fear
and her repulsion grew together.

And " Svengali, Svengali, Svengali ! " went ringing in
her head and ears till it became an obsession, a dirge, a
knell, an unendurable burden, almost as hard to bear as
the pain in her eyes.

" *Svengali, Svengali, Svengali !* "

At last she asked Durien if he knew him.

" Parbleu ! Si je connais Svengali ! "

" Qu'est-ce que t'en penses ? "

" Quand il sera mort, ça fera une fameuse crapule de
moins ! "

" CHEZ CARREL."

Carrel's atelier (or painting-school) was in the Rue
Notre Dame des Potirons St. Michel, at the end of a large
courtyard, where there were many large dirty windows

facing north, and each window let the light of heaven into a large dirty studio.

"'ÇA FERA UNE FAMEUSE CRAPULE DE MOINS'"

The largest of these studios, and the dirtiest, was Carrel's, where some thirty or forty art students drew and painted from the nude model every day but Sunday from eight till twelve, and for two hours in the afternoon, except on Saturdays, when the afternoon was devoted to much-needed Augean sweepings and cleanings.

One week the model was male, the next female, and so on, alternating through the year.

A stove, a model-throne, stools, boxes, some fifty strongly-built low chairs with backs, a couple of score easels and many drawing-boards, completed the *mobilier*.

The bare walls were adorned with endless caricatures—*des charges*—in charcoal and white chalk; and also the scrapings of many palettes—a polychromous decoration not unpleasing.

For the freedom of the studio and the use of the model each student paid ten francs a month to the *massier*, or senior student, the responsible bell-wether of the flock; besides this, it was expected of you, on your entrance or initiation, that you should pay for your footing—your *bienvenue*—some thirty, forty, or fifty francs, to be spent on cakes and rum punch all round.

Every Friday Monsieur Carrel, a great artist, and also a stately, well-dressed, and most courteous gentleman (duly decorated with the red rosette of the Legion of Honour), came for two or three hours and went the round, spending a few minutes at each drawing-board or easel— ten or even twelve when the pupil was an industrious and promising one.

He did this for love, not money, and deserved all the reverence with which he inspired this somewhat irreverent and most unruly company, which was made up of all sorts.

Graybeards who had been drawing and painting there for thirty years and more, and remembered other masters than Carrel, and who could draw and paint a torso almost as well as Titian or Velasquez—almost, but not quite— and who could never do anything else, and were fixtures at Carrel's for life.

Younger men who in a year or two, or three or five, or ten or twenty, were bound to make their mark, and perhaps follow in the footsteps of the master; others as conspicuously singled out for failure and future mischance— for the hospital, the garret, the river, the Morgue, or, worse, the traveller's bag, the road, or even the paternal counter.

Irresponsible boys, mere *rapins*, all laugh and chaff and mischief—*blague et bagout Parisien ;* little lords of misrule —wits, butts, bullies ; the idle and industrious apprentice, the good and the bad, the clean and the dirty (especially the latter)—all more or less animated by a certain *esprit de corps,* and working very happily and genially together, on the whole, and always willing to help each other with sincere artistic counsel if it was asked for seriously, though it was not always couched in terms very flattering to one's self-love.

Before Little Billee became one of this band of brothers he had been working for three or four years in a London art school, drawing and painting from the life; he had also worked from the antique in the British Museum—so that he was no novice.

As he made his début at Carrel's one Monday morning he felt somewhat shy and ill at ease. He had studied French most earnestly at home in England, and could read it pretty well, and even write it and speak it after a fashion; but he spoke it with much difficulty, and found studio French a different language altogether from the formal and polite language he had been at such pains to acquire. Ollendorff does not cater for the Quartier Latin. Acting on Taffy's advice—for Taffy had worked under Carrel—Little Billee handed sixty francs to the *massier* for his *bienvenue*—a lordly sum—and this liberality made a most favourable impression, and went far to destroy any little prejudice that might have been caused by the daintiness of his dress, the cleanliness of his person, and the politeness of his manners. A place was assigned to him, and an easel and a board; for he elected to stand at his work and begin with a chalk drawing. The model (a male) was posed, and work began in silence. Monday morning is always rather sulky everywhere (except perhaps in Judee). During the ten minutes' rest three or four students came and looked at Little Billee's beginnings, and saw at a glance that he thoroughly well knew what he was about, and respected him for it.

Nature had given him a singularly light hand—or rather two, for he was ambidextrous, and could use both with equal skill; and a few months' practice at a London life school had quite cured him of that purposeless indecision of touch which often characterises the prentice hand for years of apprenticeship, and remains with the amateur for life. The lightest and most careless of his pencil strokes had a precision that was inimitable, and a charm that specially belonged to him, and was easy to recognise at a glance. His touch on either canvas or paper was like Svengali's on the keyboard—unique.

As the morning ripened little attempts at conversation were made—little breakings of the ice of silence. It was

Lambert, a youth with a singularly facetious face, who first woke the stillness with the following uncalled-for remarks in English very badly pronounced :

" Av you seen my fahzere's ole shoes ? "

" I av not seen your fahzere's ole shoes."

Then, after a pause :

" Av you seen my fahzere's ole 'at ? "

" I av not seen your fahzere's ole 'at ! "

Presently another said, " Je trouve qu'il a une jolie tête, l'Anglais."

But I will put it all into English :

" I find that he has a pretty head—the Englishman ! What say *you*, Barizel ? "

" Yes; but why has he got eyes like brandy-balls, two a penny ? "

" Because he's an Englishman ! "

" Yes; but why has he got a mouth like a guinea-pig, with two big teeth in front like the double blank at dominoes ? "

" Because he's an Englishman ! "

" Yes; but why has he got a back without any bend in it. as if he'd swallowed the Colonne Vendôme as far up as the battle of Austerlitz ? "

" Because he's an Englishman ! "

And so on, till all the supposed characteristics of Little Billee's outer man were exhausted. Then :

" Papelard ! "

" What ? "

" *I* should like to know if the Englishman says his prayers before going to bed."

" Ask him."

" Ask him yourself ! "

" *I* should like to know if the Englishman has sisters; and if so, how old and how many and what sex."

" Ask him."

" Ask him yourself ! "

" *I* should like to know the detailed and circumstantial history of the Englishman's first love, and how he lost his innocence ! "

" Ask him," etc. etc. etc.

Little Billee, conscious that he was the subject of con-

"'AV YOU SEEN MY FAHZERE'S OLE SHOES?'"

versation, grew somewhat nervous. Soon he was addressed directly.

"Dites donc, l'Anglais?"

"Kwaw?" said Little Billee.

"Avez-vous une sœur?"

"Wee."

"Est-ce qu'elle vous ressemble?"

"Nong."

"C'est bien dommage! Est-ce qu'elle dit ses prières, le soir, en se couchant?"

A fierce look came into Little Billee's eyes and a redness to his cheeks, and this particular form of overture to friendship was abandoned.

Presently Lambert said, "Si nous mettions l'Anglais à l'échelle?"

Little Billee, who had been warned, knew what this ordeal meant.

They tied you to a ladder, and carried you in procession up and down the courtyard, and if you were nasty about it they put you under the pump.

During the next rest it was explained to him that he must submit to this indignity, and the ladder (which was used for reaching the high shelves round the studio) was got ready.

Little Billee smiled a singularly winning smile, and suffered himself to be bound with such good-humour that they voted it wasn't amusing, and unbound him, and he escaped the ordeal by ladder.

Taffy had also escaped, but in another way. When they tried to seize him he took up the first *rapin* that came to hand, and using him as a kind of club, he swung him about so freely and knocked down so many students and easels and drawing-boards with him, and made such a terrific rumpus, that the whole studio had to cry for "pax!" Then he performed feats of strength of such a surprising kind that the memory of him remained in Carrel's studio for years, and he became a legend, a tradition, a myth! It is now said (in what still remains of the Quartier Latin) that he was seven feet high, and used to juggle with the *massier* and model as with a pair of billiard balls, using only his left hand!

TAFFY À L'ÉCHELLE !

To return to Little Billee. When it struck twelve, the cakes and rum punch arrived—a very goodly sight that put every one in a good temper.

The cakes were of three kinds—Babas, Madeleines, and Savarins—three sous apiece, fourpence-halfpenny the set of three. No nicer cakes are made in France, and they are as good in the Quartier Latin as anywhere else; no nicer cakes are made in the whole world, that I know of. You must begin with the Madeleine, which is rich and rather heavy; then the Baba; and finish up with the Savarin, which is shaped like a ring, very light, and flavoured with rum. And then you must really leave off.

The rum punch was tepid, very sweet, and not a bit too strong.

They dragged the model-throne into the middle, and a chair was put on for Little Billee, who dispensed his hospitality in a very polite and attractive manner, helping the *massier* first, and then the other graybeards in the order of their grayness, and so on down to the model.

Presently, just as he was about to help himself, he was asked to sing them an English song. After a little pressing he sung them a song about a gay cavalier who went to serenade his mistress (and a ladder of ropes, and a pair of masculine gloves that didn't belong to the gay cavalier, but which he found in his lady's bower)—a poor sort of song, but it was the nearest approach to a comic song he knew. There are four verses to it, and each verse is rather long. It does not sound at all funny to a French audience, and even with an English one Little Billee was not good at comic songs.

He was, however, much applauded at the end of each verse. When he had finished, he was asked if he were *quite* sure there wasn't any more of it, and they expressed a deep regret; and then each student, straddling on his little thick-set chair as on a horse, and clasping the back of it in both hands, galloped round Little Billee's throne quite seriously—the strangest procession he had ever seen. It made him laugh till he cried, so that he could not eat or drink.

Then he served more punch and cake all round; and just as he was going to begin himself, Papelard said:

"Say, you others, I find that the Englishman has
something of truly distinguished in the voice, something
of sympathetic, of touching—something of *je ne sais quoi !*"
Bouchardy : " Yes, yes—something of *je ne sais quoi !*
That's the very phrase—n'est-ce pas, vous autres?—that
is a good phrase that Papelard has just invented to describe
the voice of the Englishman. He is very intelligent—
Papelard."
Chorus : " Perfect, perfect; he has the genius of
characterisation—Papelard. Dites donc, l'Anglais ! once
more that beautiful song—*hein ?* Nous vous en prions
tous."
Little Billee willingly sang it again, with even greater
applause, and again they galloped, but the other way
round and faster, so that Little Billee became quite
hysterical, and laughed till his sides ached.
Then Dubosc : " I find there is something of very
capitous and exciting in English music—of very stimulat-
ing. And you, Bouchardy? "
Bouchardy : " Oh me ! It is above all the *words* that
I admire ; they have something of passionate, of romantic
—' ze-ese glâ-âves, zese glâ-âves, zey do not belong to
me.' I don't know what that means, but I love that sort
of—of—of—of—*je ne sais quoi*, in short ! Just *once* more,
l'Anglais ; only *once*, the *four* couplets."
So he sang it a third time, all four verses, while they
leisurely ate and drank and smoked and looked at each
other, nodding solemn commendation of certain phrases
in the song : " Très bien ! " " Très bien ! " " Ah ! voilà
qui est bien réussi ! " " Épatant, ça ! " " Très fin ! "
etc. etc. For, stimulated by success, and rising to the
occasion, he did his very utmost to surpass himself in
emphasis of gesture and accent and histrionic drollery—
heedless of the fact that not one of his listeners had the
slightest notion what his song was about.
It was a sorry performance.
And it was not till he had sung it four times that he
discovered the whole thing was an elaborate impromptu
farce, of which he was the butt, and that of all his royal
spread not a crumb or a drop was left for himself.
It was the old fable of the fox and the crow ! And to

"THE FOX AND THE CROW"

do him justice, he laughed as heartily as any one, as if he
thoroughly enjoyed the joke—and when you take jokes in
that way people soon leave off poking fun at you. It is
almost as good as being very big, like Taffy, and having a
choleric blue eye !

Such was Little Billee's first experience of Carrel's
studio, where he spent many happy mornings and made
many good friends.

No more popular student had ever worked there within
the memory of the grayest graybeards; none more
amiable, more genial, more cheerful, self-respecting,
considerate, and polite, and certainly none with greater
gifts for art.

Carrel would devote at least fifteen minutes to him, and
invited him often to his own private studio. And often,
on the fourth or fifth day of the week, a group of admiring
students would be gathered by his easel watching him as
he worked.

"C'est un rude lapin, l'Anglais ! au moins il sait son
orthographe en peinture, ce coco-là ! "

Such was the verdict on Little Billee at Carrel's studio;
and I can conceive no much loftier praise,

.   .   .   .   .   .

Young as she was (seventeen or eighteen, or thereabouts), and also tender (like Little Billee), Trilby had
singularly clear and quick perceptions in all matters that
concerned her tastes, fancies, or affections, and thoroughly
knew her own mind, and never lost much time in making
it up.

On the occasion of her first visit to the studio in the
Place St. Anatole des Arts, it took her just five minutes
to decide that it was quite the nicest, homeliest, genialest,
jolliest studio in the whole Quartier Latin, or out of it,
and its three inhabitants, individually and collectively,
were more to her taste than any one else she had ever
met.

In the first place, they were English, and she loved to
hear her mother-tongue and speak it. It awoke all manner
of tender recollections, sweet reminiscences of her childhood, her parents, her old home—such a home as it was—
or, rather, such homes; for there had been many flittings

from one poor nest to another. The O'Ferralls had been
as birds on the bough.

She had loved her parents very dearly; and, indeed,
with all their faults, they had many endearing qualities—
the qualities that so often go with those particular faults
—charm, geniality, kindness, warmth of heart, the constant
wish to please, the generosity that comes before justice,
and lends its last sixpence and forgets to pay its debts !

She knew other English and American artists, and
had sat to them frequently for the head and hands; but
none of these, for general agreeableness of aspect or manner,
could compare in her mind with the stalwart and magnificent Taffy, the jolly fat Laird of Cockpen, the refined,
sympathetic, and elegant Little Billee; and she resolved
that she would see as much of them as she could, that she
would make herself at home in that particular studio, and
necessary to its *locataires ;* and without being the least bit
vain or self-conscious, she had no doubts whatever of her
power to please—to make herself both useful and orna-
mental if it suited her purpose to do so.

Her first step in this direction was to borrow Père
Martin's basket and lantern and pick (he had more than one
set of these trade properties) for the use of Taffy, whom
she feared she might have offended by the freedom of her
comments on his picture.

Then, as often as she felt it to be discreet, she sounded
her war-cry at the studio door and went in and made kind
inquiries, and, sitting cross-legged on the model-throne,
ate her bread and cheese and smoked her cigarette and
" passed the time of day," as she chose to call it; telling
them all such news of the Quartier as had come within her
own immediate ken. She was always full of little stories
of other studios, which, to do her justice, were always
good-natured, and probably true—quite so, as far as she
was concerned; she was the most literal person alive;
and she told all these *ragots, cancans, et potins d'atelier* in
a quaint and amusing manner. The slightest look of
gravity or boredom on one of those three faces, and she
made herself scarce at once.

She soon found opportunities for usefulness also. If
a costume were wanted, for instance, she knew where to

borrow it, or hire it or buy it cheaper than any one anywhere else. She procured stuffs for them at cost price,
as it seemed, and made them into draperies and female
garments of any kind that was wanted, and sat in them for
the toreador's sweetheart (she made the mantilla herself),
for Taffy's starving dressmaker about to throw herself into
the Seine, for Little Billee's studies of the beautiful French

peasant girl in his picture,
now so famous, called "The
Pitcher Goes to the Well."

Then she darned their
socks and mended their
clothes, and got all their
washing done properly and
cheaply at her friend
Madame Boisse's, in the Rue
des Cloîtres Ste. Pétronille.

And then again, when
they were hard up and

THE LATIN QUARTER

wanted a good round sum of money for some little pleasure
excursion, such as a trip to Fontainebleau or Barbizon for
two or three days, it was she who took their watches and
scarf-pins and things to the Mount of Piety in the Street
of the Well of Love (where dwelt *ma tante,* which is
French for "my uncle" in this connection), in order to
raise the necessary funds.

She was, of course, most liberally paid for all these little
services, rendered with such pleasure and goodwill—far

too liberally, she thought. She would have been really happier doing them for love.

Thus in a very short time she became a *persona gratissima*—a sunny and ever-welcome vision of health and grace and liveliness and unalterable good-humour, always ready to take any trouble to please her beloved " Angliches," as they were called by Madame Vinard, the handsome shrill-voiced *concierge*, who was almost jealous; for she was devoted to the Angliches too—and so was Monsieur Vinard—and so were the little Vinards.

She knew when to talk and when to laugh and when to hold her tongue; and the sight of her sitting cross-legged on the model-throne darning the Laird's socks or sewing buttons on his shirts or repairing the smoke-holes in his trousers was so pleasant that it was painted by all three. One of these sketches (in water-colour by Little Billee) sold the other day at Christie's for a sum so large that I hardly dare to mention it. It was done in an afternoon.

Sometimes on a rainy day, when it was decided they should dine at home, she would fetch the food and cook it, and lay the cloth, and even make the salad. She was a better saladist than Taffy, a better cook than the Laird, a better caterer than Little Billee. And she would be invited to take her share in the banquet. And on these occasions her tremulous happiness was so immense that it would be quite pathetic to see—almost painful; and their three British hearts were touched by thoughts of all the loneliness and homelessness, the expatriation, the half-conscious loss of caste, that all this eager childish clinging revealed.

And that is why (no doubt) that with all this familiar intimacy there was never any hint of gallantry or flirtation in any shape or form whatever—*bonne camaraderie voilà tout*. Had she been Little Billee's sister she could not have been treated with more real respect. And her deep gratitude for this unwonted compliment transcended any passion she had ever felt. As the good Lafontaine so prettily says—

> " Ces animaux vivaient entre eux comme cousins;
> Cette union si douce, et presque fraternelle,
> Edifiait tous les voisins ! "

CUISINE BOURGEOISE EN BOHÊME

And then their talk ! It was to her as the talk of the gods in Olympus, save that it was easier to understand, and she could always understand it. For she was a very intelligent person, in spite of her woefully neglected education, and most ambitious to learn—a new ambition for her.

So they lent her books—English books : Dickens, Thackeray, Walter Scott—which she devoured in the silence of the night, the solitude of her little attic in the Rue des Pousse-Cailloux, and new worlds were revealed to her. She grew more English every day; and that was a good thing.

Trilby speaking English and Trilby speaking French were two different beings. Trilby's English was more or less that of her father, a highly-educated man; her mother, who was a Scotchwoman, although an uneducated one, had none of the ungainliness that mars the speech of so many Englishwomen in that humble rank—no droppings of the *h*, no broadening of the *o*'s and *a*'s.

Trilby's French was that of the Quartier Latin—droll, slangy, piquant, quaint, picturesque—quite the reverse of ungainly, but in which there was scarcely a turn of phrase that would not stamp the speaker as being hopelessly, emphatically " no lady ! " Though it was funny without being vulgar, it was perhaps a little *too* funny !

And she handled her knife and fork in the dainty English way, as no doubt her father had done—and his ; and, indeed, when alone with them she was so absolutely " like a lady " that it seemed quite odd (though very seductive) to see her in a grisette's cap and dress and apron. So much for her English training.

But enter a Frenchman or two, and a transformation effected itself immediately—a new incarnation of Trilby-ness—so droll and amusing that it was difficult to decide which of her two incarnations was the more attractive.

It must be admitted that she had her faults—like Little Billee.

For instance, she would be miserably jealous of any other woman who came to the studio, to sit or scrub or sweep or do anything else, even of the dirty tipsy old hag who sat for Taffy's " Found drowned "—" as if she couldn't have sat for it herself ! "

And then she would be cross and sulky, but not for long—an injured martyr, soon ready to forgive and be forgiven.

She would give up any sitting to come and sit to her three English friends. Even Durien had serious cause for complaint.

Then her affection was exacting : she always wanted to be told one was fond of her, and she dearly loved her own way, even in the sewing on of buttons and the darning of socks, which was innocent enough. But when it came to the cutting and fashioning of garments for a toreador's bride, it was a nuisance not to be borne !

" What could *she* know of toreadors' brides and their wedding-dresses ? " the Laird would indignantly ask—as if he were a toreador himself; and this was the aggravating side of her irrepressible Trilbyness.

In the caressing, demonstrative tenderness of her friendship she " made the soft eyes " at all three indiscriminately. But sometimes Little Billee would look up from his work as she was sitting to Taffy or the Laird, and find her gray eyes fixed on him with an all-enfolding gaze, so piercingly, penetratingly, unutterably sweet and kind and tender, such a brooding, dovelike look of soft and warm solicitude, that he would feel a flutter at his heart, and his hand would shake so that he could not paint; and in a waking dream he would remember that his mother had often looked at him like that when he was a small boy, and she a beautiful young woman untouched by care or sorrow; and the tear that always lay in readiness so close to the corner of Little Billee's eye would find it very difficult to keep itself in its proper place—unshed.

And at such moments the thought that Trilby sat for the figure would go through him like a knife.

She did not sit promiscuously to anybody who asked, it is true. But she still sat to Durien; to the great Gérôme; to M. Carrel, who scarcely used any other model.

It was poor Trilby's sad distinction that she surpassed all other models as Calypso surpassed her nymphs; and whether by long habit, or through some obtuseness in her nature, or lack of imagination, she was equally unconscious of self with her clothes on or without ! Truly, she could be naked and unashamed—in this respect an absolute savage.

She would have ridden through Coventry, like Lady Godiva—but without giving it a thought beyond wondering why the streets were empty and the shops closed and the blinds pulled down—would even have looked up to Peeping Tom's shutter with a friendly nod, had she known he was behind it.

In fact, she was abso-

" THE SOFT EYES "

lutely without that kind of shame, as she was without any kind of fear. But she was destined soon to know both fear and shame.

And here it would not be amiss for me to state a fact well known to all painters and sculptors who have used the nude model (except a few shady pretenders, whose purity, not being of the right sort, has gone rank from too much watching), namely, that nothing is so chaste as nudity. Venus herself, as she drops her garments and steps on to the model-throne, leaves behind her on the floor every weapon in her armoury by which she can pierce to the grosser passions of man. The more perfect her unveiled beauty, the more keenly it appeals to his higher instincts. And where her beauty fails (as it almost always does somewhere in the Venuses who sit for hire), the failure is so lamentably conspicuous in the studio light— the fierce light that beats on this particular throne—that Don Juan himself, who has not got to paint, were fain to hide his eyes in sorrow and disenchantment, and fly to other climes.

All beauty is sexless in the eyes of the artist at his work—the beauty of man, the beauty of woman, the heavenly beauty of the child, which is the sweetest and best of all.

Indeed it is woman, lovely woman, whose beauty falls the shortest, for sheer lack of proper physical training.

As for Trilby, G——, to whom she sat for his Phryne, once told me that the sight of her thus was a thing to melt Sir Galahad, yet sober Silenus, and chasten Jove himself— a thing to Quixotise a modern French masher ! I can well believe him. For myself, I only speak of Trilby as I have seen her—clothed and in her right mind. She never sat to me for any Phryne, never bared herself to me, nor did I ever dream of asking her. I would as soon have asked the Queen of Spain to let me paint her legs ! But I have worked from many female models in many countries, some of them the best of their kind. I have also, like Svengali, seen Taffy " trying to get himself clean," either at home or in the swimming-baths of the Seine ; and never a sitting woman among them all who could match for grace or finish or splendour of outward form that mighty York- shireman sitting in his tub, or sunning himself, like Ilyssus, at the Bains Henri Quatre, or taking his running header *à la hussarde*, off the springboard at the Bains Deligny, with a group of wondering Frenchmen gathered round.

Up he shot himself into mid-air with a sounding double downward kick, parabolically ; then, turning a splendid semi-demi-somersault against the sky, down he came headlong, his body straight and stiff as an arrow, and made his clean hole in the water without splash or sound, to reappear a hundred yards farther on !

" Sac à papier ! quel gaillard que cet Anglais, hein ? "

" A-t-on jamais vu un torse pareil ! "

" Et les bras, donc ! "

" Et les jambes, nom d'un tonnerre ! "

" Mâtin !   J'aimerais mieux être en colère contre lui qu'il ne soit en colère contre moi ! " etc. etc. etc.

Omne ignotum pro magnifico !

If our climate were such that we could go about without any clothes on, we probably should; in which case, although we should still murder and lie and steal and bear

ILYSSUS

false witness against our neighbour, and break the Sabbath Day, and take the Lord's name in vain, much deplorable wickedness of another kind would cease to exist for sheer lack of mystery; and Christianity would be relieved of its hardest task in this sinful world, and Venus Aphrodite (*alias* Aselgeia) would have to go a-begging along with the tailors and dresssmakers and bootmakers, and perhaps our bodies and limbs would be as those of the Theseus and Venus of Milo; who was no Venus, except in good looks !

At all events, there would be no cunning, cruel deceptions, no artful taking in of artless inexperience, no unduly hurried waking-up from Love's young dream, no handing down to posterity of hidden uglinesses and weaknesses, and worse !

And also many a flower, now born to blush unseen, would be reclaimed from its desert, and suffered to hold its own, and flaunt away with the best in the inner garden of roses ! And poor Miss Gale, the figure-model, would be permitted to eke out her slender earnings by teaching calisthenics and deportment to the daughters of the British upper middle-class at Miss Pinkerton's academy for young ladies, The Mall, Chiswick.

And here let me humbly apologise to the casual reader for the length and possible irrelevancy of this digression, and for its subject. To those who may find matter for sincere disapprobation or even grave offence in a thing that has always seemed to me so simple, so commonplace, as to be hardly worth talking or writing about, I can only plead sincerity equal to theirs, and as deep a love and reverence for the gracious, goodly shape that God is said to have made after His own image for inscrutable purposes of His own.

Nor, indeed, am I pleading for such a subversive and revolutionary measure as the wholesale abolition of clothes, being the chilliest of mortals, and quite unlike Mr. Theseus or Mr. Ilyssus either.

Sometimes Trilby would bring her little brother to the studio in the Place St. Anatole des Arts, in his *beaux habits de Pâques*, his hair well curled and pomatumed, his hands and face well washed.

He was a very engaging little mortal. The Laird would fill his pockets full of Scotch goodies, and paint him as a little Spaniard, in " Le Fils du Toréador," a sweet little Spaniard with blue eyes, and curly locks as light as tow, and a complexion of milk and roses, in singular and piquant contrast to his swarthy progenitors.

Taffy would use him as an Indian club or a dumb-bell, to the child's infinite delight, and swing him on the trapeze, and teach him *la boxe*.

And the sweetness and fun of his shrill, happy, infantile laughter (which was like an echo of Trilby's, only an octave higher) so moved and touched and tickled one that Taffy had to look quite fierce, so he might hide the strange delight of tenderness that somehow filled his manly bosom at the mere sound of it (lest Little Billee and the Laird should think him goody-goody); and the fiercer Taffy looked, the less this small mite was afraid of him.

Little Billee made a beautiful water-colour sketch of him, just as he was, and gave it to Trilby, who gave it to le père Martin, who gave it to his wife with strict injunctions not to sell it as an old master. Alas ! it *is* an old master now, and Heaven only knows who has got it !

Those were happy days for Trilby's little brother, happy days for Trilby, who was immensely fond of him, and very proud. And the happiest day of all was when the *trois Angliches* took Trilby and Jeannot (for so the mite was called) to spend the Sunday in the woods at Meudon, and breakfast and dine at the *garde champêtre's*. Swings, peep-shows, donkey-rides ; shooting at a mark with cross-bows and little pellets of clay, and smashing little plaster figures and winning macaroons ; losing one's self in the beautiful forest ; catching newts and tadpoles and young frogs ; making music on *mirlitons*. Trilby singing " Ben Bolt " into a *mirliton* was a thing to be remembered, whether one would or no !

Trilby on this occasion came out in a new character, *en demoiselle*, with a little black bonnet, and a gray jacket of her own making.

To look at (but for her loose, square-toed, heel-less silk boots laced up the inner side), she might have been the daughter of an English dean—until she undertook to teach the Laird some favourite cancan steps. And then the Laird himself, it must be admitted, no longer looked like the son of a worthy, God-fearing, Sabbath-keeping Scotch solicitor.

This was after dinner, in the garden, at *la loge du garde champêtre*. Taffy and Jeannot and Little Billee made the necessary music on their *mirlitons*, and the dancing soon became general, with plenty also to look on, for the *garde* had many customers who dined there on summer Sundays.

It is no exaggeration to say that Trilby was far and away the belle of that particular ball, and there have been worse balls in much finer company, and far plainer women !

Trilby lightly dancing the cancan (there are cancans and cancans) was a singularly gainly and seductive person—*et vera incessu patuit dea !* Here, again, she was funny without

" ' VOILÀ L'ESPAYCE DE HOM KER JER SWEE ! ' "

being vulgar. And for mere gracé (even in the cancan), she was the forerunner of Miss Kate Vaughan ; and for sheer fun, the precursor of Miss Nelly Farren !

And the Laird, trying to dance after her (" dongsong le konkong," as he called it), was too funny for words ; and if genuine popular success is a true test of humour, no greater humorist ever danced a *pas seul*.

What Englishmen could do in France during the fifties,

and yet manage to preserve their self-respect, and even the respect of their respectable French friends !

" Voilà l'espayce de hom ker jer swee ! " said the Laird, every time he bowed in acknowledgment of the applause that greeted his performance of various solo steps of his own—Scotch reels and sword-dances that came in admirably. . . .

Then, one fine day (as a judgment on him, no doubt), the Laird fell ill, and the doctor had to be sent for, and he ordered a nurse. But Trilby would hear of no nurses, not even a Sister of Charity ! She did all the nursing herself, and never slept a wink for three successive days and nights.

On the third day the Laird was out of all danger, the delirium was past, and the doctor found poor Trilby fast asleep by the bedside.

Madame Vinard, at the bedroom door, put her finger to her lips, and whispered : " Quel bonheur ! il est sauvé, M. le Docteur ; écoutez ! il dit ses prières en Anglais, ce brave garçon ! "

The good old doctor, who didn't understand a word of English, listened, and heard the Laird's voice, weak and low, but quite clear, and full of heartfelt fervour, intoning, solemnly :

" ' Green herbs, red peppers, mussels, saffron,
    Soles, onions, garlic, roach, and dace—
    All these you eat at Terré's Tavern
    In that one dish of bouillabaisse ! ' "

" Ah ! mais c'est très bien de sa part, ce brave jeune homme ! rendre grâces au ciel comme cela, quand le danger est passé ! très bien, très bien ! "

Sceptic and Voltairian as he was, and not the friend of prayer, the good doctor was touched, for he was old, and therefore kind and tolerant, and made allowances.

And afterwards he said such sweet things to Trilby about it all, and about her admirable care of his patient, that she positively wept with delight—like sweet Alice with hair so brown, whenever Ben Bolt gave her a smile.

All this sounds very goody-goody, but it's true.

So it will be easily understood how the *trois* Angliches

came in time to feel for Trilby quite a peculiar regard, and
looked forward with sorrowful forebodings to the day when
this singular and pleasant little quartet would have to be
broken up, each of them to spread his wings and fly away
on his own account, and poor Trilby to be left behind all by
herself. They would even frame little plans whereby she
might better herself in life, and avoid the many snares and
pitfalls that would beset her lonely path in the Quartier
Latin when they were gone.

Trilby never thought of such things as these; she took
short views of life, and troubled herself about no morrows.

There was, however, one jarring figure in her little fool's
paradise, a baleful and most ominous figure that constantly
crossed her path, and came between her and the sun, and
threw its shadow over her, and that was Svengali.

He also was a frequent visitor at the studio in the Place
St. Anatole, where much was forgiven him for the sake of
his music, especially when he came with Gecko and they
made music together. But it soon became apparent that
they did not come there to play to the three Angliches;
it was to see Trilby, whom they both had taken it into their
heads to adore, each in a different fashion :

Gecko, with a humble, doglike worship that expressed
itself in mute, pathetic deference and looks of lowly self-
depreciation, of apology for his own unworthy existence, as
though the only requital he would ever dare to dream
of were a word of decent politeness, a glance of tolerance
or good-will—a mere bone to a dog.

Svengali was a bolder wooer. When he cringed, it was
with a mock humility full of sardonic threats ; when he was
playful, it was with a terrible playfulness, like that of a cat
with a mouse—a weird, ungainly cat, and most unclean ;
a sticky, haunting, long, lean, uncanny, black spider-cat,
if there is such an animal outside a bad dream.

It was a great grievance to him that she had suffered
from no more pains in her eyes. She had; but preferred
to endure them rather than seek relief from *him*.

So he would playfully try to mesmerise her with his
glance, and sidle up nearer and nearer to her, making
passes and counter-passes, with stern command in his eyes,
till she would shake and shiver and almost sicken with fear,

and all but feel the spell come over her, as in a nightmare, and rouse herself with a great effort and escape.

If Taffy were there he would interfere with a friendly " Now then, old fellow, none of that ! " and a jolly slap on the back, which would make Svengali cough for an hour, and paralyse his mesmeric powers for a week.

Svengali had a stroke of good-fortune. He played at three grand concerts with Gecko, and had a well-deserved success. He even gave a concert of his own, which made a furore, and blossomed out into beautiful and costly clothes of quite original colour and shape and pattern, so that people would turn round and stare at him in the street— a thing he loved. He felt his fortune was secure, and ran into debt with tailors, hatters, shoemakers, jewellers, but paid none of his old debts to his friends. His pockets were always full of printed slips—things that had been written about him in the papers—and he would read them aloud to everybody he knew, especially to Trilby, as she sat darning socks on the model-throne while the fencing and boxing were in train. And he would lay his fame and his fortune at her feet, on condition that she should share her life with him.

" Ach, himmel, Drilpy ! " he would say, " you don't know what it is to be a great pianist like me—*hein ?* What is your Little Billee, with his stinking oil-bladders, sitting mum in his corner, his mahlstick and his palette in one hand, and his twiddling little footle pig's-hair brush in the other ! What noise does *he* make ? When his little fool of a picture is finished he will send it to London, and they will hang it on a wall with a lot of others, all in a line, like recruits called out for inspection, and the yawning public will walk by in procession and inspect, and say ' damn ! ' Svengali will go to London *himself.* Ha ! ha ! He will be all alone on a platform, and play as nobody else can play ; and hundreds of beautiful Engländerinnen will see and hear and go mad with love for him—Prinzessen, Comtessen, Serene English Altessen. They will soon lose their Serenity and their Highness when they hear Svengali ! They will invite him to their palaces, and pay him a thousand francs to play for them ; and after, he will loll in the best armchair, and they will sit all round him on footstools,

and bring him tea and gin and *küchen* and *marrons glacés,*
and lean over him and fan him—for he is tired after playing them for a thousand francs of Chopin ! Ha, ha ! I
know all about it—*hein ?*

" And he will not look at them, even ! He will look
inward, at his own dream—and his dream will be about
Drilpy—to lay his talent, his glory, his thousand francs at
her beautiful white feet !

" Their stupid, big, fat, tow-headed, putty-nosed
husbands will be mad with jealousy, and long to box him,
but they will be afraid. Ach ! those beautiful Anclaises !
they will think it an honour to mend his shirts, to sew
buttons on his pantaloons ; to darn his socks, as you are
doing now for that sacred imbecile of a Scotchman who is
always trying to paint toréadors, or that sweating, pig-
headed bullock of an Englander who is always trying to get
himself dirty and then to get himself clean again !—*e da
capo !*

" Himmel ! what big socks are those ! what potato-
sacks !

" Look at your Taffy ! what is he good for but to bang
great musicians on the back with his big bear's paw ! He
finds that droll, the bullock ! . . . .

" Look at your Frenchmen there—your damned conceited *verfluchte* pig-dogs of Frenchmen—Durien, Barizel,
Bouchardy ! What can a Frenchman talk of, *hein ?*
Only himself, and run down everybody else ! His vanity
makes me sick ! He always thinks the world is talking
about *him,* the fool ! He forgets that there is a fellow
called *Svengali* for the world to talk about ! I tell you,
Drilpy, it is about *me* the world is talking—me and nobody
else—me, me, me !

" Listen what they say in the *Figaro* (reads it).

" What do you think of that, *hein ?* What would
your Durien say if people wrote of *him* like that ?

" But you are not listening, sapperment ! great big she-
fool that you are—sheep's-head ! Dummkopf ! Donnerwetter ! you are looking at the chimney-pots when
Svengali talks ! Look a little lower down between the
houses, on the other side of the river ! There is a little
ugly gray building there, and inside are eight slanting

slabs of brass, all of a row, like beds in a school dormitory, and one fine day you shall lie asleep on one of those slabs— you, Drilpy, who would not listen to Svengali, and there- fore lost him ! . . . And over the middle of you will be a little leather apron, and over your head a little brass tap, and all day long and all night the cold water shall trickle, trickle, trickle all the way down your beautiful white body to your beautiful white feet till they turn green, and your poor, damp, draggled, muddy rags will hang above you from the ceiling for your friends to know you by; drip, drip, drip ! But you will have no friends. . . .

"And people of all sorts, strangers, will stare at you through the big plate-glass window—Englanders, chiffon- niers, painters and sculptors, workmen, piou-pious, old hags of washerwomen—and say, 'Ah ! what a beautiful woman was that ! Look at her ! She ought to be rolling in her carriage and pair !' And just then who should come by, rolling in his carriage and pair, smothered in furs, and smoking a big cigar of the Havana, but Sven- gali, who will jump out, and push the canaille aside, and say, 'Ha ! ha ! that is la grande Drilpy, who would not listen to Svengali, but looked at the chimney-pots when he told her of his manly love, and——' "

" Hi ! damn it, Svengali, what the devil are you talking to Trilby about ? You're making her sick ; can't you see ? Leave off, and go to the piano, man, or I'll come and slap you on the back again ! "

Thus would that sweating, pig-headed bullock of an Englander stop Svengali's love-making and release Trilby from bad quarters of an hour.

Then Svengali, who had a wholesome dread of the pig- headed bullock, would go to the piano and make impossible discords, and say : " Dear Drilpy, come and sing ' Pen Polt !' I am thirsting for those so beautiful chest notes ! Come ! "

Poor Trilby needed little pressing when she was asked to sing, and would go through her lamentable performance, to the great discomfort of Little Billee. It lost nothing of its grotesqueness from Svengali's accompaniment, which was a triumph of cacophony, and he would encourage her— *Très pien, très pien, ça y est !*

TIT FOR TAT

When it was over, Svengali would test her ear, as he called it, and strike the C in the middle and then the F just above, and ask which was the highest; and she would declare they were both exactly the same. It was only when he struck a note in the bass and another in the treble that she could perceive any difference, and said that the first sounded like Père Martin blowing up his wife, and the second like her little godson trying to make the peace between them.

She was quite tone-deaf, and didn't know it; and he would pay her extravagant compliments on her musical talent, till Taffy would say: "Look here, Svengali, let's hear *you* sing a song!"

And he would tickle him so masterfully under the ribs that the creature howled and became quite hysterical.

Then Svengali would vent his love of teasing on Little Billee, and pin his arms behind his back and swing him round, saying: "Himmel! what's this for an arm? It's like a girl's!"

"It's strong enough to paint!" said Little Billee.

"And what's this for a leg? It's like a mahlstick!"

"It's strong enough to kick, if you don't leave off!"

And Little Billee, the young and tender, would let out his little heel and kick the German's shins; and just as the German was going to retaliate, big Taffy would pin *his* arms and make him sing another song, more discordant than Trilby's—for he didn't dream of kicking Taffy: of that you may be sure!

Such was Svengali—only to be endured for the sake of his music—always ready to vex, frighten, bully, or torment anybody or anything smaller and weaker than himself—from a woman or a child to a mouse or a fly.

PART THIRD

" Par deçà, ne dela la mer
Ne sçay dame ni damoiselle
Qui soit en tous biens parfaits telle—
C'est un songe que d'y penser :
Dieu ! qu'il fait bon la regarder ! "

ONE lovely Monday morning in late September, at about
eleven or so, Taffy and the Laird sat in the studio—each
opposite his picture, smoking, nursing his knee, and saying
nothing. The heaviness of Monday weighed on their
spirits more than usual, for the three friends had returned
late on the previous night from a week spent at Barbizon
and in the forest of Fontainebleau—a heavenly week
among the painters; Rousseau, Millet, Corot, Daubigny,
let us suppose, and others less known to fame this day.
Little Billee, especially, had been fascinated by all this
artistic life in blouses and sabots and immense straw hats
and panamas, and had sworn to himself and to his friends
that he would some day live and die there—painting the
forest as it is, and peopling it with beautiful people out of
his own fancy—leading a healthy outdoor life of simple
wants and lofty aspirations.

At length Taffy said : " Bother work this morning !
I feel much more like a stroll in the Luxembourg Gardens
and lunch at the Café de l'Odén, where the omelets are
good and the wine isn't blue."

" The very thing I was thinking of myself," said the
Laird.

So Taffy slipped on his old shooting-jacket and his old
Harrow cricket cap, with the peak turned the wrong way,
and the Laird put on an old greatcoat of Taffy's that
reached to his heels, and a battered straw hat they had
found in the studio when they took it ; and both sallied
forth into the mellow sunshine on the way to Carrel's.
For they meant to seduce Little Billee from his work, that
he might share in their laziness, greediness, and general
demoralisation.

THE HAPPY LIFE

And whom should they meet coming down the narrow turreted Rue Vielle des Trois Mauvais Ladres but Little Billee himself, with an air of general demoralisation so tragic that they were quite alarmed. He had his paint-box and field-easel in one hand and his little valise in the other. He was pale, his hat on the back of his head, his hair starting all at sixes and sevens, like a sick Scotch terrier's.

"Good Lord! what's the matter?" said Taffy.

"Oh! oh! oh! she's sitting at Carrel's!"

"Who's sitting at Carrel's?"

"Trilby! sitting to all those ruffians! There she was, just as I opened the door; I saw her, I tell you! The sight of her was like a blow between the eyes, and I bolted! I shall never go back to that beastly hole again! I'm off to Barbizon, to paint the forest; I was coming round to tell you. Good-bye! . . ."

"Stop a minute—are you mad?" said Taffy, collaring him.

"Let me go, Taffy—let me go, damn it! I'll come back in a week—but I'm going now! Let me go; do you hear?"

" ' LET ME GO, TAFFY . . . ' "

" But look here—I'll go with you."

" No; I want to be alone—quite alone. Let me go, I tell you ! "

" I shan't let you go unless you swear to me, on your honour, that you'll write directly you get there, and every day till you come back. Swear ! "

" All right; I swear—honour bright ! Now there ! Good-bye—good-bye; back on Sunday—good-bye ! " And he was off.

" Now, what the devil does all that mean ? " asked Taffy, much perturbed.

" I suppose he's shocked at seeing Trilby in that guise, or disguise, or unguise, sitting at Carrel's—he's such an odd little chap. And I must say, I'm surprised at Trilby. It's a bad thing for her when we're away. What could have induced her ? She never sat in a studio of that kind before. I thought she only sat to Durien and old Carrel."

They walked for a while in silence.

" Do you know, I've got a horrid idea that the little fool's in love with her ! "

" I've long had a horrid idea that *she's* in love with *him*."

" That would be a very stupid business," said Taffy.

They walked on, brooding over those two horrid ideas, and the more they brooded, considered, and remembered, the more convinced they became that both were right.

" Here's a pretty kettle of fish ! " said the Laird—" and talking of fish, let's go and lunch."

And so demoralised were they that Taffy ate three omelets without thinking, and the Laird drank two half-bottles of wine, and Taffy three, and they walked about the whole of that afternoon for fear Trilby should come to the studio—and were very unhappy.

This is how Trilby came to sit at Carrel's studio :

Carrel had suddenly taken it into his head that he would spend a week there, and paint a figure among his pupils, that they might see and paint with—and if possible like —him. And he had asked Trilby as a great favour to be the model, and Trilby was so devoted to the great Carrel that she readily consented. So that Monday morning found her there, and Carrel posed her as Ingres's famous

figure in his picture called "La Source," holding an
earthenware pitcher on her shoulder.

And the work began in religious silence. Then in five
minutes or so Little Billee came bursting in, and as soon
as he caught sight of her he stopped and stood as one petri-
fied, his shoulders up, his
eyes staring. Then lifting
his arms, he turned and
fled.

"Qu'est ce qu'il a donc,
ce Litrebili?" exclaimed
one or two students (for
they had turned his Eng-
lish nickname into French).

"Perhaps he's forgotten
something," said another.
"Perhaps he's forgotten
to brush his teeth and
part his hair!"

"Perhaps he's forgot
ten to say his prayers!"
said Barizel.

"He'll come back, I
hope!" exclaimed the
master.

And the incident gave
rise to no further com-
ment.

But Trilby was much
disquieted, and fell to
wondering what on earth
was the matter.

"'QU'EST CE QU'IL A DONC,
CE LITREBILI?'"

At first she wondered in French : French of the Quartier
Latin. She had not seen Little Billee for a week, and
wondered if he were ill. She had looked forward so much
to his painting her—painting her beautifully—and hoped
he would soon come back, and lose no time.

Then she began to wonder in English—nice clean English
of the studio in the Place St. Anatole des Arts—her father's
English—and suddenly a quick thought pierced her through
and through, and made the flesh tingle on her insteps and

the backs of her hands, and bathed her brow and temples with sweat.

She had good eyes, and Little Billee had a singularly expressive face.

Could it possibly be that he was *shocked* at seeing her sitting there?

She knew that he was peculiar in many ways. She remembered that neither he nor Taffy nor the Laird had ever asked her to sit for the figure, though she would have been only too delighted to do so for them. She also remembered how Little Billee had always been silent whenever she alluded to her posing for the " altogether," as she called it, and had sometimes looked pained and always very grave.

She turned alternately pale and red, pale and red all over, again and again, as the thought grew up in her—and soon the growing thought became a torment.

This new-born feeling of shame was unendurable—its birth a travail that racked and rent every fibre of her moral being, and she suffered agonies beyond anything she had ever felt in her life.

" What is the matter with you, my child? Are you ill? " asked Carrel, who, like every one else, was very fond of her, and to whom she had sat as a child (" L'Enfance de Psyché," now in the Luxembourg Gallery, was painted from her).

She shook her head, and the work went on.

Presently she dropped her pitcher, that broke into bits; and putting her two hands to her face she burst into tears and sobs—and there, to the amazement of everybody, she stood crying like a big baby—*La source aux larmes ?*

" What *is* the matter, my poor dear child? " said Carrel, jumping up and helping her off the throne.

" Oh, I don't know—I don't know—I'm ill—very ill—let me go home ! "

And with kind solicitude and despatch they helped her on with her clothes, and Carrel sent for a cab and took her home.

And on the way she dropped her head on his shoulder, and wept, and told him all about it as well as she could, and Monsieur Carrel had tears in his eyes too, and wished

REPENTANCE

to Heaven he had never induced her to sit for the figure, either then or at any other time. And pondering deeply and sorrowfully on such terrible responsibility (he had grown-up daughters of his own), he went back to the studio; and in an hour's time they got another model and another pitcher, and went to work again. So the pitcher went to the well once more.

And Trilby, as she lay disconsolate on her bed all that day and all the next, and all the next again, thought of her past life with agonies of shame and remorse that made the pain in her eyes seem as a light and welcome relief. For it came, and tortured worse and lasted longer than it had ever done before. But she soon found, to her miserable bewilderment, that mind-aches are the worst of all.

Then she decided that she must write to one of the *trois* Angliches, and chose the Laird.

She was more familiar with him than with the other two : it was impossible not to be familiar with the Laird if he liked one, as he was so easy-going and demonstrative, for all that he was such a canny Scot ! Then she had nursed him through his illness; she had often hugged and kissed him before the whole studio full of people—and even when alone with him it had always seemed quite natural for her to do so. It was like a child caressing a favourite young uncle or elder brother. And though the good Laird was the least susceptible of mortals, he would often find these innocent blandishments a somewhat trying ordeal ! She had never taken such a liberty with Taffy; and as for Little Billee, she would sooner have died !

So she wrote to the Laird. I give her letter without the spelling, which was often faulty, although her nightly readings had much improved it :

" MY DEAR FRIEND—I am very unhappy. I was sitting at Carrel's, in the Rue des Potirons, and Little Billee came in, and was so shocked and disgusted that he ran away and never came back.

" I saw it all in his face.

" I sat there because M. Carrel asked me to. He has

always been very kind to me—M. Carrel—ever since I was
a child; and I would do anything to please him, but never
that again.

" He was there too.

" I never thought anything about sitting before. I sat
first as a child to M. Carrel. Mamma made me, and made
me promise not to tell papa, and so I didn't. It soon
seemed as natural to sit for people as to run errands for
them, or wash and mend their clothes. Papa wouldn't
have liked my doing that either, though we wanted the
money badly. And so he never knew.

" I have sat for the ' altogether ' to several other people
besides—M. Gérôme, Durien, the two Hennequins, and
Émile Baratier; and for the head and hands to lots of
people, and for the feet only to Charles Faure, André
Besson, Mathieu Dumoulin, and Collinet. Nobody else.

" It seemed as natural for me to sit as for a man. Now I
see the awful difference.

" And I have done dreadful things besides, as you must
know—as all the Quartier knows. Baratier and Besson;
but not Durien, though people think so. Nobody else, I
swear—except old Monsieur Penque at the beginning, who
was mamma's friend.

" It makes me almost die of shame and misery to think
of it; for that's not like sitting. I knew how wrong it was
all along—and there's no excuse for me, none. Though
lots of people do as bad, and nobody in the Quartier seems
to think any the worse of them.

" If you and Taffy and Little Billee cut me, I really
think I shall go mad and die. Without your friendship
I shouldn't care to live a bit. Dear Sandy, I love your
little finger better than any man or woman I ever met;
and Taffy's and Little Billee's little fingers too.

" What shall I do? I daren't go out for fear of meeting
one of you. Will you come and see me?

" I am never going to sit again, not even for the face and
hands. I am going back to be a *blanchisseuse de fin* with
my old friend Angèle Boisse, who is getting on very well
indeed, in the Rue des Cloîtres Ste. Pétronille.

" You *will* come and see me, won't you? I shall be in
all day till you do. Or else I will meet yousome where,

if you will tell me where and when; or else I will go and
see you in the studio, if you are sure to be alone. Please
don't keep me waiting long for an answer.

" You don't know what I'm suffering.

" Your ever loving, faithful friend,

"TRILBY O'FERRALL."

She sent this letter by hand, and the Laird came in
less than ten minutes after she had sent it; and she hugged
and kissed and cried over him so that he was almost ready
to cry himself; but he burst out laughing instead—which
was better and more in his line, and very much more
comforting—and talked to her so nicely and kindly and
naturally that by the time he left her humble attic in the
Rue des Pousse-Cailloux her very aspect, which had quite
shocked him when he first saw her, had almost become what
it usually was.

The little room under the leads, with its sloping roof and
mansard window, was as scrupulously neat and clean as if
its tenant had been a holy sister who taught the noble
daughters of France at some Convent of the Sacred Heart.
There were nasturtiums and mignonette on the outer
window-sill, and convolvulus was trained to climb round
the window.

As she sat by his side on the narrow white bed, clasping
and stroking his painty, turpentiny hand, and kissing it
every five minutes, he talked to her like a father—as he
told Taffy afterwards—and scolded her for having been so
silly as not to send for him directly, or come to the studio.
He said how glad he was, how glad they would all be, that
she was going to give up sitting for the figure—not, of
course, that there was any real harm in it, but it was
better not—and especially how happy it would make them
to feel she intended to live straight for the future. Little
Billee was to remain at Barbizon for a little while; but she
must promise to come and dine with Taffy and himself that
very day, and cook the dinner; and when he went back to
his picture, " Les Noces du Toréador "—saying to her as
he left, " à ce soir donc, mille sacrés tonnerres de nong de
Dew ! "—he left the happiest woman in the whole Latin
Quarter behind him : she had confessed and been forgiven.

CONFESSION

And with shame and repentance and confession and forgiveness had come a strange new feeling—that of a dawning self-respect.

Hitherto, for Trilby, self-respect had meant little more than the mere cleanliness of her body, in which she had always revelled; alas! it was one of the conditions of her humble calling. It now meant another kind of cleanliness, and she would luxuriate in it for evermore; and the dreadful past—never to be forgotten by her—should be so lived down as in time, perhaps, to be forgotten by others.

The dinner that evening was a memorable one for Trilby. After she had washed up the knives and forks and plates and dishes, and put them by, she sat and sewed. She wouldn't even smoke her cigarette, it reminded her so of things and scenes she now hated. No more cigarettes for Trilby O'Ferrall.

They all talked of Little Billee. She heard about the way he had been brought up, about his mother and sister, the people he had always lived among. She also heard (and her heart alternately rose and sank as she listened) what his future was likely to be, and how rare his genius was, and how great—if his friends were to be trusted. Fame and Fortune would soon be his—such fame and fortune as fall to the lot of very few—unless anything should happen to spoil his promise and mar his prospects in life, and ruin a splendid career; and the rising of the heart was all for him, the sinking for herself. How could she ever hope to be even the friend of such a man? Might she ever hope to be his servant—his faithful, humble servant?

Little Billee spent a month at Barbizon, and when he came back it was with such a brown face that his friends hardly knew him; and he brought with him such studies as made his friends " sit up."

The crushing sense of their own hopeless inferiority was lost in wonder at his work, in love and enthusiasm for the workman.

Their Little Billee, so young and tender, so weak of body, so strong of purpose, so warm of heart, so light of hand, so keen and quick and piercing of brain and eye, was their master, to be stuck on a pedestal and looked up to and bowed down to, to be watched and warded and worshipped for evermore.

When Trilby came in from her work at six, and he shook hands with her and said " Hullo, Trilby ! " her face turned pale to the lips, her under lip quivered, and she gazed down at him (for she was among the tallest of her sex) with such a moist, hungry, wide-eyed look of humble craving adoration that the Laird felt his worst fears were realised : and the look Little Billee sent up in return filled the manly bosom of Taffy with an equal apprehension.

Then they all four went and dined together at le père Trin's, and Trilby went back to her *blanchisserie de fin.*

Next day Little Billee took his work to show Carrel, and Carrel invited him to come and finish his picture " The Pitcher Goes to the Well " at his own private studio—an unheard-of favour, which the boy accepted with a thrill of proud gratitude and affectionate reverence.

So little was seen for some time of Little Billee at the studio in the Place St. Anatole des Arts, and little of Trilby ; a *blanchisseuse de fin* has not many minutes to spare from her irons. But they often met at dinner. And on Sunday mornings Trilby came to repair the Laird's linen and darn his socks and look after his little comforts, as usual, and spend a happy day. And on Sunday afternoons the studio would be as lively as ever, with the fencing and boxing, the piano-playing and fiddling—all as it used to be.

And week by week the friends noticed a gradual and subtle change in Trilby. She was no longer slangy in French, unless it were now and then by a slip of the tongue, no longer so facetious and droll, and yet she seemed even happier than she had ever seemed before.

Also, she grew thinner, especially in the face, where the bones of her cheeks and jaws began to show themselves, and these bones were constructed on such right principles (as were those of her brow and chin and the bridge of her nose) that the improvement was astonishing, almost inexplicable.

Also, she lost her freckles as the summer waned and she herself went less into the open air. And she let her hair grow, and made of it a small knot at the back of her head,

and showed her little flat ears, which were charming, and just in the right place, very far back and rather high; Little Billee could not have placed them better himself. Also, her mouth, always too large, took on a firmer and sweeter outline, and her big British teeth were so white and regular that even Frenchmen forgave them their British bigness. And a new soft brightness came into her eyes that no one had ever seen there before. They were stars, just twin gray stars—or rather planets just thrown off by some new sun, for the steady mellow light they gave out was not entirely their own.

Favourite types of beauty change with each succeeding generation. These were the days of Buckner's aristocratic Album beauties, with lofty foreheads, oval faces, little aquiline noses, heart-shaped little mouths, soft dimpled chins, drooping shoulders, and long side ringlets that fell over them —the Lady Arabellas and the Lady Clementinas, Musidoras and Medoras ! A type that will perhaps come back to us some day. May the present scribe be dead !

" TWIN GRAY STARS "

Trilby's type would be infinitely more admired now than in the fifties. Her photograph would be in the shop-windows. Sir Edward Burne-Jones—if I may make so bold as to say so—would perhaps have marked her for his own, in spite of her almost too exuberant joyousness and irrepressible vitality. Rossetti might have evolved another new formula from her; Sir John Millais another old one of the kind that is always new and never sates nor palls— like Clytie, let us say—ever old and ever new as love itself !

Trilby's type was in singular contrast to the type Gavarni had made so popular in the Latin Quarter at the period we are writing of, so that those who fell so readily under her charm were rather apt to wonder why. More-

over, she was thought much too tall for her sex, and her
day, and her station in life, and especially for the country
she lived in. She hardly looked up to a bold gendarme !
and a bold gendarme was nearly as tall as a *dragon de la
garde,* who was nearly as tall as an average English policeman. Not that she was a giantess, by any means. She
was about as tall as Miss Ellen Terry—and that is a
charming height, *I* think.

One day Taffy remarked to the Laird : "Hang it !
I'm blest if Trilby isn't the handsomest woman I know !
She looks like a grande dame masquerading as a grisette—
almost like a joyful saint at times. She's lovely ! By
Jove ! I couldn't stand her hugging me as she does you !
There'd be a tragedy—say the slaughter of Little Billee."

"Ah ! Taffy, my boy," rejoined the Laird, " when those
long sisterly arms are round my neck it isn't *me* she's
hugging."

" And then," said Taffy, " what a trump she is ! Why,
she's as upright and straight and honourable as a man !
And what she says to one about one's self is always so
pleasant to hear ! That's Irish, I suppose. And, what's
more, it's always true."

" Ah, that's Scotch ! " said the Laird, and tried to wink
at Little Billee, but Little Billee wasn't there.

Even Svengali perceived the strange metamorphosis.
" Ach, Drilpy," he would say, on a Sunday-afternoon,
" how beautiful you are ! It drives me mad ! I adore
you. I like you thinner; you have such beautiful bones !
Why do you not answer my letters ? What ! you do not
read them ? You *burn* them ? And yet I—— Donnerwetter ! I forgot ! The grisettes of the Quartier Latin
have not learned how to read or write; they have only
learned how to dance the cancan with the dirty little pig-
dog monkeys they call men. Sacrement ! *We* will teach
the little pig-dog monkeys to dance something else some
day, we Germans. We will make music for them to dance
to ! Boum ! boum ! Better than the waiter at the Café
de la Rotonde, *hein ?* And the grisettes of the Quartier
Latin shall pour us out your little white wine—*fotre betit
fin planc,* as your pig-dog monkey of a poet says, your
rotten *verfluchter* De Musset, ' who has got such a splendid

future behind him!' Bah! What do *you* know of Monsieur Alfred de Musset? We have got a poet too, my Drilpy. His name is Heinrich Heine. If he's still alive, he lives in Paris, in a little street off the Champs Élysées. He lies in bed all day long, and only sees out of one eye, like the Countess Hahn-Hahn, ha! ha! He adores French grisettes. He married one. Her name is Mathilde, and she has got *süssen füssen*, like you. He would adore you too, for your beautiful bones; he would like to count them one by one, for he is very playful, like me. And, ach! what a beautiful skeleton you will make! And very soon, too, because you do not smile on your madly-loving Svengali. You burn his letters without reading them! You shall have a nice little mahogany glass case all to yourself in the museum of the École de Médecine, and Svengali shall come in his new fur-lined coat, smoking his big cigar of the Havana, and push the dirty carabins out of the way, and look through the holes of your eyes into your stupid empty skull, and up the nostrils of your high, bony sounding-board of a nose without either a tip or a lip to it, and into the roof of your big mouth, with your thirty-two big English teeth, and between your big ribs into your big chest, where the big leather lungs used to be, and say, ' Ach! what a pity she had no more music in her than a big tom-cat!' And then he will look all down your bones to your poor crumbling feet, and say, ' Ach! what a fool she was not to answer Svengali's letters!' and the dirty carabins shall——"

"Shut up, you sacred fool, or I'll precious soon spoil *your* skeleton for you."

Thus the short-tempered Taffy, who had been listening.

Then Svengali, scowling, would play Chopin's funeral march more divinely than ever; and where the pretty soft part comes in, he would whisper to Trilby, "That is Svengali coming to look at you in your little mahogany glass case!"

And here let me say that these vicious imaginations of Svengali's, which look so tame in English print, sounded much more ghastly in French, pronounced with a Hebrew-German accent, and uttered in his hoarse, rasping, nasal, throaty rook's caw, his big yellow teeth baring themselves in a mongrel canine snarl, his heavy upper eyelids drooping over his insolent black eyes.

Besides which, as he played the lovely melody he would go through a ghoulish pantomime, as though he were taking stock of the different bones in her skeleton with greedy but discriminating approval. And when he came down to the feet, he was almost droll in the intensity of his terrible realism. But Trilby did not appreciate this exquisite fooling, and felt cold all over.

He seemed to her a dread powerful demon, who, but for Taffy (who alone could hold him in check), oppressed and weighed on her like an incubus—and she dreamed of him oftener than she dreamed of Taffy, the Laird, or even Little Billee !

" AN INCUBUS "

Thus pleasantly and smoothly, and without much change or adventure, things went on till Christmas-time.

Little Billee seldom spoke of Trilby, or Trilby of him. Work went on every morning at the studio in the Place St. Anatole des Arts, and pictures were begun and finished —little pictures that didn't take long to paint—the Laird's Spanish bull-fighting scenes, in which the bull never appeared, and which he sent to his native Dundee and sold there; Taffy's tragic little dramas of life in the slums of Paris—starvings, drownings—suicides by charcoal and poison—which he sent everywhere, but did not sell.

Little Billee was painting all this time at Carrel's studio —his private one—and seemed preoccupied and happy when they all met at meal-time, and less talkative even than usual.

He had always been the least talkative of the three; more prone to listen, and no doubt to think the more.

In the afternoon people came and went as usual, and boxed and fenced and did gymnastic feats, and felt Taffy's biceps, which by this time equalled Mr. Sandow's!

Some of these people were very pleasant and remarkable, and have become famous since then in England, France, America—or have died, or married, and come to grief or glory in other ways. It is the Ballad of the Bouillabaisse all over again!

It might be worth while my trying to sketch some of the more noteworthy, now that my story is slowing for a while —like a French train when the engine-driver sees a long curved tunnel in front of him, as I do—and no light at the other end!

My humble attempts at characterisation might be useful as *mémoires pour servir* to future biographers. Besides, there are other reasons, as the reader will soon discover.

There was Durien, for instance—Trilby's especial French adorer, *pour le bon motif!* a son of the people, a splendid sculptor, a very fine character in every way—so perfect, indeed, that there is less to say about him than any of the others—modest, earnest, simple, frugal, chaste, and of untiring industry; living for his art, and perhaps also a little for Trilby, whom he would have been only too glad to marry. He was Pygmalion; she was his Galatea —a Galatea whose marble heart would never beat for *him!*

Durien's house is now the finest in the Parc Monceau; his wife and daughters are the best-dressed women in Paris, and he one of the happiest of men; but he will never quite forget poor Galatea:

" La belle aux pieds d'albâtre—aux deux talons de rose!"

Then there was Vincent, a Yankee medical student, who could both work and play.

He is now one of the greatest oculists in the world, and Europeans cross the Atlantic to consult him. He can still play, and when he crosses the Atlantic himself for that purpose he has to travel incognito like a royalty, lest his play should be marred by work. And his daughters are so beautiful and accomplished that British dukes have sighed after them in vain. Indeed, these fair young ladies spend their autumn holiday in refusing the British aristocracy. We are told so in the society papers, and I can quite believe it. Love is not always blind; and if he is, Vincent is the man to cure him.

In those days he prescribed for us all round, and punched and stethoscoped us, and looked at our tongues for love, and told us what to eat, drink, and avoid, and even where to go for it.

For instance : late one night Little Billee woke up in a cold sweat, and thought himself a dying man—he had felt seedy all day and taken no food; so he dressed and dragged himself to Vincent's hotel, and woke him up, and said, " Oh, Vincent, Vincent ! I'm a dying man ! " and all but fainted on his bed. Vincent felt him all over with the greatest care, and asked him many questions. Then, looking at his watch, he delivered himself thus : " Humph! 3.30 ! rather late—but still—look here, Little Billee—do you know the Halle, on the other side of the water, where they sell vegetables ? "

" Oh yes ! yes ! What vegetable shall I——"

" Listen ! On the north side are two restaurants— Bordier and Baratte. They remain open all night. Now go straight off to one of those tuck shops, and tuck in as big a supper as you possibly can. Some people prefer Baratte. I prefer Bordier myself. Perhaps you'd better try Bordier first and Baratte after. At all events, lose no time; so off you go ! "

Thus he saved Little Billee from an early grave.

Then there was the Greek, a boy of only sixteen, but six feet high, and looking ten years older than he was, and able to smoke even stronger tobacco than Taffy himself, and colour pipes divinely ; he was a great favourite in the Place St. Anatole, for his *bonhommie*, his niceness, his warm geniality. He was the capitalist of this select circle (and nobly lavish of his capital). He went by the name of Poluphloisboiospaleapologos Petrilopetrolicoconose—for so he was christened by the Laird—because his real name was thought much too long; and much too lovely for the Quartier Latin, and reminded one too much of the Isles of Greece—where burnîng Sappho loved and sang. What was he learning in the Latin Quarter? French? He spoke French like a native! Nobody knows. But when his Paris friends transferred their Bohemia to London, where were they ever made happier and more at home than in his lordly parental abode—or fed with nicer things?

That abode is now his, and lordlier than ever, as becomes the dwelling of a millionaire and city magnate; and its gray-bearded owner is as genial, as jolly, and as hospitable as in the old Paris days, but he no longer colours pipes.

Then there was Carnegie, fresh from Balliol, redolent of the 'varsity. He intended himself then for the diplomatic service, and came to Paris to learn French as it is spoke; and spent most of his time with his fashionable English friends on the right side of the river, and the rest with Taffy, the Laird, and Little Billee on the left. Perhaps that is why he has not become an ambassador. He is now only a rural dean, and speaks the worst French I know, and speaks it wherever and whenever he can.

It serves him right, I think.

He was fond of lords, and knew some (at least, he gave one that impression), and often talked of them, and dressed so beautifully that even Little Billee was abashed in his presence. Only Taffy, in his threadbare, out-at-elbow shooting-jacket and cricket-cap, and the Laird, in his tattered straw hat and Taffy's old overcoat down to his heels, dared to walk arm-in-arm with him—nay, insisted on doing so—as they listened to the band in the Luxembourg Gardens.

And his whiskers were even longer and thicker and more golden than Taffy's own. But the mere sight of a boxing-glove made him sick.

Then there was the yellow-haired Antony, a Swiss—the idle apprentice, *le roi des truands*, as we called him—to whom everything was forgiven, as to François Villon, *à cause de ses gentillesses*—surely, for all his reprehensible

THE CAPITALIST AND THE SWELL

pranks, the gentlest and most lovable creature that ever
lived in Bohemia, or out of it.

Always in debt, like Svengali, for he had no more notion
of the value of money than a humming-bird, and gave away
in reckless generosity to friends what in strictness belonged
to his endless creditors; like Svengali, humorous, witty,
and a most exquisite and original artist, and also somewhat
eccentric in his attire (though scrupulously clean), so that
people would stare at him as he walked along—a thing that
always gave him dire offence ! But, unlike Svengali, full
of delicacy, refinement, and distinction of mind and
manner, void of any self-conceit; and, in spite of the
irregularities of his life, the very soul of truth and honour,
as gentle as he was chivalrous and brave; the warmest,
staunchest, sincerest, most unselfish friend in the world;
and, as long as his purse was full, the best and drollest
boon companion in the world—but that was not for
ever !

When the money was gone, then would Antony hie
him to some beggearly attic in some lost Parisian slum,
and write his own epitaph in lovely French or German
verse—or even English (for he was an astounding linguist);
and telling himself that he was forsaken by family, friends,
and mistress alike, look out of his casement over the Paris
chimney-pots for the last time, and listen once more to
" the harmonies of nature," as he called it, and " aspire
towards the infinite," and bewail " the cruel deceptions of
his life," and finally lay himself down to die of sheer
starvation.

And as he lay and waited for his release, that was so long
in coming, he would beguile the weary hours by mumbling
a crust " watered with his own salt tears," and decorating
his epitaph with fanciful designs of the most exquisite
humour, pathos, and beauty; these early illustrated
epitaphs of the young Antony, of which there still exist
a goodly number, are now priceless, as all collectors know
all over the world.

Fainter and fainter would he grow, and finally, on the
third day or thereabouts, a remittance would reach him
from some long-suffering sister or aunt in far Lausanne;
or else the fickle mistress or faithless friend (who had been

looking for him all over Paris) would discover his hiding-place, the beautiful epitaph would be walked off in triumph to le père Marcas in the Rue du Ghette and sold for twenty, fifty, a hundred francs; and then *vogue la galère!* and back again to Bohemia, dear Bohemia and all its joys, as long as the money lasted . . . *e poi, da capo!*

And now that his name is a household word in two hemispheres, and he himself an honour and a glory to the land he has adopted as his own, he loves to remember all this, and look back from the lofty pinnacle on which he sits perched up aloft to the impecunious days of his idle apprenticeship—*le bon temps où l'on était si malheureux!*

And with all that Quixotic dignity of his, so famous is he as a wit that when he jokes (and he is always joking), people laugh first, and then ask what he was joking about, and you can make your own mild funniments raise a roar by merely prefacing them " as Antony once said ! "

The present scribe has often done so. And if by a happy fluke you should some day hit upon a really good thing of your own—good enough to be quoted—be sure it will come back to you after many days prefaced " as Antony once said ! "

And these jokes are so good-natured that you almost resent their being made at anybody's expense but your own! Never from Antony :

> " The aimless jest that striking has caused pain,
> The idle word that he'd wish back again ! "

Indeed, in spite of his success, I don't suppose he ever made an enemy in his life.

And here let me add (lest there be any doubt as to his identity) that he is now tall and stout and strikingly handsome, though rather bald ; and such an aristocrat in bearing, aspect, and manner, that you would take him for a blue-blooded descendant of the Crusaders instead of the son of a respectable burgher in Lausanne.

Then there was Lorrimer, the industrious apprentice, who is now also well pinnacled on high; himself a pillar of the Royal Academy—probably, if he lives long enough, its future president—the duly knighted or baroneted Lord Mayor of " all the plastic arts " (except one or two perhaps, here and there, that are not altogether without some importance).

May this not be for many, many years ! Lorrimer himself would be the first to say so !

Tall, thin, red-haired, and well-favoured, he was a most eager, earnest, and painstaking young enthusiast, of precocious culture, who read improving books, and did not share in the amusements of the Quartier Latin, but spent his evenings at home with Handel, Michael Angelo, and Dante, on the respectable side of the river. Also, he went into good society sometimes, with dress-coat on, and a white tie, and his hair parted in the middle !

THE TWO APPRENTICES

But in spite of these blemishes on his otherwise exemplary record as an art student, he was the most delightful companion—the most affectionate, helpful, and sympathetic of friends. May he live long and prosper !

Enthusiast as he was, he could only worship one god at a time. It was either Michael Angelo, Phidias, Paul Veronese, Tintoret, Raphael, or Titian—never a modern

—moderns didn't exist ! And so thoroughgoing was he in his worship, and so persistent in voicing it, that he made those immortals quite unpopular in the Place St. Anatole des Arts. We grew to dread their very names. Each of them would last him a couple of months or so; then he would give us a month's holiday, and take up another.

Antony did not think much of Lorrimer in those days, nor Lorrimer of him, for all they were such good friends. And neither of them thought much of Little Billee, whose pinnacle (of pure unadulterated fame) is now the highest of all—the highest probably that can be for a mere painter of pictures !

And what is so nice about Lorrimer, now that he is a graybeard, an Academician, an accomplished man of the world and society, is that he admires Antony's genius more than he can say—and reads Mr. Rudyard Kipling's delightful stories as well as Dante's *Inferno*—and can listen with delight to the lovely songs of Signor Tosti, who has not precisely founded himself on Handel—can even scream with laughter at a comic song—even a nigger melody—so, at least, that it but be sung in well-bred and distinguished company—for Lorrimer is no Bohemian.

> " Shoo, fly ! don'tcher bother me !
> For I belong to the Comp'ny G ! "

Both these famous men are happily (and most beautifully) married—grandfathers for all I know—and " move in the very best society " (Lorrimer always, I'm told; Antony now and then); *la haute,* as it used to be called in French Bohemia—meaning dukes and lords and even royalties, I suppose, and those who love them, and whom they love !

That *is* the best society, isn't it? At all events, we are assured it used to be ; but that must have been before the present scribe (a meek and somewhat innocent outsider) had been privileged to see it with his own little eye.

And when they happen to meet there (Antony and Lorrimer, I mean), I don't expect they rush very wildly into each other's arms, or talk very fluently about old times. Nor do I suppose their wives are very intimate. None of our wives are. Not even Taffy's and the Laird's.

Oh, Orestes ! Oh, Pylades !

Oh, ye impecunious, unpinnacled young inseparables of eighteen, nineteen, twenty, even twenty-five, who share each other's thoughts and purses, and wear each other's clothes, and swear each other's oaths, and smoke each other's pipes, and respect each other's lights o' love, and keep each other's secrets, and tell each other's jokes, and pawn each other's watches and merrymake together on the proceeds, and sit all night by each other's bedsides in sickness, and comfort each other in sorrow and disappointment with silent, manly sympathy—"wait till you get to forty year ! "

Wait even till each or either of you gets himself a little pinnacle of his own—be it ever so humble !

Nay, wait till either or each of you gets himself a wife !

History goes on repeating itself, and so do novels, and this s a platitude, and there's nothing new under the sun.

May too cecee (as the idiomatic Laird would say in the language he adores)—may too cecee ay nee eecee nee lâh !

Then there was Dodor, the handsome young *dragon de la garde*—a full private, if you please, with a beardless face, and damask-rosy cheeks, and a small waist, and narrow feet like a lady's, and who, strange to say, spoke English just like an Englishman.

And his friend Gontran, *alias* l'Zouzou—a corporal in the Zouaves.

Both of these worthies had met Taffy in the Crimea, and frequented the studios in the Quartier Latin, where they adored (and were adored by) the grisettes and models, especially Trilby.

Both of them were distinguished for being the worst subjects (*les plus mauvais garnements*) of their respective regiments ; yet both were special favourites not only with their fellow-rankers, but with those in command, from their colonels downward.

Both were in the habit of being promoted to the rank of corporal or brigadier, and degraded to the rank of private next day for general misconduct, the result of a too exuberant delight in their promotion.

"'I WILL NOT! I WILL NOT!'"

Neither of them knew fear, envy, malice, temper, or
low spirits; ever said or did an ill-natured thing; ever
even thought one; ever had an enemy but himself.
Both had the best or the worst manners going, according
to their company, whose manners they reflected; they
were true chameleons !

Both were always ready to share their last ten-sou
piece (not that they ever seemed to have one) with each
other or anybody else, or anybody else's last ten-sou
piece with you; to offer you a friend's cigar; to invite
you to dine with any friend they had; to fight with you,
or for you, at a moment's notice. And they made up for
all the anxiety, tribulation, and sorrow they caused at
home by the endless fun and amusement they gave to
all outside.

It was a pretty dance they led; but our three friends
of the Place St. Anatole (who hadn't got to pay the
pipers) loved them both, especially Dodor.

One fine Sunday afternoon Little Billee found himself
studying life and character in that most delightful and
festive scene la Fête de St. Cloud, and met Dodor and
l'Zouzou there, who hailed him with delight, saying :

" Nous allons joliment jubiler, nom d'une pipe ! " and
insisted on his joining in their amusements and paying
for them—round-abouts, swings, the giant, the dwarf, the
strong man, the fat woman—to whom they made love
and were taken too seriously, and turned out—the
menagerie of wild beasts, whom they teased and aggravated
till the police had to interfere. Also *al fresco* dances, where
their cancan step was of the wildest and most unbridled
character, till a *sous-officier* or a gendarme came in sight,
and then they danced quite mincingly and demurely, *en
maître d'école,* as they called it, to the huge delight of an
immense and ever-increasing crowd, and the disgust of
all truly respectable men.

They also insisted on Little Billee's walking between
them, arm-in-arm, and talking to them in English whenever they saw coming towards them a respectable English
family with daughters. It was the dragoon's delight to
get himself stared at by fair daughters of Albion for
speaking as good English as themselves—a rare accom-

plishment in a French trooper—and Zouzou's happiness to be thought English too, though the only English he knew was the phrase, "I will not! I will not!" which he had picked up in the Crimea, and repeated over and over again when he came within ear-shot of a pretty English girl.

Little Billee was not happy in these circumstances. He was no snob. But he was a respectably-brought-up young Briton of the higher middle class, and it was not quite pleasant for him to be seen (by fair country-women of his own) walking arm-in-arm on a Sunday afternoon with a couple of French private soldiers, and uncommonly rowdy ones at that.

Later, they came back to Paris together on the top of an omnibus, among a very proletarian crowd; and there the two facetious warriors

DODOR IN HIS GLORY

immediately made themselves pleasant all round and
became very popular, especially with the women and
children; but not, I regret to say, through the propriety,
refinement, and discretion of their behaviour. Little
Billee resolved that he would not go a-pleasuring with
them any more.

However, they stuck to him through thick and thin,
and insisted on escorting him all the way back to the
Quartier Latin by the Pont de la Concorde and the Rue
de Lille in the Faubourg St. Germain.

Little Billee loved the Faubourg St. Germain, especially
the Rue de Lille. He was fond of gazing at the magnificent old mansions, the *hôtels* of the old French noblesse,
or rather the outside walls thereof, the grand sculptured
portals with the armorial bearings and the splendid old
historic names above them—Hôtel de This, Hôtel de
That, Rohan-Chabot, Montmorency, La Rochefoucauld-
Liancourt, La Tour d'Auvergne.

He would forget himself in romantic dreams of past and
forgotten French chivalry which these glorious names
called up; for he knew a little of French history, loving to
read Froissart and Saint Simon and the genial Brantôme.

Halting opposite one of the finest and oldest of all these
gateways, his especial favourite, labelled " Hôtel de la
Rochemartel " in letters of faded gold over a ducal
coronet and a huge escutcheon of stone, he began to
descant upon its architectural beauties and noble propor-
tions to l'Zouzou.

" *Parbleu !* " said l'Zouzou, " *connu, farceur !* why, I
was *born* there, on the 6th of March 1834, at 5.30 in the
morning. Lucky day for France—*hein ?* "

" Born there? what do you mean—in the porter's
lodge ? "

At this juncture the two great gates rolled back, a
liveried *Suisse* appeared, and an open carriage and pair
came out, and in it were two elderly ladies and a younger
one.

To Little Billee's indignation, the two incorrigible
warriors made the military salute, and the three ladies
bowed stiffly and gravely.

And then (to Little Billee's horror this time) one of

HÔTEL DE LA ROCHEMARTEL

them happened to look back, and Zouzou actually kissed his hand to her.

" Do you *know* that lady? " asked Little Billee, very sternly.

" *Parbleu! si je la connais!* Why, it's my mother! Isn't she nice? She's rather cross with me just now."

" Your *mother!* Why, what do you mean? What on earth would your mother be doing in that big carriage and at that big house? "

" *Parbleu, farceur!* She lives there! "

" *Lives* there? Why, who and what is she, your mother? "

" The Duchesse de la Rochemartel, *parbleu!* and that's my sister; and that's my aunt, Princesse de Chevagné-Bauffremont! She's the ' *patronne* ' of that *chic* equipage. She's a millionaire, my aunt Chevagné! "

" Well, I never! What's *your* name, then? "

" Oh, *my* name! Hang it—let me see! Well—Gontran—Xavier—François—Marie—Joseph d'Amaury de Brissac de Roncesvaulx de la Rochemartel-Boisségur, at your service! "

" Quite correct! " said Dodor; " *l'enfant dit vrai!* "

" Well—I—never! And what's *your* name, Dodor? "

" Oh! I'm only a humble individual, and answer to the one-horse name of Théodore Rigolot de Lafarce. But Zouzou's an awful swell, you know—his brother's the Duke! "

Little Billee was no snob. But he was a respectably-brought-up young Briton of the higher middle class, and these revelations, which he could not but believe, astounded him so that he could hardly speak. Much as he flattered himself that he scorned the bloated aristocracy, titles are titles—even French titles!—and when it comes to dukes and princesses who live in houses like the Hôtel de la Rochemartel . . . !

It's enough to take a respectably-brought-up young Briton's breath away.

When he saw Taffy that evening, he exclaimed: " I say, Zouzou's mother's a duchess! "

" Yes—the Duchesse de la Rochemartel-Boisségur."

" You never told me! "

" You never asked me. It's one of the greatest names in France. They're very poor, I believe."

" Poor ! You should see the house they live in ! "

" I've been there, to dinner; and the dinner wasn't very good. They let a great part of it, and live mostly in the country. The Duke is Zouzou's brother; very unlike Zouzou; he's consumptive and unmarried, and the most respectable man in Paris. Zouzou will be the Duke some day."

" And Dodor—he's a swell, too, I suppose—he says he's *de* something or other ! "

" Yes—Rigolot de Lafarce. I've no doubt he descends from the Crusaders too; the name seems to favour it, anyhow; and such lots of them do in this country. His mother was English, and bore the worthy name of Brown. He was at school in England; that's why he speaks English so well—and behaves so badly, perhaps ! He's got a very beautiful sister, married to a man in the 60th Rifles—Jack Reeve, a son of Lord Reevely's; a selfish sort of chap. I don't suppose he gets on very well with his brother-in-law. Poor Dodor ! His sister's about the only living thing he cares for—except Zouzou."

I wonder if the bland and genial Monsieur Théodore —" notre Sieur Theodore "—now junior partner in the great haberdashery firm of " Passefil et Rigolot," on the Boulevard des Capucines, and a pillar of the English chapel in the Rue Marbœuf, is very hard on his employés and employées if they are a little late at their counters on a Monday morning?

I wonder if that stuck-up, stingy, stodgy, communard-shooting, church-going, time-serving, place-hunting, pious-eyed, pompous old prig, martinet, and philistine, Monsieur le Maréchal-Duc de la Rochemartel-Boisségur, ever tells Madame la Maréchale-Duchesse (*née* Hunks, of Chicago) how once upon a time Dodor and he—

We will tell no tales out of school.

The present scribe is no snob. He is a respectably-brought-up old Briton of the higher middle class—at least, he flatters himself so. And he writes for just such old philistines as himself, who date from a time when titles were not thought so cheap as to-day. Alas! all reverence for all that is high and time-honoured and beautiful seems at a discount.

So he has kept his blackguard ducal Zouave for the bouquet of this little show—the final *bonne bouche* in his Bohemian *menu*—that he may make it palatable to those who only look upon the good old Quartier Latin (now no more to speak of) as a very low, common, vulgar quarter indeed, deservedly swept away, where misters the students (shocking bounders and cads) had nothing better to do, day and night, than mount up to a horrid place called the thatched house—*la chaumière*—

> " Pour y danser le cancan
> Ou le Robert Macaire—
> Toujours—toujours—toujours—
> La nuit comme le jour . . .
> Et youp! youp! youp!
> Tra la la la la . . . la la la! "

. . . . . .

Christmas was drawing near.

There were days when the whole Quartier Latin would veil its iniquities under fogs almost worthy of the Thames Valley between London Bridge and Westminster, and out of the studio window the prospect was a dreary blank. No Morgue! no towers of Notre Dame! not even the chimney-pots over the way—not even the little mediæval toy turret at the corner of the Rue Vieille des Trois Mauvais Ladres, Little Billee's delight!

The stove had to be crammed till its sides grew a dull deep red before one's fingers could hold a brush or squeeze a bladder; one had to box or fence at nine in the morning, that one might recover from the cold bath, and get warm for the rest of the day!

Taffy and the Laird grew pensive and dreamy, child-like and bland; and when they talked it was generally about Christmas at home in Merry England and the distant Land of Cakes, and how good it was to be there at such a time—hunting, shooting, curling, and endless carouse!

It was Ho! for the jolly West Riding, and Hey! for the bonnets of Bonnie Dundee, till they grew quite homesick, and wanted to start by the very next train.

They didn't do anything so foolish. They wrote over to friends in London for the biggest Turkey, the biggest plum-pudding, that could be got for love or money, with mince-pies, and holly and mistletoe, and sturdy, short, thick English sausages; half a Stilton cheese, and a sirloin of beef—two sirloins, in case one should not be enough.

For they meant to have a Homeric feast in the studio on Christmas Day—Taffy, the Laird, and Little Billee— and invite all the delightful chums I have been trying to describe; and that is just why I tried to describe them— Durien, Vincent, Antony, Lorrimer, Carnegie, Petrolicoco- nose, l'Zouzou, and Dodor !

The cooking and waiting should be done by Trilby, her friend Angèle Boisse, M. et Mme. Vinard, and such little Vinards as could be trusted with glass and crockery and mince-pies; and if that was not enough, they would also cook themselves, and wait upon each other.

When dinner should be over, supper was to follow with scarcely any interval to speak of; and to partake of this other guests should be bidden—Svengali and Gecko, and perhaps one or two more. No ladies !

For, as the unsusceptible Laird expressed it, in the language of a gillie he had once met at a servant's dance in a Highland country-house, " Them wimmen spiles the ball ! "

Elaborate cards of invitation were sent out, in the designing and ornamentation of which the Laird and Taffy exhausted all their fancy (Little Billee had no time).

Wines and spirits and English beers were procured at great cost from M. E. Delevingne's, in the Rue St. Honoré, and liqueurs of every description—chartreuse, curaçoa, *ratafia de cassis*, and anisette; no expense was spared.

Also, truffled galantines of turkey, tongues, hams, *rillettes de Tours, pâtés de foie gras, fromage d'Italie* (which has nothing to do with cheese), *saucissons d'Arles et de Lyon*, with and without garlic, cold jellies peppery and salt — everything that French *charcutiers* and their wives can make out of French pigs, or any other animal whatever, beast, bird, or fowl (even cats and rats), for the

CHRISTMAS EVE

supper; and sweet jellies, and cakes, and sweetmeats, and confections of all kinds, from the famous pastry-cook at the corner of the Rue Castiglione.

Mouths went watering all day long in joyful anticipation. They water somewhat sadly now at the mere remembrance of these delicious things—the mere immediate sight or scent of which in these degenerate latter days would no longer avail to promote any such delectable secretion. *Hélas! ahimè! ach weh! ay de mi! eheu!* οἴμοι—in point of fact, *alas!*

That is the very exclamation I wanted.

Christmas Eve came round. The pieces of resistance and plum-pudding and mince-pies had not yet arrived from London—but there was plenty of time.

Les trois Angliches dined at le père Trin's, as usual, and played billiards and dominoes at the Café du Luxembourg, and possessed their souls in patience till it was time to go and hear the midnight mass at the Madeleine, where Roucouly, the great baritone of the Opéra Comique, was retained to sing Adam's famous Noël.

The whole Quartier seemed alive with the *réveillon.* It was a clear, frosty night, with a splendid moon just past the full, and most exhilarating was the walk along the quays on the Rive Gauche, over the Pont de la Concorde and across the Place thereof, and up the thronged Rue de la Madeleine to the massive Parthenaic place of worship that always has such a pagan, worldly look of smug and prosperous modernity.

They struggled manfully, and found standing and kneeling room among that fervent crowd, and heard the impressive service with mixed feelings, as became true Britons of very advanced liberal and religious opinions; not with the unmixed contempt of the proper British Orthodox (who were there in full force, one may be sure).

But their susceptible hearts soon melted at the beautiful music, and in mere sensuous *attendrissement* they were quickly in unison with all the rest.

For as the clock struck twelve out pealed the organ, and up rose the finest voice in France:

> " Minuit, Chrétiens ! c'est l'heure solennelle
> Où l'Homme-Dieu descendit parmi nous ! "

And a wave of religious emotion rolled over Little
Billee and submerged him; swept him off his little legs,
swept him out of his little self, drowned him in a great
seething surge of love—love of his kind, love of love, love of
life, love of death, love of all that is and ever was and ever
will be—a very large order indeed, even for Little Billee.

" ' ALLONS, GLYCÈRE ! ROUGIS MON VERRE. . . .''

And it seemed to him that he stretched out his arms
for love to one figure especially beloved beyond all the
rest—one figure erect on high with arms outstretched to
him, in more than common fellowship of need; not the
sorrowful figure crowned with thorns, for it was in the
likeness of a woman; but never that of the Virgin Mother
of Our Lord.

It was Trilby, Trilby, Trilby ! a poor fallen sinner and

waif all but lost amid the scum of the most corrupt city
on earth. Trilby weak and mortal like himself, and in
woeful want of pardon ! and in her gray dove-like eyes he
saw the shining of so great a love that he was abashed;
for well he knew that all that love was his, and would be
his for ever, come what would or could.

> " Peuple, debout ! Chante ta délivrance !
> *Noël ! Noël ! Voici le Rédempteur !* "

So sang and rang and pealed and echoed the big, deep,
metallic baritone bass—above the organ, above the
incense, above everything else in the world—till the very
universe seemed to shake with the rolling thunder of that
great message of love and forgiveness !

Thus at least felt Little Billee, whose way it was to
magnify and exaggerate all things under the subtle
stimulus of sound, and the singing human voice had
especially strange power to penetrate into his inmost
depths—even the voice of man !

And what voice but the deepest and gravest and grandest
there is can give worthy utterance to such a message as
that, the epitome, the abstract, the very essence of all
collective humanity's wisdom at its best !

Little Billee reached the Hôtel Corneille that night in
a very exalted frame of mind indeed; the loftiest, lowliest
mood of all.

Now see what sport we are of trivial, base, ignoble
earthly things !

Sitting on the doorstep, and smoking two cigars at
once he found Ribot, one of his fellow-lodgers, whose
room was just under his own. Ribot was so tipsy that
he could not ring. But he could still sing, and did so at
the top of his voice. It was not the Noël of Adam that
he sang. He had not spent his *réveillon* in any church.

With the help of a sleepy waiter, Little Billee got the
bacchanalian into his room and lit his candle for him,
and, disengaging himself from his maudlin embraces, left
him to wallow in solitude.

As he lay awake in his bed, trying to recall the deep
and high emotions of the evening, he heard the tipsy hog
below tumbling about his room and still trying to sing
his senseless ditty:

" Allons, Gycère !
Rougis mon verre
Du jus divin dont mon cœur est toujours jaloux ; ; ;
Et puis à table,
Bacchante aimable !
Enivrons-nous (hic) Les g'glougloux sont des rendez-
vous ! . . ."

Then the song ceased for a while, and soon there were
other sounds, as on a Channel steamer. Glougloux
indeed !

Then the fear arose in Little Billee's mind lest the
drunken beast should set fire to his bedroom curtains.
All heavenly visions were chased away for the night. . . .

Our hero, half crazed with fear, disgust, and irritation,
lay wide awake, his nostrils on the watch for the smell of
burning chintz or muslin, and wondered how an educated
man—for Ribot was a law-student—could ever make
such a filthy beast of himself as that ! It was a scandal
—a disgrace; it was not to be borne; there should be
no forgiveness for such as Ribot—not even on Christmas
Day ! He would complain to Madame Paul, the *patronne* ;
he would have Ribot turned out into the street; he would
leave the hotel himself the very next morning ! At last
he fell asleep, thinking of all he would do; and thus,
ridiculously and ignominiously for Little Billee, ended
the *réveillon.*

Next morning he complained to Madame Paul; and
though he did not give her warning, nor even insist on
the expulsion of Ribot (who, as he heard with a hard
heart, was *bien malade ce matin*), he expressed himself
very severely on the conduct of that gentleman, and on
the dangers from fire that might arise from a tipsy man
being trusted alone in a small bedroom with chintz
curtains and a lighted candle. If it hadn't been for
himself, he told her, Ribot would have slept on the door-
step, and serve him right ! He was really grand in his
virtuous indignation, in spite of his imperfect French;
and Madame Paul was deeply contrite for her peccant
lodger, and profuse in her apologies; and Little Billee
began his twenty-first Christmas Day like a Pharisee,
thanking his star that he was not as Ribot !

PART FOURTH

" Félicité passée
Qui ne peux revenir,
Tourment de ma pensée,
Que n'ay-je, en te perdant, perdu le souvenir ! "

MID-DAY had struck. The expected hamper had not turned up in the Place St. Anatole des Arts.

All Madame Vinard's kitchen battery was in readiness ; Trilby and Madame Angèle Boisse were in the studio, their sleeves turned up, and ready to begin.

At twelve the *trois* Angliches and the two fair *blanchisseuses* sat down to lunch in a very anxious frame of mind, and finished a *pâté de foie gras* and two bottles of Burgundy between them, such was their disquietude.

The guests had been invited for six o'clock.

Most elaborately they laid the cloth on the table they had borrowed from the Hôtel de Seine, and settled who was to sit next to whom, and then unsettled it, and quarrelled over it—Trilby, as was her wont in such matters, assuming an authority that did not rightly belong to her, and of course getting her own way in the end.

And that, as the Laird remarked, was her confounded Trilbyness.

Two o'clock—three—four—but no hamper ! Darkness had almost set in. It was simply maddening. They knelt on the divan, with their elbows on the window-sill, and watched the street-lamps popping into life along the quays—and looked out through the gathering dusk for the van from the Chemin de Fer du Nord—and gloomily thought of the Morgue, which they could still make out across the river.

At length the Laird and Trilby went off in a cab to the station—a long drive—and, lo ! before they came back the long-expected hamper arrived, at six o'clock.

And with it Durien, Vincent, Antony, Lorrimer, Car-

SOUVENIR

negie, Petrolicoconose, Dodor, and l'Zouzou— the last two in uniform, as usual.

And suddenly the studio, which had been so silent, dark, and dull, with Taffy and Little Billee sitting hopeless and despondent round the stove, became a scene of the noisiest, busiest, and cheerfullest animation. The three big lamps were lit, and all the Chinese lanterns. The pieces of resistance and the pudding were whisked off by Trilby, Angèle, and Madame Vinard to other regions—the porter's lodge and Durien's studio (which had been lent for the purpose); and every one was pressed into the preparations for the banquet. There was plenty for idle hands to do. Sausages to be fried for the turkey, stuffing made, and sauces, salads mixed, and punch—holly hung in festoons all round and about—a thousand things. Everybody was so clever and good-humoured that nobody got in anybody's way—not even Carnegie, who was in evening dress (to the Laird's delight). So they made him do the scullion's work—cleaning, rinsing, peeling, etc.

The cooking of the dinner was almost better fun than the eating of it. And though there were so many cooks, not even the broth was spoiled (cockaleekie, from a receipt of the Laird's).

It was ten o'clock before they sat down to that most memorable repast.

Zouzou and Dodor, who had been the most useful and energetic of all its cooks, apparently quite forgot they were due at their respective barracks at that very moment; they had only been able to obtain *la permission de dix heures*. If they remembered it, the certainty that next day Zouzou would be reduced to the ranks for the fifth time, and Dodor confined to his barracks for a month, did not trouble them in the least.

The waiting was as good as the cooking. The handsome, quick, authoritative Madame Vinard was in a dozen places at once, and openly prompted, rebuked, and bully-ragged her husband into a proper smartness. The pretty little Madame Angèle moved about as deftly and as quietly as a mouse; which of course did not prevent them both from genially joining in the general conversation whenever it wandered into French.

Trilby, tall, graceful, and stately, and also swift of action, though more like Juno or Diana than Hebe, devoted herself more especially to her own particular favourites— Durien, Taffy, the Laird, Little Billee—and Dodor and Zouzou, whom she loved, and *tutoyé'd en bonne camarade* as she served them with all there was of the choicest.

The two little Vinards did their little best—they scrupulously respected the mince-pies, and only broke two bottles of oil and one of Harvey sauce, which made their mother furious. To console them, the Laird took one of them on each knee and gave them of his share of plum-pudding and many other unaccustomed good things, so bad for their little French tumtums.

The genteel Carnegie had never been at such a queer scene in his life. It opened his mind—and Dodor and Zouzou, between whom he sat (the Laird thought it would do him good to sit between a private soldier and a humble corporal), taught him more French than he had learned during the three months he had spent in Paris. It was

a specialty of theirs. It was more colloquial than what
is generally used in diplomatic circles, and stuck longer in
the memory; but it hasn't interfered with his preferment
in the Church.

He quite unbent. He was the first to volunteer a song
(without being asked) when the pipes and cigars were lit,
and after the usual toasts had been drunk—Her Majesty's
health, Tennyson, Thackeray, and Dickens; and John
Leech.

He sang, with a very cracked and rather hiccupy voice,
his only song (it seems)—an English one, of which the
burden, he explained, was French :

> " Veeverler veeverler veeverler vee
> Veeverler companyee ! "

And Zouzou and Dodor complimented him so profusely on his French accent that he was with difficulty
prevented from singing it all over again.

Then everybody sang in rotation.

The Laird, with a capital baritone, sang

> " Hie diddle dee for the Lowlands low,"

which was encored.

Little Billee sang " Little Billee."

Vincent sang.

> " Old Joe kicking up behind and afore,
> And the yaller gal a-kicking up behind old Joe."

A capital song, with words of quite a masterly scansion.

Antony sang " Le Sire de Framboisy." Enthusiastic
encore.

Lorrimer, inspired no doubt by the occasion, sang the
" Hallelujah Chorus," and accompanied himself on the
piano, but failed to obtain an encore.

Durien sang.

> " Plaisir d'amour ne dure qu'un moment;
> Chagrin d'amour dure toute la vie. . . ."

It was his favourite song, and is one of the beautiful songs
of the world, and he sang it very well—and it became
popular in the Quartier Latin ever after.

The Greek couldn't sing, and very wisely didn't.

Zouzou sang capitally a capital song in praise of *le vin à quat' sous !*

Taffy, in a voice like a high wind (and with a very good imitation of the Yorkshire brogue), sang a Somersetshire hunting ditty, ending :

> " Of this 'ere song should I be axed the reason for to show,
> I don't exactly know, I don't exactly know !
> But all my fancy dwells upon Nancy,
> And I sing Tally-ho ! "

It is a quite super-excellent ditty, and haunts my memory to this day ; and one felt sure that Nancy was a dear and a sweet, wherever she lived, and when. So Taffy was encored twice—once for her sake, once for his own.

And finally, to the surprise of all, the bold dragoon sang (in English) " My Sister Dear," out of *Masaniello,* with such pathos, and in a voice so sweet and high and well in tune, that his audience felt almost weepy in the midst of their jollification ; and grew quite sentimental, as Englishmen abroad are apt to do when they are rather tipsy and hear pretty music, and think of their dear sisters across the sea, or their friends' dear sisters.

Madame Vinard interrupted her Christmas dinner on the model-throne to listen, and wept and wiped her eyes quite openly, and remarked to Madame Boisse, who stood modestly close by : " Il est gentil tout plein, ce dragon ! Mon Dieu ! comme il chante bien ! Il est Angliche aussi, il paraît. Ils sont joliment bien élevés, tous ces Angliches—tous plus gentils les uns que les autres ! et quant à Monsieur Litrebili, on lui donnerait le bon Dieu sans confession ! "

And Madame Boisse agreed.

Then Svengali and Gecko came, and the table had to be laid and decorated anew, for it was supper-time.

Supper was even jollier than dinner, which had taken off the keen edge of the appetites, so that every one talked at once—the true test of a successful supper— except when Antony told some of his experiences of Bohemia ; for instance, how, after staying at home all

"MY SISTER DEAR"

day for a month to avoid his creditors, he became reckless
one Sunday morning, and went to the Bains Deligny,
and jumped into a deep part by mistake, and was saved
from a watery grave by a bold swimmer, who turned out
to be his bootmaker, Satory, to whom he owed sixty
francs—of all his duns the one he dreaded the most, and
who didn't let him go in a hurry.

Whereupon Svengali remarked that he also owed
sixty francs to Satory—" Mais comme che ne me baigne
chamais, che n'ai rien à craindre ! "

Whereupon there was such a laugh that Svengali felt
he had scored off Antony at last, and had a prettier wit,
He flattered himself that he'd got the laugh of Antony
this time.

And after supper Svengali and Gecko made such lovely
music that everybody was sobered and athirst again, and
the punch-bowl, wreathed with holly and mistletoe, was
placed in the middle of the table, and clean glasses set all
round it.

Then Dodor and l'Zouzou stood up to dance with
Trilby and Madame Angèle, and executed a series of
cancan steps, which, though they were so inimitably droll
that they had each and all to be encored, were such that
not one of them need have brought the blush of shame to
the cheek of modesty.

Then the Laird danced a sword-dance over two T-squares
and broke them both. And Taffy, baring his mighty arms
to the admiring gaze of all, did dumb-bell exercises, with
Little Billee for a dumb-bell, and all but dropped him
into the punch-bowl; and tried to cut a pewter ladle in
two with Dodor's sabre, and sent it through the window;
and this made him cross, so that he abused French sabres,
and said they were made of worse pewter than even
French ladles; and the Laird sententiously opined that
they managed these things better in England, and winked
at Little Billee.

Then they played at " cock-fighting," with their wrists
tied across their shins, and a broomstick thrust in between;
thus manacled, you are placed opposite your antagonist,
and try to upset him with your feet, and he you. It is a
very good game. The cuirassier and the Zouave playing

at this got so angry, and were so irresistibly funny a sight, that the shouts of laughter could be heard on the other side of the river, so that a *sergent-de-ville* came in and civilly requested them not to make so much noise. They were disturbing the whole Quartier, he said, and there was quite a *rassemblement* outside. So they made him tipsy, and also another policeman, who came to look after his comrade, and yet another; and these guardians of the peace of Paris were trussed and made to play at cock-fighting, and were still funnier than the two soldiers,

A DUCAL FRENCH FIGHTING COCK

and laughed louder and made more noise than any one else, so that Madame Vinard had to remonstrate with them, till they got too tipsy to speak, and fell fast asleep, and were laid next to each other behind the stove.

The *fin-de-siècle* reader, disgusted at the thought of such an orgy as I have been trying to describe, must remember that it happened in the fifties, when men calling themselves gentlemen, and being called so, still wrenched off door-knockers and came back drunk from the Derby, and even drank too much after dinner before joining the ladies, as is all duly chronicled and set down in John Leech's immortal pictures of life and character out of *Punch*.

Then M. and Mme. Vinard and Trilby and Angèle Boisse bade the company good-night, Trilby being the last of them to leave.

Little Billee took her to the top of the staircase, and there he said to her:

"Trilby, I have asked you nineteen times, and you have refused. Trilby, once more, on Christmas night, for the twentieth time—*will* you marry me? If not, I leave Paris to-morrow morning, and never come back. I swear it on my word of honour!"

Trilby turned very pale, and leaned her back against the wall, and covered her face with her hands.

Little Billee pulled them away.

"Answer me, Trilby!"

"God forgive me, *yes!*" said Trilby, and she ran down-stairs, weeping.

It was now very late.

It soon became evident that Little Billee was in extra-ordinarily high spirits—in an abnormal state of excitement.

He challenged Svengali to spar, and made his nose bleed, and frightened him out of his sardonic wits. He performed wonderful and quite unsuspected feats of strength. He swore eternal friendship to Dodor and Zouzou, and filled their glasses again and again, and also (in his innocence) his own, and *trinquéd* with them many times running. They were the last to leave (except the three helpless policemen); and at about five or six in the morning, to his surprise, he found himself walking between Dodor and Zouzou by a late windy moonlight in the Rue Vieille des Trois Mauvais Ladres, now on one side of the frozen gutter, now on the other, now in the middle of it, stopping them now and then to tell them how jolly they were and how dearly he loved them.

Presently his hat flew away, and went rolling and skipping and bounding up the narrow street, and they discovered that as soon as they let each other go to run after it, they all three sat down.

" ' ANSWER ME, TRILBY ! ' "

So Dodor and Little Billee remained sitting, with their
arms round each other's necks and their feet in the gutter,
while Zouzou went after the hat on all fours, and caught it,
and brought it back in his mouth like a tipsy retriever.
Little Billee wept for sheer love and gratitude, and called
him a cary*hat*ide (in English), and laughed loudly at his own
wit, which was quite thrown away on Zouzou! " No man
ever *had* such dear, dear frenge! no man ever *was* s'happy! "

After sitting for a while in love and amity, they
managed to get up on their feet again, each helping the
other; and in some never-to-be-remembered way they
reached the Hôtel Corneille.

There they sat Little Billee on the door-step and rang
the bell, and seeing some one coming up the Place de
l'Odéon, and fearing he might be a *sergent-de-ville*, they
bid Little Billee a most affectionate but hasty farewell,
kissing him on both cheeks in French fashion, and con-
trived to get themselves round the corner and out of sight.

Little Billee tried to sing Zouzou's drinking-song:

> " Quoi de plus doux
> Que les glougloux—
> Les glougloux du vin à quat' sous. . . ."

The stranger came up.
Fortunately, it was no
sergent-de-ville, but Ribot,

A CARY*HAT*IDE

just back from a Christmas-tree and a little family dance
at his aunt's, Madame Kolb (the Alsatian banker's wife,
in the Rue de la Chaussée d'Antin).

Next morning poor Little Billee was dreadfully ill.

He had passed a terrible night. His bed had heaved
like the ocean, with oceanic results. He had forgotten to

"'LES GLOUGLOUX DU VIN À QUAT' SOUS. . . .'"

put out his candle, but fortunately Ribot had blown it out
for him, after putting him to bed and tucking him up
like a real good Samaritan.

And next morning, when Madame Paul brought him
a cup of *tisane de chiendent* (which does not happen to
mean a hair of the dog that bit him), she was kind, but
very severe on the dangers and disgrace of intoxication,
and talked to him like a mother.

"If it had not been for kind Monsieur Ribot" (she told him), "the doorstep would have been his portion; and who could say he didn't deserve it? And then think of the danger of fire from a tipsy man all alone in a small bed-room with chintz curtains and a lighted candle!"

"Ribot was kind enough to blow out my candle," said Little Billee, humbly.

"Ah, Dame!" said Madame Paul, with much meaning —"au moins il a *bon cœur*, Monsieur Ribot!"

And the cruellest sting of all was when the good-natured and incorrigibly festive Ribot came and sat by his bedside, and was kind and tenderly sympathetic, and got him a pick-me-up from the chemist's (unbeknown to Madame Paul).

"Credieu! vous vous êtes crânement bien amusé, hier soir! quelle bosse, hein! je parie que c'était plus drôle que chez ma tante Kolb!"

All of which, of course, it is unnecessary to translate; except, perhaps, the word *bosse*, which stands for *noce*, which stands for a "jolly good spree."

In all his innocent little life Little Billee had never dreamed of such humiliation as this—such ignominious depths of shame and misery and remorse! He did not care to live. He had but one longing: that Trilby, dear Trilby, kind Trilby, would come and pillow his head on her beautiful white English bosom, and lay her soft, cool, tender hand on his aching brow, and there let him go to sleep, and sleeping, die!

He slept and slept, with no better rest for his aching brow than the pillow of his bed in the Hôtel Corneille, and failed to die this time. And when, after some forty-eight hours or so, he had quite slept off the fumes of that memorable Christmas debauch, he found that a sad thing had happened to him, and a strange!

It was as though a tarnishing breath had swept over the reminiscent mirror of his mind and left a little film behind it, so that no past thing he wished to see therein was reflected with quite the old pristine clearness. As though the keen, quick, razor-like edge of his power to reach and re-evoke the bygone charm and glamour and essence of things had been blunted and coarsened. As though the bloom of that special joy, the gift he unconsciously had of recalling past emotions and sensations and situations, and making them actual once more by a mere effort of the will, had been brushed away.

And he never recovered the full use of that most precious faculty, the boon of youth and happy childhood, and which he had once possessed, without knowing it, in such singular and exceptional completeness. He was to lose other precious faculties of his over-rich and complex nature—to be pruned and clipped and thinned—that his one supreme faculty of painting might have elbow-room to reach its fullest, or else you could never have seen the wood for the trees (or *vice versa*—which is it?).

On New Year's Day Taffy and the Laird were at their work in the studio, when there was a knock at the door, and Monsieur Vinard, cap in hand, respectfully introduced a pair of visitors, an English lady and gentleman.

The gentleman was a clergyman, small, thin, round-shouldered, with a long neck; weak-eyed and dryly polite. The lady was middle-aged, though still young-looking; very pretty, with gray hair; very well dressed; very small, full of nervous energy, with tiny hands and feet. It was Little Billee's mother; and the clergyman, the Rev. Thomas Bagot, was her brother-in-law.

Their faces were full of trouble—so much so that the two painters did not even apologise for the carelessness of their attire, or for the odour of tobacco that filled the room. Little Billee's mother recognised the two painters at a glance, from the sketches and descriptions of which her son's letters were always full.

They all sat down.

After a moment's embarrassed silence, Mrs. Bagot exclaimed, addressing Taffy: "Mr. Wynne, we are in terrible distress of mind. I don't know if my son has told you, but on Christmas day he engaged himself to be married!"

"To—be—*married!*" exclaimed Taffy and the Laird, for whom this was news indeed.

"Yes—to be married to a Miss Trilby O'Ferrall, who, from what he implies, is in quite a different position in life from himself. Do you know the lady, Mr. Wynne?"

"Oh yes! I know her very well indeed; we *all* know her."

"Is she English?"

"She's an English subject, I believe."

"Is she a Protestant or a Roman Catholic?" inquired the clergyman.

"A—a—upon my word. I really don't know!"

"' IS SHE A *LADY*, MR. WYNNE?'"

"You know her very well indeed, and you *don't—know—that*, Mr. Wynne!" exclaimed Mr. Bagot.

"Is she a *lady*, Mr. Wynne?" asked Mrs. Bagot, somewhat impatiently, as if that were a much more important matter.

By this time the Laird had managed to basely desert his friend; had got himself into his bedroom, and from thence, by another door, into the street and away.

"A lady?" said Taffy; "a—it so much depends upon

what that word exactly means, you know; things are so
—a—so different here. Her father was a gentleman, I
believe—a Fellow of Trinity, Cambridge—and a clergyman, if *that* means anything ! . . . he was unfortunate
and all that—a—intemperate, I fear, and not successful
in life. He has been dead six or seven years."

" And her mother ? "

" I really know very little about her mother, except
that she was very handsome, I believe, and of inferior
social rank to her husband. She's also dead; she died
soon after him."

" What is the young lady, then ? An English governess,
or something of that sort ? "

" Oh no, no—a—nothing of *that* sort," said Taffy (and
inwardly, " You coward—you cad of a Scotch thief of a
sneak of a Laird—to leave all this to me ! ").

"What ? Has she independent means of her own,then ?"

" A—not that I know of; I should even say, decidedly
not ! "

" What *is* she, then? She's at least respectable, I
hope ? "

" At present she's a—a *blanchisseuse de fin*—that is
considered respectable here."

" Why, that's a washerwoman, isn't it ? "

" Well—rather better than that, perhaps—*de fin*, you
know !—things are so different in Paris ! I don't think
you'd say she was very much like a washerwoman—to
look at ! "

" Is she so good-looking, then ? "

" Oh yes; extremely so. You may well say that—
very beautiful, indeed—about that, at least, there is no
doubt whatever ! "

" And of unblemished character ? "

Taffy, red and perspiring as if he were going through
his Indian-club exercise, was silent — and his face
expressed a miserable perplexity. But nothing could
equal the anxious misery of those two maternal eyes, so
wistfully fixed on his.

After some seconds of a most painful stillness, the
lady said, " Can't you—oh, *can't* you give me an answer,
Mr. Wynne ? "

"Oh, Mrs. Bagot, you have placed me in a terrible position! I—I love your son just as if he were my own brother! This engagement is a complete surprise to me —a most painful surprise! I'd thought of many possible things, but never of *that!* I cannot—I really *must* not conceal from you that it would be an unfortunate marriage for your son—from a—a worldly point of view, you know —although both I and M'Allister have a very deep and warm regard for poor Trilby O'Ferrall—indeed, a great admiration and affection and respect. She was once a model."

"A *model*, Mr. Wynne? What *sort* of a model—there are models and models, of course."

"Well, a model of every sort, in every possible sense of the word—head, hands, feet, everything!"

"A model for the *figure?*"

"Well—yes!"

"Oh, my God! my God! my God!" cried Mrs. Bagot —and she got up and walked up and down the studio in a most terrible state of agitation, her brother-in-law following her and begging her to control herself. Her exclamations seemed to shock him, and she didn't seem to care.

"Oh! Mr. Wynne! Mr. Wynne! If you only *knew* what my son is to me—to all of us—always has been! He has been with us all his life, till he came to this wicked, accursed city! My poor husband would never hear of his going to any school, for fear of all the harm he might learn there. My son was as innocent and pure-minded as any girl, Mr. Wynne—I could have trusted him any-where—and that's why I gave way and allowed him to come *here*, of all places in the world—all alone. Oh! I should have come with him! Fool—fool—fool that I was! . . .

"Oh, Mr. Wynne, he won't see either his mother or his uncle! I found a letter from him at the hotel, saying he'd left Paris—and I don't even know where he's gone! . . . Can't *you*, can't Mr. M'Allister do *anything* to avert this miserable disaster? You don't know how he loves you both—you should see his letters to me and to his sister! they are always full of you!"

"Indeed, Mrs. Bagot—you can count on M'Allister and me for doing everything in our power! But it is of no use our trying to influence your son—I feel quite sure of *that!* It is to *her* we must make our appeal."

"Oh, Mr. Wynne! to a washerwoman—a figure model —and Heaven knows what besides! and with such a chance as this!"

"Mrs. Bagot, you don't know her! She may have been all that. But strange as it may seem to you—and seems to me, for that matter—she's a—she's—upon my word of honour, I really think she's about the best woman I ever met—the most unselfish—the most——"

"Ah! She's a *beautiful* woman—I can well see *that!*"

"She has a beautiful nature, Mrs. Bagot—you may believe me or not as you like—and it is to that I shall make my appeal, as your son's friend, who has his interests at heart. And let me tell you that deeply as I grieve for you in your present distress, my grief and concern for her are far greater!"

"What! grief for her if she marries my son!"

"No, indeed—but if she refuses to marry him. She may not do so, of course—but my instinct tells me she will!"

"Oh! Mr. Wynne, is that likely?"

"I will do my best to make it so—with such an utter trust in her unselfish goodness of heart and her passionate affection for your son as——"

"How do you know she has all this passionate affection for him?"

"Oh, M'Allister and I have long guessed it—though we never thought this particular thing would come of it. I think, perhaps, that first of all you ought to see her yourself—you would get quite a new idea of what she really is—you would be surprised, I assure you."

Mrs. Bagot shrugged her shoulders impatiently, and there was silence for a minute or two.

And then, just as in a play, Trilby's "Milk below!" was sounded at the door, and Trilby came into the little antechamber, and seeing strangers, was about to turn back. She was dressed as a grisette, in her Sunday gown and pretty white cap (for it was New Year's Day), and looking her very best.

Taffy called out, " Come in, Trilby ! "

And Trilby came into the studio.

As soon as she saw Mrs. Bagot's face she stopped short—erect, her shoulders a little high, her mouth a little open, her eyes wide with fright—and pale to the lips—a pathetic, yet commanding, magnificent, and most distinguished apparition, in spite of her humble attire.

The little lady got up and walked straight to her, and looked up into her face, that seemed to tower so. Trilby breathed hard.

At length Mrs. Bagot said, in her high accents, " You are Miss Trilby O'Ferrall ? "

" Oh yes—yes—I am Trilby O'Ferrall, and you are Mrs. Bagot; I can see that ! "

A new tone had come into her large, deep, soft voice, so tragic, so touching, so strangely in accord with her whole aspect just then—so strangely in accord with the whole situation—that Taffy felt his cheeks and lips turn cold, and his big spine thrill and tickle all down his back.

" Oh yes ; you are very, very beautiful—there's no doubt about *that !* You wish to marry my son ? "

" I've refused to marry him nineteen times—for his own sake; he will tell you so himself. I am not the right person for him to marry. I know that. On Christmas night he asked me for the twentieth time; he swore he would leave Paris next day for ever if I refused him. I hadn't the courage. I was weak, you see ! It was a dreadful mistake."

" Are you so fond of him ? "

" *Fond* of him ? Aren't *you ?* "

" I'm his mother, my good girl ! "

To this Trilby seemed to have nothing to say.

" You have just said yourself you are not a fit wife for him. If you are so *fond* of him, will you ruin him by marrying him; drag him down; prevent him from getting on in life; separate him from his sister, his family, his friends ? "

Trilby turned her miserable eyes to Taffy's miserable face, and said, " Will it really be all that, Taffy ? "

" Oh, Trilby, things have got all wrong, and can't be
righted ! I'm afraid it might be so. Dear Trilby—I
can't tell you what I feel—but I can't tell you lies, you
know ! "

" Oh no—Taffy—you don't tell lies ! "

Then Trilby began to tremble very much, and Taffy
tried to make her sit down, but she wouldn't. Mrs. Bagot

" ' FOND OF HIM ? AREN'T YOU ? ' "

looked up into her face, herself breathless with keen suspense and cruel anxiety—almost imploring.

Trilby looked down at Mrs. Bagot very kindly, put
out her shaking hand, and said : " Good-bye, Mrs. Bagot.
I will not marry your son. I *promise* you. I will never
see him again."

Mrs. Bagot caught and clasped her hand and tried to
kiss it, and said : " Don't go yet, my dear good girl. I

want to talk to you. I want to tell you how deeply
I——"

"Good-bye, Mrs. Bagot," said Trilby, once more; and
disengaging her hand, she walked swiftly out of the room.

Mrs. Bagot seemed stupefied, and only half content
with her quick triumph.

"She will not marry your son, Mrs. Bagot. I only
wish to God she'd marry *me !*"

"Oh, Mr. Wynne !" said Mrs. Bagot, and burst into
tears.

"Ah !" exclaimed the clergyman, with a feebly satirical
smile and a little cough and sniff that were not sympathetic, "now if *that* could be arranged—and I've no
doubt there wouldn't be much opposition on the part of
the lady " (here he made a little complimentary bow), " it
would be a very desirable thing all round ! "

"It's tremendously good of you, I'm sure—to interest
yourself in *my* humble affairs," said Taffy.   " Look here,
sir—I'm not a great genius like your nephew—and it
doesn't much matter to any one but myself what I make
of my life—but I can assure you that if Trilby's heart
were set on me as it is on him, I would gladly cast in my
lot with hers for life. She's one in a thousand. She's
the one sinner that repenteth, you know ? "

"Ah, yes—to be sure !—to be sure ! I know all about
that; still, facts are facts, and the world is the world, and
we've got to live in it," said Mr. Bagot, whose satirical
smile had died away under the gleam of Taffy's choleric
blue eye.

Then said the good Taffy, frowning down on the parson
(who looked mean and foolish, as people can sometimes do
even with right on their side): "And now, Mr. Bagot—I
can't tell you how very keenly I have suffered during this—
a—this most painful interview—on account of my very
deep regard for Trilby O'Ferrall. I congratulate you and
your sister-in-law on its complete success. I also feel very
deeply for your nephew. I'm not sure that he has not
lost more than he will gain by—a—by the—a—the
success of this—a—this interview, in short ! "

Taffy's eloquence was exhausted, and his quick temper
was getting the better of him.

Then Mrs. Bagot, drying her eyes, came and took his
hand in a very charming and simple manner, and said :
" Mr. Wynne, I think I know what you are feeling just
now. You must try and make some allowance for us.
You will, I am sure, when we are gone, and you have had
time to think a little. As for that noble and beautiful
girl, I only wish that she were such that my son *could*
marry her—in her past life, I mean. It is not her
humble rank that would frighten me ; *pray* believe that I
am quite sincere in this—and don't think too hardly of
your friend's mother. Think of all I shall have to go
through with my poor son—who is deeply in love—and
no wonder ! and who has won the love of such a woman
as that ! and who cannot see at present how fatal to him
such a marriage would be. I can see all the charm and
believe in all the goodness, in spite of all. And, oh, how
beautiful she is, and what a voice ! All that counts for so
much, doesn't it ? I cannot tell you how I grieve for her.
I can make no amends—who could, for such a thing ?
There are no amends, and I shall not even try. I will
only write and tell her all I think and feel. You will
forgive us, won't you ? "

And in the quick, impulsive warmth and grace and
sincerity of her manner as she said all this, Mrs. Bagot was
so absurdly like Little Billee that it touched big Taffy's
heart, and he would have forgiven anything, and there
was nothing to forgive.

" Oh, Mrs. Bagot, there's no question of forgiveness.
Good heavens ! it is all so unfortunate, you know ! Nobody's to blame, that I can see. Good-bye, Mrs. Bagot ;
good-bye, sir," and so saying, he saw them down to their
remise, in which sat a singularly pretty young lady of
seventeen or so, pale and anxious, and so like Little Billee
that it was quite funny, and touched big Taffy's heart
again.

When Trilby went out into the courtyard in the Place
St. Anatole des Arts, she saw Miss Bagot looking out of
the carriage window, and in the young lady's face, as she
caught her eye, an expression of sweet surprise and sympathetic admiration, with lifted eyebrows and parted lips

—just such a look as she had often got from Little Billee !
She knew her for his sister at once.   It was a sharp pang.

She turned away, saying to herself : "Oh no ; I will
not separate him from his sister, his family, his friends !
That would *never* do !   *That's* settled, anyhow ! "

Feeling a little dazed, and wishing to think, she turned
up the Rue Vieille des Mauvais Ladres, which was always
deserted at this hour.   It was empty, but for a solitary
figure sitting on a post, with its legs dangling, its hands
in its trousers-pockets, an inverted pipe in its mouth, a

" SO LIKE LITTLE BILLEE "

tattered straw hat on the back of its head, and a long gray
coat down to its heels.   It was the Laird.

As soon as he saw her he jumped off his post and came
to her, saying : "Oh, Trilby—what's it all about?   I
couldn't stand it !   I ran away !   Little Billee's mother's
there ! "

"Yes, Sandy dear, I've just seen her."

"Well, what's up ? "

"I've promised her never to see Little Billee any
more.   I was foolish enough to promise to marry him.
I refused many times these last three months, and then
he said he'd leave Paris and never come back, and so,
like a fool, I gave way.   I've offered to live with him
and take care of him and be his servant—to be every-

thing he wished but his wife! But he wouldn't hear of
it. Dear, dear Little Billee! he's an angel—and I'll
take precious good care no harm shall ever come to him
through me! I shall leave this hateful place and go and
live in the country: I suppose I must manage to get
through life somehow. . . . Days are so long—*aren't* they!
and there's *such* a lot of 'em! I know of some poor
people who were once very fond of me, and I could live
with them and help them and keep myself. The difficulty
is about Jeannot. I thought it all out before it came to
this. I was well prepared, you see."

She smiled in a forlorn sort of way, with her upper
lip drawn tight against her teeth, as if some one were
pulling her back by the lobes of her ears.

"Oh! but, Trilby—what shall we do without you?
Taffy and I, you know! You've become one of us!"

"Now, how good and kind of you to say that!"
exclaimed poor Trilby, her eyes filling. "Why, that's
just all I lived for, till all this happened. But it can't
be any more now, can it? Everything is changed for
me—the very sky seems different. Ah! Durien's little
song—'*Plaisir d'amour—chagrin d'amour!*' it's all quite
true, isn't it? I shall start immediately, and take
Jeannot with me, I think."

"But where do you think of going?"

"Ah! I mayn't tell you that, Sandy dear—not for a long
time! Think of all the trouble there'd be. Well, there's
no time to be lost. I must take the bull by the horns."

She tried to laugh, and took him by his big side whiskers
and kissed him on the eyes and mouth, and her tears fell
on his face.

Then, feeling unable to speak, she nodded farewell,
and walked quickly up the narrow winding street. When
she came to the first bend she turned round and waved
her hand, and kissed it two or three times, and then
disappeared.

The Laird stared for several minutes up the empty
thoroughfare—wretched, full of sorrow and compassion.
Then he filled himself another pipe and lit it, and hitched
himself on to another post, and sat there dangling his
legs and kicking his heels, and waited for the Bagots'

"'I MUST TAKE THE BULL BY THE HORNS'"

cab to depart, that he might go up and face the righteous wrath of Taffy like a man, and bear up against his bitter reproaches for cowardice and desertion before the foe.

Next morning Taffy received two letters: one, a very long one, was from Mrs. Bagot. He read it twice over, and was forced to acknowledge that it was a very good letter—the letter of a clever, warm-hearted woman, but a woman also whose son was to her as the very apple of her eye. One felt she was ready to flay her dearest friend alive in order to make Little Billee a pair of gloves out of the skin, if he wanted a pair; but one also felt she would be genuinely sorry for the friend. Taffy's own mother had been a little like that, and he missed her every day of his life.

Full justice was done by Mrs. Bagot to all Trilby's qualities of head and heart and person; but at the same time she pointed out, with all the cunning and ingeniously casuistic logic of her sex, when it takes to special pleading (even when it has right on its side), what the consequences of such a marriage must inevitably be in a few years— even sooner! The quick disenchantment, the lifelong regret, on both sides!

He could not have found a word to controvert her arguments, save perhaps in his own private belief that Trilby and Little Billee were both exceptional people; and how could he hope to know Little Billee's nature better than the boy's own mother!

And if he had been the boy's elder brother in blood, as he already was in heart and affection, would he, should he, could he have given his fraternal sanction to such a match?

Both as his friend and his brother he felt it was out of the question.

The other letter was from Trilby, in her bold, careless handwriting, that sprawled all over the page, and her occasionally imperfect spelling. It ran thus:—

"MY DEAR, DEAR TAFFY—This is to say good-bye. I'm going away, to put an end to all this misery, for which nobody's to blame but myself.

"The very moment after I'd said *yes* to Little Billee I knew perfectly well what a stupid fool I was, and I've been ashamed of myself ever since. I had a miserable week, I can tell you. I knew how it would all turn out.

"I am dreadfully unhappy, but not half so unhappy as if I married him and he were ever to regret it and be ashamed of me; and of course he would, really, even if he didn't show it—good and kind as he is—an angel!

"Besides—of course I could never be a lady—how could I?—though I ought to have been one, I suppose. But everything seems to have gone wrong with me, though I never found it out before—and it can't be righted!

"Poor papa!

"I am going away with Jeannot. I've been neglecting him shamefully. I mean to make up for it all now.

"You mustn't try and find out where I am going; I know you won't if I beg you, nor any one else. It would make everything so much harder for me.

"Angèle knows; she has promised me not to tell. I should like to have a line from you very much. If you send it to her she will send it on to me.

"Dear Taffy, next to Little Billee, I love you and the Laird better than any one else in the whole world. I've never known real happiness till I met you. You have changed me into another person—you and Sandy and Little Billee.

"Oh, it *has* been a jolly time, though it didn't last long. It will have to do for me for life. So good-bye. I shall never, never forget; and remain, with dearest love, your ever faithful and most affectionate friend,

"TRILBY O'FERRALL.

"*P.S.*—When it has all blown over and settled again, if it ever does, I shall come back to Paris, perhaps, and see you again some day."

The good Taffy pondered deeply over this letter—read it half a dozen times at least; and then he kissed it, and put it back into its envelope and locked it up.

He knew what very deep anguish underlay this somewhat trivial expression of her sorrow.

He guessed how Trilby, so childishly impulsive and demonstrative in the ordinary intercourse of friendship, would be more reticent than most women in such a case as this.

He wrote to her warmly, affectionately, at great length, and sent the letter as she had told him.

The Laird also wrote a long letter full of tenderly-worded friendship and sincere regard. Both expressed their hope and belief that they would soon see her again, when the first bitterness of her grief would be over, and that the old pleasant relations would be renewed.

And then, feeling wretched, they went and silently lunched together at the Café de l'Odéon, where the omelets were good and the wine wasn't blue.

Late that evening they sat together in the studio, reading. They found they could not talk to each other very readily without Little Billee to listen—three's company sometimes and two's none !

Suddenly there was a tremendous getting up the dark stairs outside in a violent hurry, and Little Billee burst into the room like a small whirlwind—haggard, out of breath, almost speechless at first with excitement.

" Trilby ! where is she ? . . . what's become of her ? . . . She's run away . . . oh ! She's written me such a letter ! . . . We were to have been married . . . at the Embassy . . . my mother . . . she's been meddling ; and that cursed old ass . . . that beast . . . my uncle ! . . . They've been here ! I know all about it. . . . Why didn't you stick up for her ? . . ."

" I did . . . as well as I could. Sandy couldn't stand it, and cut."

" *You* stuck up for her . . . *you*—why, you agreed with my mother that she oughtn't to marry me—you— you false friend—*you !* . . . Why, she's an angel—far too good for the likes of *me* . . . you know she is. As . . . as for her social position and all that, what degrading rot ! Her father was as much a gentleman as mine . . . besides . . . what the devil do I care for her father ? . . . it's *her* I want—*her*—*her*—*her*, I tell you . . . I can't *live* without her . . . I must have her *back*—I must have her *back* . . . do you *hear ?* We were to have lived together at

Barbizon ⟨ ⟨ ⟨ all our lives—and I was to have painted stunning pictures . . . like those other fellows there. Who cares for *their* social position, I should like to know ⟨ . . or that of their wives? *Damn* social position! . . ⟨ we've often said so—over and over again. An artist's life should be *away* from the world above all that meanness and paltriness ⟨ . ⟨ all in his work. Social position,

"' TRILBY! WHERE IS SHE?'"

indeed! Over and over again we've said what fetid, bestial rot it all was—a thing to make one sick and shut one's self away from the world. . . . Why say one thing and act another? . . . Love comes before all—love levels all—love and art . . . and beauty—before such beauty as Trilby's rank doesn't exist. Such rank as mine, too! Good God! I'll never paint another stroke till I've got her back . . . never, never, never, I tell you—I can't—I won't! . . ."

And so the poor boy went on, tearing and raving about in his rampage, knocking over chairs and easels, stammering and shrieking, mad with excitement.

They tried to reason with him, to make him listen, to point out that it was not her social position alone that unfitted her to be his wife and the mother of his children, etc.

It was no good. He grew more and more uncontrollable, became almost unintelligible, he stammered so—a pitiable sight and pitiable to hear.

"Oh! oh! good heavens! are you so precious immaculate, you two, that you should throw stones at poor Trilby! What a shame, what a hideous shame it is that there should be one law for the woman and another for the man! . . . poor weak women—poor, soft, affectionate things that beasts of men are always running after, and pestering, and ruining, and trampling under foot.

LA SŒUR DE LITREBILI

. . . Oh! oh! it makes me sick—it makes me sick!" And finally he gasped and screamed and fell down in a fit on the floor.

The doctor was sent for; Taffy went in a cab to the Hôtel de Lille et d'Albion to fetch his mother; and poor Little Billee, quite unconscious, was undressed by Sandy and Madame Vinard and put into the Laird's bed.

The doctor came, and not long after Mrs. Bagot and her daughter. It was a serious case. Another doctor was called in. Beds were got and made up in the studio for the two grief-stricken ladies, and thus closed the eve of what was to have been poor Little Billee's wedding-day, it seems.

Little Billee's attack appears to have been a kind of epileptic seizure. It ended in brain fever and other complications—a long and tedious illness. It was many weeks before he was out of danger, and his convalescence was long and tedious too.

His nature seemed changed. He lay languid and listless—never even mentioned Trilby, except once to ask if she had come back, and if any one knew where she was, and if she had been written to.

She had not, it appears. Mrs. Bagot had thought it was better not, and Taffy and the Laird agreed with her that no good could come of writing.

Mrs. Bagot felt bitterly against the woman who had been the cause of all this trouble, and bitterly against herself for her injustice. It was an unhappy time for everybody.

There was more unhappiness still to come.

One day in February Madame Angèle Boisse called on Taffy and the Laird in the temporary studio where they worked. She was in terrible tribulation.

Trilby's little brother had died of scarlet fever and was buried, and Trilby had left her hiding-place the day after the funeral and had never come back, and this was a week ago. She and Jeannot had been living at a village called Vibraye, in La Sarthe, lodging with some poor people she knew—she washing and working with her needle till her brother fell ill.

She had never left his bedside for a moment, night or day, and when he died her grief was so terrible that people thought she would go out of her mind; and the day after he was buried she was not to be found anywhere—she had disappeared, taking nothing with her, not even her clothes—simply vanished and left no sign, no message of any kind.

All the ponds had been searched—all the wells, and the small stream that flows through Vibraye—and the old forest.

Taffy went to Vibraye, cross-examined everybody he could, communicated with the Paris police, but with no result; and every afternoon, with a beating heart, he went to the Morgue. . . .

The news was of course kept from Little Billee. There was no difficulty about this. He never asked a question, hardly ever spoke.

When he first got up and was carried into the studio he asked for his picture " The Pitcher Goes to the Well," and looked at it for a while, and then shrugged his shoulders and laughed—a miserable sort of laugh, painful to hear and see—the laugh of a cold old man, who laughs so as not to cry ! Then he looked at his mother and sister, and saw the sad havoc that grief and anxiety had wrought in them.

It seemed to him, as in a bad dream, that he had been mad for many years—a cause of endless sickening terror and distress; and that his poor weak wandering wits had come back at last, bringing in their train cruel remorse, and the remembrance of all the patient love and kindness that had been lavished on him; for many, many years ! His sweet sister—his dear, long-suffering mother ! what had really happened to make them look like this ?

And taking them both in his feeble arms, he fell a-weeping, quite desperately and for a long time.

And when his weeping-fit was over, when he had quite wept himself out, he fell asleep.

And when he awoke he was conscious that another sad thing had happened to him, and that for some mysterious cause his power of loving had not come back with his wandering wits—had been left behind—and it seemed to him that it was gone for ever and ever—would never come back again—not even his love for his mother and sister, not even his love for Trilby—where all *that* had once been was a void, a gap, a blankness. . . .

Truly, if Trilby had suffered much, she had also been the innocent cause of terrible suffering. Poor Mrs. Bagot, in her heart, could not forgive her.

I feel this is getting to be quite a sad story, and that it is high time to cut this part of it short.

As the warmer weather came, and Little Billee got stronger, the studio became more lively. The ladies' beds were removed to another studio on the next landing, which was vacant, and the friends came to see Little Billee, and make life more easy for him and his mother and sister.

As for Taffy and the Laird, they had already long been to Mrs. Bagot as a pair of crutches, without whose

"HE FELL A-WEEPING, QUITE DESPERATELY"

invaluable help she could never have held herself upright to pick her way in all this maze of trouble.

Then M. Carrel came every day to chat with his favourite pupil and gladden Mrs. Bagot's heart. And also Durien, Carnegie, Petrolicoconose, Vincent, Antony, Lorrimer, Dodor, and l'Zouzou; Mrs. Bagot thought the last two irresistible, when she had once been satisfied that they were "gentlemen," in spite of appearances. And, indeed, they showed themselves to great advantage; and though they were so much the opposite to Little Billee in every-

thing, she felt almost maternal towards them, and gave
them innocent, good, motherly advice, which they swallowed *avec attendrissement*, not even stealing a look at each
other. And they held Mrs. Bagot's wool, and listened to
Miss Bagot's sacred music with upturned pious eyes, and
mealy mouths that butter wouldn't melt in !

It is good to be a soldier and a detrimental; you touch
the hearts of women and charm them—old and young,
high or low (excepting, perhaps, a few worldly mothers of
marriageable daughters). They take the sticking of your
tongue in the cheek for the wearing of your heart on the
sleeve.

Indeed, good women all over the world, and ever since
it began, have loved to be bamboozled by these genial,
roistering dare-devils, who haven't got a penny to bless
themselves with (which is so touching), and are supposed
to carry their lives in their hands, even in piping times of
peace. Nay, even a few rare *bad* women sometimes;
such women as the best and wisest of us are often ready
to sell our souls for !

> " A lightsome eye, a soldier's mien,
>   A feather of the blue,
> A doublet of the Lincoln green—
>   No more of me you knew,
>   My love !
> No more of me you knew. . . ."

As if that wasn't enough, and to spare !

Little Billee could hardly realise that these two polite
and gentle and sympathetic sons of Mars were the lively
grigs who had made themselves so pleasant all round,
and in such a singular manner, on the top of that St.
Cloud omnibus; and he admired how they added hypocrisy
to their other crimes !

Svengali had gone back to Germany, it seemed, with
his pockets full of napoleons and big Havana cigars, and
wrapped in an immense fur-lined coat, which he meant to
wear all through the summer. But little Gecko often
came with his violin and made lovely music, and that
seemed to do Little Billee more good than anything else.

It made him realise in his brain all the love he could
no longer feel in his heart. The sweet melodic phrase,

"THE SWEET MELODIC PHRASE"

rendered by a master, was as wholesome, refreshing balm
to him while it lasted—as manna in the wilderness. It
was the one good thing within his reach, never to be
taken from him as long as his ear-drums remained and he
could hear a master play.

Poor Gecko treated the two English ladies *de bas en
haut* as if they had been goddesses, even when they accompanied him on the piano ! He begged their pardon for
every wrong note they struck, and adopted their " tempi "
—that is the proper technical term, I believe—and turned
scherzos and allegrettos into funeral dirges to please
them ; and agreed with them, poor little traitor, that it all
sounded much better like that !

O Beethoven ! O Mozart ! did you turn in your graves ?

Then, on fine afternoons, Little Billee was taken for
drives to the Bois de Boulogne with his mother and sister
in an open fly, and generally Taffy as a fourth ; to Passy,
Auteuil, Boulogne, St. Cloud, Meudon—there are many
charming places within an easy drive of Paris.

And sometimes Taffy or the Laird would escort Mrs.
and Miss Bagot to the Luxembourg Gallery, the Louvre,
the Palais Royal ; to the Comédie Française once or
twice ; and on Sundays, now and then, to the English
chapel in the Rue Marbœuf. It was all very pleasant ;
and Miss Bagot looks back on the days of her brother's
convalescence as among the happiest in her life.

And they would all five dine together in the studio,
with Madame Vinard to wait, and her mother (a cordon
bleu) for cook ; and the whole aspect of the place was
changed and made fragrant, sweet, and charming by all
this new feminine invasion and occupation.

And what is sweeter to watch than the dawn and
growth of love's young dream, when strength and beauty
meet together by the couch of a beloved invalid ?

Of course the sympathetic reader will foresee how
readily the stalwart Taffy fell a victim to the charms of
his friend's sweet sister, and how she grew to return his
more than brotherly regard ! and how, one lovely evening,
just as March was going out like a lamb (to make room for
the first of April), Little Billee joined their hands together,
and gave them his brotherly blessing !

As a matter of fact, however, nothing of this kind happened. Nothing ever happens but the *un*foreseen. Pazienza !

Then at length one day—it was a fine, sunny, showery day in April, by the bye, and the big studio window was open at the top and let in a pleasant breeze from the north-west, just as when our little story began—a railway omnibus drew up at the porte cochère in the Place St. Anatole des Arts, and carried away to the station of the Chemin de Fer du Nord Little Billee and his mother and sister, and all their belongings (the famous picture had gone before); and Taffy and the Laird rode with them, their faces very long, to see the last of the dear people, and of the train that was to bear them away from Paris; and Little Billee, with his quick, prehensile, æsthetic eye, took many a long and wistful parting gaze at many a French thing he loved, from the gray towers of Notre Dame downward—Heaven only knew when he might see them again !—so he tried to get their aspect well by heart, that he might have the better store of beloved shape and colour memories to chew the cud of when his lost powers of loving and remembering clearly should come back, and he lay awake at night and listened to the wash of the Atlantic along the beautiful red sandstone coast at home.

He had a faint hope that he should feel sorry at parting with Taffy and the Laird.

But when the time came for saying good-bye he couldn't feel sorry in the least, for all he tried and strained so hard !

So he thanked them so earnestly and profusely for all their kindness and patience and sympathy (as did also his mother and sister) that their hearts were too full to speak, and their manner was quite gruff—it was a way they had when they were deeply moved and didn't want to show it.

And as he gazed out of the carriage window at their two forlorn figures looking after him when the train steamed out of the station, his sorrow at not feeling sorry made him look so haggard and so woe-begone that they could scarcely bear the sight of him departing without them, and almost felt as if they must follow by the next train, and go and cheer him up in Devonshire, and themselves too.

"SORROWFULLY, ARM IN ARM"

They did not yield to this amiable weakness. Sorrowfully, arm-in-arm, with trailing umbrellas, they recrossed
the river, and found their way to the Café de l'Odéon,
where they ate many omelets in silence, and dejectedly
drank of the best they could get, and were very sad indeed.

. . . . . .

Nearly five years have elapsed since we bade farewell
and *au revoir* to Taffy and the Laird at the Paris station
of the Chemin de Fer du Nord, and wished Little Billee
and his mother and sister Godspeed on their way to
Devonshire, where the poor sufferer was to rest and lie
fallow for a few months, and recruit his lost strength and
energy, that he might follow up his first and well-deserved
success, which perhaps contributed just a little to his
recovery.

Many of my readers will remember his splendid *début*
at the Royal Academy in Trafalgar Square with that now
so famous canvas " The Pitcher Goes to the Well," and
how it was sold three times over on the morning of the
private view, the third time for a thousand pounds—
just five times what he got for it himself. And that
was thought a large sum in those days for a beginner's
picture two feet by four.

I am well aware that such a vulgar test is no criterion
whatever of a picture's real merit. But this picture is
well known to all the world by this time, and sold only
last year at Christie's (more than thirty-six years after it
was painted) for three thousand pounds.

Thirty-six years ! That goes a long way to redeem
even three thousand pounds of all their cumulative
vulgarity.

" The Pitcher " is now in the National Gallery, with
that other canvas by the same hand, " The Moon-Dial."
There they hang together for all who care to see them,
his first and his last—the blossom and the fruit.

He had not long to live himself, and it was his good
fortune, so rare among those whose work is probably
destined to live for ever, that he succeeded at his first
go off.

And his success was of the best and most flattering
kind.

It began high up, where it should, among the masters
of his own craft. But his fame filtered quickly down
to those immediately beneath, and through these to wider
circles. And there was quite enough of opposition and
vilification and coarse abuse of him to clear it of any
suspicion of cheapness or evanescence. What better
antiseptic can there be than the philistine's deep hate?
what sweeter, fresher, wholesomer music than the sound
of his voice when he doth so furiously rage ?

Yes ! That is " good production "—as Svengali would
have said—" C'est un cri du cœur."

And then, when popular acclaim brings the great dealers
and the big cheques, up rises the printed howl of the
duffer, the disappointed one, the " wounded thing with
an angry cry "—the prosperous and happy bagman that
should have been, who has given up all for art, and finds
he can't paint and make himself a name, after all, and
never will, so falls to writing about those who can—and
what writing !

To write in hissing dispraise of our more successful
fellow-craftsman, and of those who admire him—that is
not a clean or pretty trade. It seems, alas ! an easy one,
and it gives pleasure to so many. It does not even want
good grammar. But it pays—well enough even to start
and run a magazine with, instead of scholarship, and
taste, and talent ! humour, sense, wit, and wisdom ! It
is something like the purveying of pornographic pictures :
some of us look at them and laugh, and even buy. To
be a purchaser is bad enough; but to be the purveyor
thereof—ugh !

A poor devil of a cracked soprano (are there such
people still ?) who has been turned out of the Pope's choir
because he can't sing in tune, *after all !*—think of him
yelling and squeaking his treble rage at Santley—Sims
Reeves—Lablache !

Poor, lost, beardless nondescript ! why not fly to other
climes, where at least thou might'st hide from us thy
woeful crack, and keep thy miserable secret to thyself !
Are there no harems still left in Stamboul for the likes of
thee to sweep and clean, no women's beds to make and
slops to empty, and doors and windows to bar—and tales

to carry, and the pasha's confidence and favour and protection to win? Even *that* is a better trade than pander-
ing for hire to the basest instinct of all—the dirty pleasure
we feel (some of us) in seeing mud and dead cats and
rotten eggs flung at those we cannot but admire—and
secretly envy!

All of which eloquence means that Little Billee was
pitched into right and left, as well as overpraised. And
it all rolled off him like water off a duck's back, both
praise and blame.

It was a happy summer for Mrs. Bagot, a sweet compensation for all the anguish of the winter that had gone
before, with her two beloved children together under her
wing, and all the world (for her) ringing with the praise
of her boy, the apple of her eye, so providentially rescued
from the very jaws of death, and from other dangers
almost as terrible to her fiercely-jealous maternal heart.

And his affection for her *seemed* to grow with his returning health; but, alas! he was never again to be quite
the same light-hearted, innocent, expansive lad he had
been before that fatal year spent in Paris.

One chapter of his life was closed, never to be reopened,
never to be spoken of again by him to her, by her to him.
She could neither forgive nor forget. She could but be
silent.

Otherwise he was pleasant and sweet to live with, and
everything was done to make his life at home as sweet
and pleasant as a loving mother could—as could a most
charming sister—and others' sisters who were charming
too, and much disposed to worship at the shrine of this
young celebrity, who woke up one morning in their little
village to find himself famous, and bore his blushing
honours so meekly. And among them the vicar's daughter,
his sister's friend and co-teacher at the Sunday-school, " a
simple, pure, and pious maiden of gentle birth," everything
he once thought a young lady should be; and her name
it was Alice, and she was sweet, and her hair was brown—
as brown! . . .

And if he no longer found the simple country pleasures,
the junketings and pic-nics, the garden-parties and inno-

cent little musical evenings, quite so exciting as of old, he
never showed it.

Indeed, there was much that he did not show, and that
his mother and sister tried in vain to guess—many things.

And among them one thing that constantly preoccupied
and distressed him—the numbness of his affections. He
could be as easily demonstrative to his mother and sister
as though nothing had ever happened to him—from the
mere force of a sweet old habit—even more so, out of
sheer gratitude and compunction.

But alas ! he felt that in his heart he could no longer
care for them in the least !—nor for Taffy, nor the Laird,
nor for himself; not even for Trilby, of whom he constantly thought, but without emotion; and of whose
strange disappearance he had been told, and the story
had been confirmed in all its details by Angèle Boisse, to
whom he had written.

It was as though some part of his brain where his
affections were seated had been paralysed, while all the
rest of it was as keen and as active as ever. He felt like
some poor live bird or beast or reptile, a part of whose
cerebrum (or cerebellum, or whatever it is) had been dug
out by the vivisector for experimental purposes; and the
strongest emotional feeling he seemed capable of was his
anxiety and alarm about this curious symptom, and his
concern as to whether he ought to mention it or not.

He did not do so, for fear of causing distress, hoping
that it would pass away in time, and redoubled his caresses
to his mother and sister, and clung to them more than
ever; and became more considerate of others in thought
and manner, word, and deed than he had ever been
before, as though by constantly assuming the virtue he
had no longer he would gradually coax it back again.
There was no trouble he would not take to give pleasure
to the humblest.

Also, his vanity about himself had become as nothing,
and he missed it almost as much as his affection.

Yet he told himself over and over again that he was a
great artist, and that he would spare no pains to make
himself a greater. But that was no merit of his own.

$2 + 2 = 4$, also $2 \times 2 = 4$: that peculiarity was no reason why 4 should be conceited; for what was 4 but a result, either way?

Well, he was like 4—just an inevitable result of circumstances over which he had no control—a mere product or sum; and though he meant to make himself as big a 4 as he could (to cultivate his peculiar *fourness*), he could no longer feel the old conceit and self-complacency; and they had been a joy, and it was hard to do without them.

At the bottom of it all was a vague, disquieting unhappiness, a constant fidget.

And it seemed to him, and much to his distress, that such mild unhappiness would be the greatest he could ever feel henceforward—but that, such as it was, it would never leave him, and that his moral existence would be for evermore one long gray gloomy blank—the glimmer of twilight—never glad, confident morning again!

So much for Little Billee's convalescence.

Then one day in the late autumn he spread his wings and flew away to London, which was very ready with open arms to welcome William Bagot, the already famous painter, *alias* Little Billee!

PART FIFTH

An Interlude

" Then the mortal coldness of the soul like death itself comes
down;
It cannot feel for others' woes, it dare not dream its own;
That heavy chill has frozen o'er the fountain of our tears,
And, though the eye may sparkle yet, 'tis where the ice
appears.

" Though wit may flash from fluent lips, and mirth distract
the breast,
Through midnight hours that yield no more their former
hope of rest :
'Tis but as ivy leaves around a ruined turret wreathe,
All green and wildly fresh without, but worn and gray
beneath."

WHEN Taffy and the Laird went back to the studio in
the Place St. Anatole des Arts, and resumed their ordinary
life there, it was with a sense of desolation and dull
bereavement beyond anything they could have imagined;
and this did not seem to lessen as the time wore on.

They realised for the first time how keen and penetrating
and unintermittent had been the charm of those two
central figures—Trilby and Little Billee—and how hard
it was to live without them, after such intimacy as had
been theirs.

" Oh, it *has* been a jolly time, though it didn't last
long ! " So Trilby had written in her farewell letter to
Taffy; and these words were true for Taffy and the
Laird as well as for her.

And that is the worst of those dear people who have
charm : they are so terrible to do without, when once
you have got accustomed to them and all their ways.

And when, besides being charming, they are simple,
clever, affectionate, constant, and sincere, like Trilby and
Little Billee ! Then the lamentable hole their disappear-

ance makes is not to be filled up! And when they are full of genius, like Little Billee—and like Trilby, funny without being vulgar! For so she always seemed to the Laird and Taffy, even in French (in spite of her Gallic audacities of thought, speech, and gesture).

All seemed to have suffered change. The very boxing and fencing were gone through perfunctorily, for mere health's sake; and a thin layer of adipose deposit began to soften the outlines of the hills and dales on Taffy's mighty forearm.

Dodor and l'Zouzou no longer came so often, now that the charming Little Billee and his charming mother and still more charming sister had gone away—nor Carnegie, nor Antony, nor Lorrimer, nor Vincent, nor the Greek. Gecko never came at all. Even Svengali was missed, little as he had been liked. It is a dismal and sulky-looking piece of furniture, a grand piano that nobody ever plays—with all its sound and its souvenirs locked up inside—a kind of mausoleum! a lop-sided coffin, trestles and all! So it went back to London by the "little quickness," just as it had come!

Thus Taffy and the Laird grew quite sad and mopy, and lunched at the Café de l'Odéon every day—till the goodness of the omelets palled, and the redness of the wine there got on their nerves and into their heads and faces, and made them sleepy till dinner-time. And then, waking up, they dressed respectably, and dined expensively, "like gentlemen," in the Palais Royal, or the Passage Choiseul, or the Passage des Panoramas—for three francs, three francs fifty, even five francs a head, and half a franc to the waiter!—and went to the theatre almost every night, on that side of the water—and more often than not they took a cab home, each smoking a Panatellas, which costs twenty-five centimes—five sous—$2\frac{1}{2}d$. !

Then they feebly drifted into quite decent society—like Lorrimer and Carnegie—with dress-coats and white ties on, and their hair parted in the middle and down the back of the head, and brought over the ears in a bunch at each side, as was the English fashion in those days; and subscribed to *Galignani's Messenger*; and had themselves proposed and seconded for the Cercle Anglais in the Rue

DEMORALISATION

Sainte-n'y Touche, a circle of British philistines of the
very deepest dye; and went to hear divine service on
Sunday mornings in Rue Marbœuf!

Indeed, by the end of the summer they had sunk into
such depths of demoralisation that they felt they must
really have a change; and decided on giving up the
studio in the Place St. Anatole des Arts, and leaving Paris
for good; and going to settle for the winter in Düsseldorf,
which is a very pleasant place for English painters who
do not wish to overwork themselves—as the Laird well
knew, having spent a year there.

It ended in Taffy's going to Antwerp for the Kermesse,
to paint the Flemish drunkard of our time just as he
really is; and the Laird's going to Spain, so that he
might study toreadors from the life.

I may as well state here that the Laird's toreador
pictures, which had had quite a vogue in Scotland as
long as he had been content to paint them in the Place

St. Anatole des Arts, quite ceased to please (or sell) after
he had been to Seville and Madrid; so he took to painting
Roman cardinals and Neapolitan pifferari from the depths
of his consciousness—and was so successful that he made
up his mind he would never spoil his market by going to
Italy !

So he went and painted his cardinals and his pifferari
in Algiers, and Taffy joined him there, and painted
Algerian Jews—just as they really are (and didn't sell
them); and then they spent a year in Munich, and then
a year in Düsseldorf, and a winter in Cairo, and so on.

And all this time, Taffy, who took everything *au grand
sérieux*—especially the claims and obligations of friendship
—corresponded regularly with Little Billee, who wrote
him long and amusing letters back again, and had plenty
to say about his life in London—which was a series of
triumphs, artistic and social—and you would have thought
from his letters, modest though they were, that no happier
young man, or more elate, was to be found anywhere in
the world.

It was a good time in England, just then, for young
artists of promise; a time of evolution, revolution, change,
and development—of the founding of new schools and
the crumbling away of old ones—a keen struggle for
existence—a surviving of the fit—a preparation, let us
hope, for the ultimate survival of the fittest.

And among the many glories of this particular period
two names stand out very conspicuously—for the immediate and (so far) lasting fame their bearers achieved, and
the wide influence they exerted, and continue to exert
still.

The world will not easily forget Frederic Walker and
William Bagot, those two singularly gifted boys, whom it
soon became the fashion to bracket together, to compare
and to contrast, as one compares and contrasts Thackeray
and Dickens, Carlyle and Macaulay, Tennyson and
Browning—a futile though pleasant practice, of which
the temptations seem irresistible !

Yet why compare the lily and the rose?

These two young masters had the genius and the luck
to be the progenitors of much of the best art work that

has been done in England during the last thirty years, in oils, in water colour, in black and white.

They were both essentially English and of their own time; both absolutely original, receiving their impressions straight from nature itself; uninfluenced by any school, ancient or modern, they founded schools instead of following any, and each was a law unto himself, and a law-giver unto many others. Both were equally great in whatever they attempted—landscape, figures, birds, beasts, or fishes. Who does not remember the fishmonger's shop, by F. Walker, or W. Bagot's little piebald piglings, and their venerable black mother, and their immense fat wallowing pink papa? An ineffable charm of poetry and refinement, of pathos and sympathy and delicate humour combined, an incomparable ease and grace and felicity of workmanship belong to each; and yet in their work are they not as wide apart as the poles; each complete in himself and yet a complement to the other?

FRED WALKER

And, oddly enough, they were both singularly alike in aspect—both small and slight, though beautifully made, with tiny hands and feet; always arrayed as the lilies of the field, for all they toiled and spun so arduously; both had regularly-featured faces of a noble cast and most winning character; both had the best and simplest manners in the world, and a way of getting themselves much and quickly and permanently liked. . . .

Que la terre leur soit légère !

And who can say that the fame of one is greater than the other's !

Their pinnacles are twin, I venture to believe—of just an equal height and width and thickness, like their bodies in this life; but unlike their frail bodies in one respect:

no taller pinnacles are to be seen, methinks, in all the
garden of the deathless dead painters of our time, and
none more built to last !

But it is not with the art of Little Billee, nor with his
fame as a painter, that we are chiefly concerned in this
unpretending little tale, except in so far as they have
some bearing on his character and his fate.

" I should like to know the detailed history of the
Englishman's first love, and how he lost his innocence ! "

" Ask him ! "

" Ask him yourself ! "

Thus Papelard and Bouchardy, on the morning of Little
Billee's first appearance at Carrel's studio, in the Rue des
Potirons St. Michel.

And that is the question the present scribe is doing his
little best to answer,

A good-looking, famous, well-bred, and well-dressed
youth finds that London society opens its doors very
readily; he hasn't long to knock; and it would be difficult
to find a youth more fortunately situated, handsomer,
more famous, better dressed or better bred, more seemingly happy and successful, with more attractive qualities
and more condonable faults, than Little Billee, as Taffy
and the Laird found him when they came to London after
their four or five years in foreign parts—their Wanderjahr.

He had a fine studio and a handsome suite of rooms
in Fitzroy Square. Beautiful specimens of his unfinished
work, endless studies, hung on his studio walls. Everything else was as nice as it could be—the furniture, the
bibelots, and bric-à-brac, the artistic foreign and Eastern
knick-knacks and draperies and hangings and curtains
and rugs—the semi-grand piano by Collard and Collard.

That immortal canvas, the " Moon-Dial " (just begun,
and already commissioned by Moses Lyon, the famous
picture-dealer), lay on his easel.

No man worked harder and with teeth more clinched
than Little Billee when he was at work—none rested or
played more discreetly when it was time to rest or play.

The glass on his mantelpiece was full of cards of invitation, reminders, pretty mauve and pink and lilac scented notes; nor were coronets wanting on many of these hospitable little missives. He had quite overcome his fancied aversion for bloated dukes and lords and the rest (we all do sooner or later, if things go well with us); especially for their wives and sisters and daughters and female cousins; even their mothers and aunts. In point of fact, and in spite of his tender years, he was in some danger (for his art) of developing into that type so adored by sympathetic women who haven't got much to do: the friend, the tame cat, the platonic lover (with many loves)—the squire of dames, the trusty one, of whom husbands and brothers have no fear!—the delicate, harmless dilettante of Eros—the dainty shepherd who dwells " dans le pays du tendre ! "—and stops there !

The woman flatters and the man confides—and there is no danger whatever, I'm told—and I'm glad !

One man loves his fiddle (or, alas ! his neighbour's sometimes) for all the melodies he can wake from it—it is but a selfish love !

PLATONIC LOVE

Another, who is no fiddler, may love a fiddle too; for its symmetry, its neatness, its colour—its delicate grainings, the lovely lines and curves of its back and front—for its own sake, so to speak. He may have a whole galleryful of fiddles to love in this innocent way—a harem ! —and yet not know a single note of music, or even care to hear one. He will dust them and stroke them, and take them down and try to put them in tune—*pizzicato !*—and put them back again, and call them ever such sweet little pet exotic names : viol, viola, viola d'amore, viol di gamba, violino mio ! and breathe his little troubles into them, and they will give back inaudible little murmurs in sympathetic response, like a damp Æolian harp; but he will never draw a bow across the strings, nor wake a single chord—or discord !

And who shall say he is not wise in his generation? It is but an old-fashioned philistine notion that fiddles were only made to be played on—the fiddles themselves are beginning to resent it ; and rightly, I wot !

In this harmless fashion Little Billee was friends with more than one fine lady *de par le monde.*

Indeed, he had been reproached by his more bohemian brothers of the brush for being something of a tuft-hunter —most unjustly. But nothing gives such keen offence to our unsuccessful brother, bohemian or bourgeois, as our sudden intimacy with the so-called great, the little lords and ladies of this little world ! Not even our fame and success, and all the joy and pride they bring us, are so hard to condone—so embittering, so humiliating, to the jealous fraternal heart.

Alas ! poor humanity—that the mere countenance of our betters (if they *are* our betters !) should be thought so priceless a boon, so consummate an achievement, so crowning a glory, as all that !

> " A dirty bit of orange-peel,
> The stump of a cigar—
> Once trod on by a princely heel,
> How beautiful they are ! "

Little Billee was no tuft-hunter—he was the tuft-hunted, or had been. No one of his kind was ever more persist-

ently, resolutely, hospitably harried than this young " hare
with many friends " by people of rank and fashion.

And at first he thought them most charming; as they
so often are, these graceful, gracious, gay, good-natured
stoics and barbarians, whose manners are as easy and
simple as their morals—but how much better !—and who,
at least, have this charm, that they can wallow in untold
gold (when they happen to possess it) without ever seeming
to stink of the same : yes, they bear wealth gracefully—
and the want of it more gracefully still ! and these are
pretty accomplishments that have yet to be learned by
our new aristocracy of the shop and counting-house, Jew
or Gentile, which is everywhere elbowing its irresistible
way to the top and front of everything, both here and
abroad.

Then he discovered that, much as you might be with
them, you could never be *of* them, unless perchance you
managed to hook on by marrying one of their ugly duck-
lings—their failures—their remnants ! and even then life
isn't all beer and skittles for a rank outsider, I'm told !
Then he discovered that he didn't want to be *of* them in
the least; especially at such a cost as that ! and that to
be very much *with* them was apt to pall, like everything
else !

Also, he found that they were very mixed—good, bad,
and indifferent; and not always very dainty or select in
their predilections, since they took unto their bosoms
such queer outsiders (just for the sake of being amused
a little while) that their capricious favour ceased to be
an honour and a glory—if it ever was ! And then, their
fickleness!

Indeed, he found, or thought he found, that they could
be just as clever, as liberal, as polite or refined—as narrow,
insolent, swaggering, coarse, and vulgar—as handsome, as
ugly—as graceful, as ungainly—as modest or conceited,
as any other upper class of the community—and indeed
some lower ones !

Beautiful young women, who had been taught how to
paint pretty little landscapes (with an ivy-mantled ruin
in the middle distance), talked technically of painting to
him, *de pair à pair*, as though they were quite on the

same artistic level, and didn't mind admitting it, in spite of the social gulf between.

Hideous old frumps (osseous or obese, yet with unduly bared necks and shoulders that made him sick) patronised him and gave him good advice, and told him to emulate Mr. Buckner both in his genius and his manners—since Mr. Buckner was the only " gentleman " who ever painted for hire; and they promised him, in time, an equal success !

Here and there some sweet old darling specially enslaved him by her kindness, grace, knowledge of life, and tender womanly sympathy, like the dowager Lady Chiselhurst— or some sweet young one, like the lovely Duchess of Towers, by her beauty, wit, good-humour, and sisterly interest in all he did, and who in some vague, distant manner constantly reminded him of Trilby, although she was such a great and fashionable lady !

But just such darlings, old or young, were to be found, with still higher ideals, in less exalted spheres; and were easier of access, with no impassable gulf between—spheres where there was no patronising, nothing but deference and warm appreciation and delicate flattery, from men and women alike—and where the aged Venuses, whose prime was of the days of Waterloo, went with their historical remains duly shrouded, like ivy-mantled ruins (and in the middle distance !).

So he actually grew tired of the great before they had time to tire of him—incredible as it may seem, and against nature; and this saved him many a heart-burning; and he ceased to be seen at fashionable drums or gatherings of any kind, except in one or two houses where he was especially liked and made welcome for his own sake; such as Lord Chiselhurst's in Piccadilly, where the " Moon-Dial " found a home for a few years before going to its last home and final resting-place in the National Gallery (*R.I.P.*); or Baron Stoppenheim's in Cavendish Square, where many lovely little water-colours signed W. B. occupied places of honour on gorgeously-gilded walls; or the gorgeously-gilded bachelor rooms of Mr. Moses Lyon, the picture-dealer in Upper Conduit Street—for Little Billee (I much grieve to say it of a hero of romance) was

"DARLINGS, OLD OR YOUNG"

an excellent man of business. That infinitesimal dose of the good old Oriental blood kept him straight, and not only made him stick to his last through thick and thin, but also to those whose foot his last was found to match (for he couldn't or wouldn't alter his last).

He loved to make as much money as he could, that he might spend it royally in pretty gifts to his mother and sister, whom it was his pleasure to load in this way, and whose circumstances had been very much altered by his

" THE MOON-DIAL "

quick success. There was never a more generous son or brother than Little Billee of the clouded heart, that couldn't love any longer !

As a set-off to all these splendours, it was also his pleasure now and again to study London life at its lower den—the eastest end of all. Whitechapel, the Minories, the Docks, Ratcliffe Highway, Rotherhithe, soon got to know him well, and he found much to interest him and much to like among their denizens, and made as many friends there among ship-carpenters, excisemen, long-

shoremen, jack-tars, and what not, as in Bayswater and
Belgravia (or Bloomsbury).

He was especially fond of frequenting sing-songs, or
" free-and-easies," where good hard-working fellows met
of an evening to relax and smoke and drink and sing,
round a table well loaded with steaming tumblers and
pewter pots, at one end of which sits Mr. Chairman in all
his glory, and at the other " Mr. Vice." They are open
to any one who can afford a pipe, a screw of tobacco, and
a pint of beer, and who is willing to do his best and sing
a song.

No introduction is needed; as soon as any one has
seated himself and made himself comfortable, Mr. Chairman taps the table with his long clay pipe, begs for
silence, and says to his vis-à-vis : " Mr. Vice, it strikes me
as the gen'l'man as is just come in 'as got a singing face.
Per'aps, Mr. Vice, you'll be so very kind as juster harsk
the aforesaid gentl'man to oblige us with a 'armony."

Mr. Vice then puts it to the new-comer, who, thus
appealed to, simulates a modest surprise, and finally pro-
fesses his willingness, like Mr. Barkis; then, clearing his
throat a good many times, looks up to the ceiling, and
after one or two unsuccessful starts in different keys,
bravely sings " Kathleen Mavourneen," let us say—perhaps in a touchingly sweet tenor voice :

> " Kathleen Mavourneen, the gry dawn is brykin,
> The 'orn of the 'unter is 'eard on the 'ill . . ."

And Little Billee didn't mind the dropping of all these
aitches if the voice was sympathetic and well in tune,
and the sentiment simple, tender, and sincere.

Or else, with a good rolling jingo bass, it was,

> " 'Earts o' hoak are our ships; 'earts o' hoak are our men;
> And we'll fight and we'll conkwer agen and agen ! "

And no imperfection of accent, in Little Billee's estima-
tion, subtracted one jot from the manly British pluck
that found expression in these noble sentiments, nor
added one tittle to their swaggering, blatant, and idiotic-
ally aggressive vulgarity !

Well, the song finishes with general applause all round.

Then the chairman says, " Your 'ealth and song, sir ! "
And drinks, and all do the same.

Then Mr. Vice asks, " What shall we 'ave the pleasure
of saying, sir, after that very nice 'armony ? "

And the blushing vocalist, if he knows the ropes, replies,
" A roast leg o' mutton in Newgate, and nobody to eat
it ! " Or else, " May 'im as is going up the 'ill o' prosperity never meet a friend coming down ! " Or else,
" 'Ere's to 'er as shares our sorrers and doubles our joys ! "
Or else, " 'Ere's to 'er as shares our joys and doubles our
expenses ! " and so forth.

More drink, more applause, and many 'ear 'ear's. And
Mr. Vice says to the singer : " You call, sir. Will you
be so good as to call on some other gen'l'man for a
'armony ? " And so the evening goes on.

And nobody was more quickly popular at such gatherings, or sang better songs, or proposed more touching
sentiments, or filled either chair or vice-chair with more
grace and dignity than Little Billee. Not even Dodor or
l'Zouzou could have beaten him at that.

And he was as happy, as genial, and polite, as much at
his ease, in these humble gatherings as in the gilded
saloons of the great, where grand-pianos are, and hired
accompanists, and highly paid singers, and a good deal of
talk while they sing.

So his powers of quick, wide, universal sympathy grew
and grew, and made up to him a little for his lost power
of being specially fond of special individuals. For he
made no close friends among men, and ruthlessly snubbed
all attempts at intimacy—all advances towards an affection which he felt he could not return ; and more than
one enthusiastic admirer of his talent and his charm was
forced to acknowledge that, with all his gifts, he seemed
heartless and capricious ; as ready to drop you as he had
been to take you up.

He loved to be wherever he could meet his kind, high
or low ; and felt as happy on a penny steamer as on the
yacht of a millionaire—on the crowded knifeboard of an
omnibus as on the box-seat of a nobleman's drag—happier ;
he liked to feel the warm contact of his fellow-man at
either shoulder and at his back, and didn't object to a

THE CHAIRMAN

little honest grime ! And I think all this genial caressing
love of his kind, this depth and breadth of human sympathy, are patent in all his work.

On the whole, however, he came to prefer for society
that of the best and cleverest of his own class—those
who live and prevail by the professional exercise of their
own specially-trained and highly-educated wits, the skilled
workmen of the brain—from the Lòrd Chief-Justice of
England downward—the salt of the earth, in his opinion;
and stuck to them.

There is no class so genial and sympathetic as *our own*,
in the long run—even if it be but the criminal class !
none where the welcome is likely to be so genuine and
sincere, so easy to win, so difficult to outstay, if we be but
decently pleasant and successful ; none where the memory
of us will be kept so green (if we leave any memory at
all !).

So Little Billee found it expedient, when he wanted
rest and play, to seek them at the houses of those whose
rest and play were like his own—little halts in a seeming
happy life-journey, full of toil and strain and endeavour ;
oases of sweet water and cooling shade, where the food
was good and plentiful, though the tents might not be of
cloth of gold ; where the talk was of something more to
his taste than court or sport or narrow party politics ;
the new beauty ; the coming match of the season ; the
coming ducal conversion to Rome ; the last elopement in
high life—the next ! and where the music was that of
the greatest music-makers that can be, who found rest
and play in making better music for love than they ever
made for hire—and were listened to as they should be,
with understanding and religious silence, and all the
fervent gratitude they deserved.

There were several such houses in London then—and
are still—thank Heaven ! And Little Billee had his little
billet there—and there he was wont to drown himself in
waves of lovely sound, or streams of clever talk, or rivers
of sweet feminine adulation, seas ! oceans !—a somewhat
relaxing bath !—and forget for a while his everlasting
chronic plague of heart-insensibility, which no doctor
could explain or cure, and to which he was becoming

gradually resigned—as one does to deafness or blindness
or locomotor ataxia—for it had lasted nearly five years !
But now and again, during sleep, and in a blissful dream,
the lost power of loving—of loving mother, sister, friend—
would be restored to him, just as with a blind man who
sometimes dreams he has recovered his sight; and the
joy of it would wake him to the sad reality : till he got
to know, even in his dream, that he was only dreaming
after all, whenever that priceless boon seemed to be his
own once more—and did his utmost not to wake. And
these were nights to be marked with a white stone, and
remembered !

And nowhere was he happier than at the houses of the
great surgeons and physicians who interested themselves
in his strange disease. When the Little Billees of this
world fall ill, the great surgeons and physicians (like the
great singers and musicians) do better for them, out of
mere love and kindness, than for the princes of the earth,
who pay them thousand-guinea fees and load them with
honours.

And of all these notable London houses none was
pleasanter than that of Cornelys, the great sculptor, and
Little Billee was such a favourite in that house that he
was able to take his friends Taffy and the Laird there the
very day they came to London.

First of all they dined together at a delightful little
Franco-Italian pothouse near Leicester Square, where
they had *bouillabaisse* (imagine the Laird's delight), and
spaghetti, and a *poulet rôti*, which is *such* a different affair
from a roast fowl ! and salad, which Taffy was allowed
to make and mix himself; and they all smoked just
where they sat, the moment they had swallowed their
food—as had been their way in the good old Paris
days.

That dinner was a happy one for Taffy and the Laird,
with their Little Billee apparently unchanged—as demonstrative, as genial and caressing as ever, and with no
swagger to speak of; and with so many things to talk
about that were new to them, and of such delightful
interest ! They also had much to say—but they didn't

A HAPPY DINNER

say very much about Paris, for fear of waking up Heaven
knows what sleeping dogs !

And every now and again, in the midst of all this
pleasant forgathering and communion of long-parted
friends, the pangs of Little Billee's miserable mind-malady
would shoot through him like poisoned arrows.

He would catch himself thinking how fat and fussy
and serious about trifles Taffy had become; and what a
shiftless, feckless, futile duffer was the Laird; and how
greedy they both were, and how red and coarse their ears
and gills and cheeks grew as they fed, and how shiny
their faces; and how little he would care, try as he might,
if they both fell down dead under the table ! And this
would make him behave more caressingly to them, more
genially and demonstratively than ever—for he knew it
was all a grewsome physical ailment of his own, which he
could no more help than a cataract in his eye !

Then, catching sight of his own face and form in a
mirror, he would curse himself for a puny, misbegotten
shrimp, an imp—an abortion—no bigger, by the side of
the herculean Taffy or the burly Laird of Cockpen, than
sixpennorth o' halfpence : a wretched little overrated
follower of a poor trivial craft—a mere light amuser !
For what did pictures matter, or whether they were good
or bad, except to the triflers who painted them, the
dealers who sold them, the idle, uneducated, purse-proud
fools who bought them and stuck them up on their walls
because they were told !

And he felt that if a dynamite shell were beneath the
table where they sat, and its fuse were smoking under
their very noses, he would neither wish to warn his friends
nor move himself. He didn't care a d—— !

And all this made him so lively and brilliant in his
talk, so fascinating and droll and witty, that Taffy and
the Laird wondered at the improvement success and the
experience of life had wrought in him, and marvelled at
the happiness of his lot, and almost found it in their
warm affectionate hearts to feel a touch of envy !

Oddly enough, in a brief flash of silence, " entre la poire
et le fromage," they heard a foreigner at an adjoining
table (one of a very noisy group) exclaim : " Mais quand

je vous dis que j'l'ai entendue, moi, La Svengali ! et même qu'elle a chanté l'Impromptu de Chopin absolument comme si c'était un piano qu'on jouait ! voyons ! . . ."

" Farceur ! la bonne blague !" said another—and then the conversation became so noisily general it was no good listening any more.

"Svengali ! how funny that name should turn up ! I wonder what's become of *our* Svengali, by the way?" observed Taffy.

" I remember *his* playing Chopin's Impromptu," said Little Billee; " what a singular coincidence !"

There were to be more coincidences that night; it never rains them but it pours !

So our three friends finished their coffee and liqueured up, and went to Cornelys's three in a hansom—

> " Like Mars,
> A-smokin' their poipes and cigyars."

Sir Louis Cornelys, as everybody knows, lives in a palace on Campden Hill, a house of many windows; and whichever window he looks out of, he sees his own garden and very little else. In spite of his eighty years, he works as hard as ever, and his hand has lost but little of its cunning. But he no longer gives those splendid parties that made him almost as famous a host as he was an artist.

When his beautiful wife died he shut himself up from the world; and now he never stirs out of his house and grounds except to fulfil his duties at the Royal Academy, and dine once a year with the Queen.

It was very different in the early sixties. There was no pleasanter or more festive house than his in London, winter or summer—no lordlier host than he—no more irresistible hostesses than Lady Cornelys and her lovely daughters; and if ever music had a right to call itself divine, it was there you heard it—on late Saturday nights during the London season—when the foreign birds of song come over to reap their harvest in London Town.

It was on one of the most brilliant of these Saturday nights that Taffy and the Laird, chaperoned by Little Billee, made their *début* at Mechelen Lodge, and were

"A-SMOKIN' THEIR POIPES AND CIGYARS"

received at the door of the immense music-room by a tall, powerful man with splendid eyes and a gray beard, and a small velvet cap on his head—and by a Greek matron so beautiful and stately and magnificently attired that they felt inclined to sink them on their bended knees as in the presence of some overwhelming Eastern royalty—and were only prevented from doing so, perhaps, by the simple, sweet, and cordial graciousness of her welcome.

And whom should they be shaking hands with next but Antony, Lorrimer, and the Greek—each with a beard and moustache of nearly five years' growth !

But they had no time for much exuberant greeting, for there was a sudden piano crash—and then an immediate silence, as though for pins to drop—and Signor Giuglini and the wondrous maiden Adelina Patti sang the " Miserere " out of Signor Verdi's most famous opera—to the delight of all but a few very superior ones who had just read Mendelssohn's letters (or misread them) and despised Italian music, and thought cheaply of " mere virtuosity," either vocal or instrumental.

When this was over, Little Billee pointed out all the lions to his friends—from the Prime Minister down to the present scribe—who was right glad to meet them again and talk of auld lang syne, and present them to the daughters of the house and other charming ladies.

Then Roucouly, the great French baritone, sang Durien's favourite song—

" Plaisir d'amour ne dure qu'un moment;
Chagrin d'amour dure toute la vie . . ."

with quite a little drawing-room voice—but quite as divinely as he had sung " Noël, noël," at the Madeleine in full blast one certain Christmas Eve our three friends remembered well.

Then there was a violin solo by young Joachim, then as now the greatest violinist of his time ; and a solo on the pianoforte by Madame Schumann, his only peeress ! and these came as a wholesome check to the levity of those for whom all music is but an agreeable pastime, a mere emotional delight, in which the intellect has no part ; and also as a well-deserved humiliation to all virtuosi who play so charmingly that they make their listeners forget the master who invented the music in the lesser master who interprets it !

For these two—man and woman—the highest of their kind, never let you forget it was Sebastian Bach they were playing—playing in absolute perfection, in absolute forgetfulness of themselves—so that if you weren't up to Bach, you didn't have a very good time !

But if you were (or wished it to be understood or thought you were), you seized your opportunity and you scored ; and by the earnestness of your rapt and tranced immobility, and the stony, gorgon-like intensity of your gaze, you rebuked the frivolous—as you had rebuked them before by the listlessness and carelessness of your bored resignation to the Signorina Patti's trills and fiori-tures, or M. Roucouly's pretty little French mannerisms.

And what added so much to the charm of this delightful concert was that the guests were not packed together sardine-wise, as they are at most concerts ; they were comparatively few and well chosen, and could get up and walk about and talk to their friends between the pieces, and wander off into other rooms and look at endless beautiful things, and stroll in the lovely grounds, by moon or star or Chinese-lantern light.

And there the frivolous could sit and chat and laugh and flirt when Bach was being played inside ; and the earnest wander up and down together in soul-communion, through darkened walks and groves and alleys where the sound of French or Italian warblings could not reach them, and talk in earnest tones of the great Zola, or Guy de Maupassant and Pierre Loti, and exult in beautiful English over the inferiority of English literature, English art, English music, English everything else.

For these high-minded ones who can only bear the sight of classical pictures and the sound of classical music do not necessarily read classical books in any language— no Shakespeares or Dantes or Molières or Goethes for *them*. They know a trick worth two of that !

And the mere fact that these three immortal French writers of light books I have just named had never been heard of at this particular period doesn't very much matter; they had cognate predecessors whose names I happen to forget. Any stick will do to beat a dog with, and history is always repeating itself.

Feydeau, or Flaubert, let us say—or for those who don't know French and cultivate an innocent mind, Miss Austen (for to be dead and buried is almost as good as to be French and immoral!)—and Sebastian Bach, and Sandro Botticelli—that all the arts should be represented. These names are rather discrepant, but they make very good sticks for dog-beating; and with a thorough knowledge and appreciation of these (or the semblance thereof), you were well equipped in those days to hold your own among the elect of intellectual London circles, and snub the philistine to rights.

Then, very late, a tall, good-looking, swarthy foreigner came in, with a roll of music in his hands, and his entrance made quite a stir; you heard all round, " Here's Glorioli," or " Ecco Glorioli," or " Voici Glorioli," till Glorioli got on your nerves. And beautiful ladies, ambassadresses, female celebrities of all kinds, fluttered up to him and cajoled and fawned;—as Svengali would have said, " Prinzessen, Comtessen, Serene English Altessen ! "—and they soon forgot their Highness and their Serenity !

For with very little pressing Glorioli stood up on the platform, with his accompanist by his side at the piano, and in his hands a sheet of music, at which he never looked. He looked at the beautiful ladies, and ogled and smiled ; and from his scarcely-parted, moist, thick, bearded lips, which he always licked before singing, there issued the most ravishing sounds that had ever been heard from throat of man or woman or boy ! He could sing both high and low and soft and loud, and the frivolous were bewitched, as was only to be expected ; but even the earnestest of all, caught, surprised, rapt, astounded, shaken, tickled, teased, harrowed, tortured, tantalised, aggravated, seduced, demoralised, degraded, corrupted into mere naturalness, forgot to dissemble their delight.

And Sebastian Bach (the especially adored of all really great musicians, and also, alas ! of many priggish outsiders who don't know a single note and can't remember a single tune) was well forgotten for the night; and who were more enthusiastic than the two great players who had been playing Bach that evening? For these, at all events, were broad and catholic and sincere, and knew what was beautiful, whatever its kind.

It was but a simple little song that Glorioli sang, as light and pretty as it could well be, almost worthy of the words it was written to, and the words are De Musset's; and I love them so much I cannot resist the temptation of setting them down here, for the mere sensuous delight of writing them, as though I had just composed them myself:

> " Bonjour, Suzon, ma fleur des bois !
>   Es-tu toujours la plus jolie ?
> Je reviens, tel que tu me vois,
>   D'un grand voyage en Italie !
> Du paradis j'ai fait le tour—
> J'ai fait des vers—j'ai fait l'amour . ; ;
>   Mais que t'importe !
> Je passe devant ta maison ;
>   Ouvre ta porte !
>   Bonjour, Suzon !

> " Je t'ai vue au temps des lilas.
>   Ton cœur joyeux venait d'éclore,
> Et tu disais : ' Je ne veux pas,
>   Je ne veux pas qu'on m'aime encore.'
> Qu'as-tu fait depuis mon départ ?
> Qui part trop tôt revient trop tard.
>   Mais que m'importe ?
> Je passe devant ta maison ;
>   Ouvre ta porte !
>   Bonjour, Suzon ! "

And when it began, and while it lasted, and after it was over, one felt really sorry for all the other singers. And nobody sang any more that night; for Glorioli was tired, and wouldn't sing again, and none were bold enough or disinterested enough to sing after him.

Some of my readers may remember that meteoric bird of song, who, though a mere amateur, would condescend to sing for a hundred guineas in the saloons of the great (as Monsieur Jourdain sold cloth); who would sing still better for love and glory in the studios of his friends.

For Glorioli—the biggest, handsomest, and most distinguished-looking Jew that ever was—one of the Sephardim (one of the Seraphim !)—hailed from Spain, where he

"BONJOUR, SUZON | "

was junior partner in the great firm of Moralés, Peralés, Gonzalés, and Glorioli, wine merchants, Malaga. He travelled for his own firm; his wine was good, and he sold much of it in England. But his voice would bring him far more gold in the month he spent here; for his wines have been equalled—if it be not libellous to say so— but there was no voice like his anywhere in the world, and no more finished singer.

Anyhow his voice got into Little Billee's head more than any wine, and the boy could talk of nothing else for days and weeks; and was so exuberant in his expressions of delight and gratitude that the great singer took a real fancy to him (especially when he was told that this fervent boyish admirer was one of the greatest of English painters); and as a mark of his esteem, privately confided to him after supper that every century two human night- ingales were born—only two ! a male and a female ; and that he, Glorioli, was the representative " male rossignol of this soi-disant dix-neuvième siècle."

" I can well believe that ! And the female, your mate that should be—*la rossignolle,* if there is such a word?" inquired Little Billee.

" Ah ! mon ami . . . it was Alboni, till la petite Adelina Patti came out a year or two ago; and now it is *La Svengali.*"

" La Svengali ? "

" Oui, mon fy ! You will hear her some day—et vous m'en direz des nouvelles ! "

" Why, you don't mean to say that she's got a better voice than Madame Alboni ? "

" Mon ami, an apple is an excellent thing—until you have tried a peach ! Her voice to that of Alboni is as a peach to an apple—I give you my word of honour ! but bah ! the voice is a detail. It's what she does with it— it's incredible ! it gives one cold all down the back ! it drives you mad ! it makes you weep hot tears by the spoonful ! Ah ! the tear, mon fy ! tenez ! I can draw everything but *that !* Ça n'est pas dans mes cordes ! *I* can only madden with *love !* But La Svengali ! . . . And then, in the middle of it all, prrrout ! . . . she makes you laugh ! Ah ! le beau rire ! faire rire avec des larmes

A HUMAN NIGHTINGALE

plein les yeux—voilà qui me passe ! . . . Mon ami, when
I heard her it made me swear that even *I* would never
try to sing any more—it seemed *too* absurd ! and I kept
my word for a month at least—and you know, je sais ce
que je vaux, moi ! "

" You are talking of La Svengali, I bet," said Signor
Spartia.

" Oui, parbleu ! You have heard her ? "

" Yes—at Vienna last winter," rejoined the greatest
singing-master in the world. " J'en suis fou ! hélas ! I
thought *I* could teach a woman how to sing, till I heard
that blackguard Svengali's pupil. He has married her,
they say ?"

" That *blackguard* Svengali ! " exclaimed Little Billee
. . . " why, that must be a Svengali I knew in Paris—a
famous pianist ! a friend of mine ! "

" That's the man ! also une fameuse crapule (sauf vot'
respect); his real name is Adler; his mother was a Polish
singer; and he was a pupil at the Leipsic Conservatorio.
But he's an immense artist, and a great singing-master,
to teach a woman like that ! and such a woman ! belle
comme un ange—mais bête comme un pot. I tried to
talk to her—all she can say is ' ja wohl,' or ' doch,' or
' nein,' or ' soh ! ' not a word of English or French or
Italian, though she sings them, oh ! but *divinely !* It is
' *il bel canto* ' come back to the world after a hundred
years. . . ."

" But what voice is it ? " asked Little Billee.

" Every voice a mortal woman can have—three octaves
—four ! and of such a quality that people who can't tell
one tune from another cry with pleasure at the mere
sound of it directly they hear her; just like anybody
else. Everything that Paganini could do with his violin,
she does with her voice—only better—and what a voice !
un vrai baume ! "

" Now I don't mind petting zat you are schbeaking of
La Sfencali," said Herr Kreutzer, the famous composer,
joining in. " Quelle merfeille, hein ? I heard her in St.
Betersburg, at ze Vinter Balace. Ze vomen all vent mat,
and pulled off zeir bearls and tiamonts and kave zem to
her—vent town on zeir knees and gried and gissed her

hants. She tit not say vun vort! She tit not efen
schmile! Ze men schnifelled in ze gorners, and looked
at ze bictures, and tissempled—efen I, Johann Kreutzer!
efen ze Emperor?"

"You're joking," said Little Billee.

"My vrent, I neffer choke ven I talk apout zinging.
You vill hear her zum tay yourzellof, and you vill acree
viz me zat zere are two classes of beoble who zing. In
ze vun class, La Sfencali; in ze ozzer, all ze ozzer
zingers!"

"And does she sing good music?"

"I ton't know. *All* music is koot ven *she* zings it. I
forket ze zong; I can only sink of ze zinger. Any koot
zinger can zing a peautiful zong and kif bleasure, I
zubboce! But I voot zooner hear La Sfencali zing a
scale zan anypotty else zing ze most peautiful zong in ze
vorldt—efen vun of my own! Zat is berhaps how zung
ze crate Italian zingers of ze last century. It vas a lost
art, and she has found it; and she must haf pecun to zing
pefore she pecan to schpeak—or else she voot not haf
hat ze time to learn all zat she knows, for she is not yet
zirty! She zings in Paris in Ogdoper, Gott sei dank!
and gums here after Christmas to zing at Trury Lane.
Chullien kifs her ten sousand bounts!"

"I wonder, now? Why, that must be the woman I
heard at Warsaw two years ago—or three," said young
Lord Witlow. "It was at Count Siloszech's. He'd heard
her sing in the streets, with a tall black-bearded ruffian,
who accompanied her on a guitar, and a little fiddling
gypsy fellow. She was a handsome woman, with hair
down to her knees, but stupid as an owl. She sang at
Siloszech's, and all the fellows went mad and gave her
their watches and diamond studs and gold scarf-pins.
By gad! I never heard or saw anything like it. I don't
know much about music myself—couldn't tell 'God save
the Queen' from 'Pop goes the Weasel,' if the people
didn't get up and stand and take their hats off; but I
was as mad as the rest—why, I gave her a little German-
silver vinaigrette I'd just bought for my wife; hanged if
I didn't—and I was only just married, you know! It's
the peculiar twang of her voice, I suppose!"

And hearing all this, Little Billee made up his mind that life had still something in store for him, since he would some day hear La Svengali. Anyhow, he wouldn't shoot himself till then !

Thus the night wore itself away. The Prinzessen, Comtessen, and Serene English Altessen (and other ladies of less exalted rank) departed home in cabs and carriages; and hostess and daughters went to bed. Late sitters of the ruder sex supped again, and smoked and chatted and listened to comic songs and recitations by celebrated actors. Noble dukes hobnobbed with low comedians; world-famous painters and sculptors sat at the feet of Hebrew capitalists and aitchless millionaires. Judges, cabinet ministers, eminent physicians and warriors and philosophers saw Sunday morning steal over Campden Hill and through the many windows of Mechelen Lodge, and listened to the pipe of half-awakened birds, and smelt the freshness of the dark summer dawn. And as Taffy and the Laird walked home to the Old Hummums by daylight, they felt that last night was ages ago, and that since then they had forgathered with "much there was of the best in London." And then they reflected that "much there was of the best in London" were still strangers to them—except by reputation—for there had not been time for many introductions : and this had made them feel a little out of it; and they found they hadn't had such a very good time after all. And there were no cabs. And they were tired, and their boots were tight.

And the last they had seen of Little Billee before leaving was a glimpse of their old friend in a corner of Lady Cornelys's boudoir, gravely playing cup and ball with Fred Walker for sixpences—both so rapt in the game that they were unconscious of anything else, and both playing so well (with either hand) that they might have been professional champions !

And that saturnine young sawbones, Jakes Talboys (now Sir Jakes, and one of the most genial of Her Majesty's physicians), who, sometimes after supper and champagne, was given to thoughtful, sympathetic, and acute observa-

CUP-AND-BALL

tion of his fellow-men, remarked to the Laird in a whisper that was almost convivial :—

"Rather an enviable pair! Their united ages amount to forty-eight or so, their united weights to about fifteen stone, and they couldn't carry you or me between them. But if you were to roll all the other brains that have been under this roof to-night into one, you wouldn't reach the sum of their united genius. . . . I wonder which of the two is the most unhappy!"

The season over, the song-birds flown, summer on the wane, his picture, the "Moon-Dial," sent to Moses Lyon's (the picture-dealer in Conduit Street), Little Billee felt the time had come to go and see his mother and sister in Devonshire, and make the sun shine twice as brightly for them during a month or so, and the dew fall softer!

So one fine August morning found him at the Great Western Station—the nicest station in all London, I think —except the stations that book you to France and far away.

It always seems so pleasant to be going west! Little Billee loved that station, and often went there for a mere stroll, to watch the people starting on their westward way, following the sun towards Heaven knows what joys or sorrows, and envy them their sorrows or their joys— any sorrows or joys that were not merely physical, like a chocolate drop or a pretty tune, a bad smell or a toothache.

And as he took a seat in a second-class carriage (it would be third in these democratic days), south corner, back to the engine, with *Silas Marner*, and Darwin's *Origin of Species* (which he was reading for the third time), and *Punch* and other literature of a lighter kind to beguile him on his journey, he felt rather bitterly how happy he could be if the little spot, or knot, or blot, or clot which paralysed that convolution of his brain where he kept his affections could but be conjured away!

The dearest mother, the dearest sister in the world, in the dearest little seaside village (or town) that ever was! and other dear people—especially Alice, sweet Alice with hair so brown, his sister's friend, the simple, pure, and pious maiden of his boyish dreams : and himself, but for that wretched little kill-joy cerebral occlusion, as sound,

as healthy, as full of life and energy, as he had ever
been !

And when he wasn't reading *Silas Marner*, or looking
out of window at the flying landscape, and watching it
revolve round its middle distance (as it always seems to
do), he was sympathetically taking stock of his fellow-
passengers, and mildly envying them, one after another,
indiscriminately !

A fat, old, wheezy philistine, with a bulbous nose and
only one eye, who had a plain, sickly daughter, to whom
he seemed devoted, body and soul; an old lady, who
still wept furtively at recollections of the parting with
her grandchildren, which had taken place at the station
(they had borne up wonderfully, as grandchildren do); a
consumptive curate, on the opposite corner seat by the
window, whose tender, anxious wife (sitting by his side)
seemed to have no thoughts in the whole world but for
him; and her patient eyes were his stars of consolation,
since he turned to look into them almost every minute,
and always seemed a little the happier for doing so.
There is no better star-gazing than that !

So Little Billee gave her up *his* corner seat, that the
poor sufferer might have those stars where he could look
into them comfortably without turning his head.

Indeed (as was his wont with everybody), Little Billee
made himself useful and pleasant to his fellow-travellers
in many ways—so many that long before they had reached
their respective journeys' ends they had almost grown to
love him as an old friend, and longed to know who this
singularly attractive and brilliant youth, this genial,
dainty, benevolent little princekin could possibly be, who
was dressed so fashionably, and yet went second class, and
took such kind thought of others; and they wondered at
the happiness that must be his at merely being alive, and
told him more of their troubles in six hours than they
told many an old friend in a year.

But he told them nothing about himself—that self he
was so sick of—and left them to wonder.

And at his own journey's end, the farthest end of all,
he found his mother and sister waiting for him, in a
beautiful little pony-carriage—his last gift—and with them

sweet Alice, and in her eyes, for one brief moment, that
unconscious look of love surprised which is not to be
forgotten for years and years and years—which can only
be seen by the eyes that meet it, and which, for the time
it lasts (just a flash), makes all women's eyes look exactly
the same (I'm told) : and it seemed to Little Billee that,
for the twentieth part of a second, Alice had looked at
him with Trilby's eyes; or his mother's, when that he
was a little tiny boy.

It all but gave him the thrill he thirsted for ! Another
twentieth part of a second, perhaps, and his brain-trouble
would have melted away; and Little Billee would have
come into his own again—the kingdom of love !

A beautiful human eye ! *Any* beautiful eye—a dog's,
a deer's, a donkey's, an owl's even ! To think of all that
it can look, and all that it can see ! all that it can even
seem, sometimes ! What a prince among gems ! what a
star !

But a beautiful eye that lets the broad white light of
infinite space (so bewildering and garish and diffused)
into one pure virgin heart, to be filtered there ! and lets
it out again, duly warmed, softened, concentrated, sub-
limated, focused to a point as in a precious stone, that
it may shed itself (a love-laden effulgence) into some
stray fellow-heart close by—through pupil and iris, entre
quatre-z-yeux—the very elixir of life !

Alas ! that such a crown-jewel should ever lose its
lustre and go blind !

Not so blind or dim, however, but it can still see well
enough to look before and after, and inward and upward,
and drown itself in tears, and yet not die ! And that's
the dreadful pity of it. And this is a quite uncalled-for
digression ; and I can't think why I should have gone out
of my way (at considerable pains) to invent it ! In fact—

" Of this 'ere song, should I be axed the reason for to show,
I don't exactly know, I don't exactly know !
But all my family dwells upon Nancy."

. . . . . .

" How pretty Alice has grown, mother ! quite lovely,
I think ! and so nice ; but she was always as nice as she
could be ! "

So observed Little Billee to his mother that evening as they sat in the garden and watched the crescent moon sink to the Atlantic.

"Ah! my darling Willie! If you *could* only guess how happy you would make your poor old mammy by growing fond of Alice. . . . And Blanche, too! what a joy for *her!*"

"Good heavens! mother . . . Alice is not for the like of *me!* She's for some splendid young Devon squire, six foot high, and acred and whiskered within an inch of his life! . . ."

"Ah, my darling Willie! you are not of those who ask for love in vain. . . . If you only *knew* how she believes in you! She almost beats your poor old mammy at *that!*"

And that night he dreamed of Alice—that he loved her as a sweet good woman should be loved; and knew, even in his dream, that it was but a dream; but, oh!

SWEET ALICE

it was good! and he managed not to wake; and it was a night to be marked with a white stone! And (still in his dream) she had kissed him, and healed him of his brain-trouble for ever. But when he woke next morning, alas! his brain-trouble was with him still, and he felt that no dream kiss would ever cure it—nothing but a real kiss from Alice's own pure lips!

And he rose thinking of Alice, and dressed and breakfasted thinking of her—and how fair she was, and how innocent, and how well and carefully trained up the way she should go—the beau ideal of a wife. . . . Could she possibly care for a shrimp like himself?

For in his love of outward form he could not understand that any woman who had eyes to see should ever quite condone the signs of physical weakness in man, in favour of any mental gifts or graces whatsoever.

Little Greek that he was, he worshipped the athlete, and opined that all women without exception—all English women especially—must see with the same eyes as himself.

He had once been vain and weak enough to believe in Trilby's love (with a Taffy standing by—a careless, unsusceptible Taffy, who was like unto the gods of Olympus !)— and Trilby had given him up at a word, a hint—for all his frantic clinging.

She would not have given up Taffy *pour si peu*, had Taffy but lifted a little finger ! It is always " just whistle, and I'll come to you, my lad ! " with the likes of Taffy . . . but Taffy hadn't even whistled ! Yet still he kept thinking of Alice—and he felt he couldn't think of her well enough till he went out for a stroll by himself on a sheep-trimmed down. So he took his pipe and his Darwin, and out he strolled into the early sunshine—up the green Red Lane, past the pretty church, Alice's father's church —and there, at the gate, patiently waiting for his mistress, sat Alice's dog—an old friend of his, whose welcome was a very warm one.

Little Billee thought of Thackeray's lovely poem in *Pendennis :*

" She comes—she's here—she's past !
May heaven go with her ! . . ."

Then he and the dog went on together to a little bench on the edge of the cliff—within sight of Alice's bedroom window. It was called " the Honeymooners' Bench."

" That look—that look—that look ! Ah—but Trilby had looked like that, too ! And there are many Taffys in Devon ! "

He sat himself down and smoked and gazed at the sea below, which the sun (still in the east) had not yet filled with glare and robbed of the lovely sapphire-blue, shot with purple and dark green, that comes over it now and again of a morning on that most beautiful coast.

There was a fresh breeze from the west, and the long, slow billows broke into creamier foam than ever, which reflected itself as a tender white gleam in the blue concavities of their shining shoreward curves as they came rolling in. The sky was all of turquoise but for the smoke of a distant steamer—a long thin horizontal streak of dun—and there were little brown or white sails here and there, dotting; and the stately ships went on. . . .

Little Billee tried hard to feel all this beauty with his heart as well as his brain—as he had so often done when a boy—and cursed his insensibility out loud for at least the thousand-and-first time.

Why couldn't these waves of air and water be turned into equivalent waves of sound, that he might feel them through the only channel that reached his emotions! That one joy was still left to him—but, alas! alas! he was only a painter of pictures—and not a maker of music!

He recited " Break, break, break," to Alice's dog, who loved him and looked up into his face with sapient, affectionate eyes—and whose name, like that of so many dogs in fiction and so few in fact, was simply Tray. For Little Billee was much given to monologues out loud, and profuse quotations from his favourite bards.

Everybody quoted that particular poem either mentally or aloud when they sat on that particular bench—except a few old-fashioned people, who still said,

" Roll on, thou deep and dark blue ocean, roll! "

or people of the very highest culture, who only quoted the nascent (and crescent) Robert Browning; or people of no culture at all, who simply held their tongues—and only felt the more !

Tray listened silently.

" Ah, Tray, the best thing but one to do with the sea is to paint it. The next best thing to that is to bathe in it. The best of all is to lie asleep at the bottom. How would *you* like that?

" MAY HEAVEN GO WITH HER ! "

" ' And on thy ribs the limpet sticks,
And in thy heart the scrawl shall play. ; ; .' "

Tray's tail became as a wagging point of interrogation, and he turned his head first on one side and then on the other—his eyes fixed on Little Billee's, his face irresistible in its genial doggy wistfulness.

" Tray, what a singularly good listener you are—and therefore what singularly good manners you've got ! I suppose all dogs have ! " said Little Billee; and then, in a very tender voice, he exclaimed,

" Alice, Alice, Alice ! "

And Tray uttered a soft, cooing, nasal croon in his head register, though he was a baritone dog by nature, with portentous, warlike chest-notes of the jingo order.

" Tray, your mistress is a parson's daughter, and therefore twice as much of a mystery as any other woman in this puzzling world !

" Tray, if my heart weren't stopped with wax, like the ears of the companions of Ulysses when they rowed past the sirens—you've heard of Ulysses, Tray? he loved a dog—if my heart weren't stopped with wax, I should be deeply in love with your mistress; perhaps she would marry me if I asked her—there's no accounting for tastes ! —and I know enough of myself to know that I should make her a good husband—that I should make her happy —and I should make two other women happy besides.

" As for myself personally, Tray, it doesn't very much matter. One good woman would do as well as another, if she's equally good-looking. You doubt it? Wait till you get a pimple inside your bump of—your bump of— wherever you keep your fondnesses, Tray.

" For that's what's the matter with me—a pimple—just a little clot of blood at the root of a nerve, and no bigger than a pin's point !

" That's a small thing to cause such a lot of wretchedness, and wreck a fellow's life, isn't it? Oh, curse it, curse it, curse it—every day and all day long.

" And just as small a thing will take it away, I'm told !

" Ah ! grains of sand are small things—and so are diamonds ! But diamond or grain of sand, only Alice has got that small thing ! Alice alone, in all the world, has got the healing touch for me now; the hands, the lips, the eyes! I know it—I feel it! I dreamed it last night! She looked me well in the face, and took my hand—both hands—and kissed me, eyes and mouth, and told me how she loved me. Ah! what a dream it was! And my little clot melted away like a snowflake on the lips, and I was my old self again, after many years—and all through that kiss of a pure woman.

" I've never been kissed by a pure woman in my life— never! except by my dear mother and sister; and mothers and sisters don't count, when it comes to kissing.

" Ah! sweet physician that she is, and better than all! It will all come back again with a rush, just as I dreamed, and we will have a good time together, we three! . . .

" But your mistress is a parson's daughter, and believes everything she's been taught from a child, just as you do— at least, I hope so. And I like her for it—and you too.

" She has believed her father—will she ever believe me, who think so differently? And if she does, will it be good for her?—and then, where will her father come in?

" Oh! it's a bad thing to live and no longer believe and trust in your father, Tray! to doubt either his honesty or his intelligence. For he (with your mother to help) has taught you all the best he knows, if he has been a good father—till some one else comes and teaches you better—or worse!

" And then, what are you to believe of what good still remains of all that early teaching—and how are you to sift the wheat from the chaff? . . .

" Kneel undisturbed, fair saint! I, for one, will never seek to undermine thy faith in any father, on earth or above it!

" Yes, there she kneels in her father's church, her pretty head bowed over her clasped hands, her cloak and skirts falling in happy folds about her: I see it all!

" And underneath, that poor, sweet, soft, pathetic thing of flesh and blood, the eternal woman—great heart and slender brain—for ever enslaved or enslaving, never self-sufficing, never free . . . that dear, weak, delicate shape, so cherishable, so perishable, that I've had to paint so often, and know so well by heart! and love . . . ah, how I love it ! Only painter-fellows and sculptor-fellows can ever quite know the fulness of that pure love.

"There she kneels and pours forth her praise or plaint, meekly and duly. Perhaps it's for me she's praying.

"'Leave thou thy sister when she prays.'

"She believes her poor little prayer will be heard and answered somewhere up aloft. The impossible will be done. She wants what she wants so badly, and prays for it so hard.

"She believes—she believes—what *doesn't* she believe, Tray?

"The world was made in six days. It is just six thousand years old. Once it all lay smothered under rain-water for many weeks, miles deep, because there were so many wicked people about somewhere down in Judea, where they didn't know everything ! A costly kind of clearance ! And then there was Noah, who *wasn't* wicked, and his most respectable family, and his ark—and Jonah and his whale—and Joshua and the sun, and what not. I remember it all, you see, and, oh ! such wonderful things that have happened since ! And there's everlasting agony for those who don't believe as she does; and yet she is happy; and good, and very kind; for the mere thought of any live creature in pain makes her wretched !

"After all, if she believes in me, she'll believe in any-thing; let her !

"Indeed, I'm not sure that it's not rather ungainly for a pretty woman *not* to believe in all these good old cosmic taradiddles, as it is for a pretty child not to believe in Little Red Riding-hood, and Jack and the Beanstalk, and Morgiana and the Forty Thieves; we learn them at our mother's knee, and how nice they are ! Let us go on believing them as long as we can, till the child grows up and the woman dies and it's all found out.

"Yes, Tray, I will be dishonest for her dear sake. I will kneel by her side if ever I have the happy chance, and ever after, night and morning, and all day long on Sundays if she wants me to ! What will I *not* do for that one pretty woman who believes in *me*? I will respect even *that* belief, and do my little best to keep it alive for

"' SO MUCH FOR ALICE, TRAY '"

ever. It is much too precious an earthly boon for *me* to play ducks and drakes with. . . .

"So much for Alice, Tray—your sweet mistress and mine.

"But then, there's Alice's papa—and that's another pair of sleeves, as we say in France.

"Ought one ever to play at make-believe with a full-grown man for any consideration whatever—even though he be a parson, and a possible father-in-law? *There's* a case of conscience for you!

"When I ask him for his daughter, as I must, and he asks me for my profession of faith, as he will, what can I tell him? The truth?"

(And now, I regret to say, the reticent Little Billee is going to show his trusty four-footed friend the least attractive side of his many-sided nature, its modernity, its dreary scepticism—his own unhappy portion of *la maladie du siècle*). . . .

"But then, what will *he* say? What allowances will *he* make for a poor little weak-kneed, well-meaning waif of a painter-fellow like me, whose only choice lay between Mr. Darwin and the Pope of Rome, and who has chosen once and for ever—and that long ago—before he'd ever even heard of Mr. Darwin's name.

"Besides, why should he make allowances for me? I don't for him. I think no more of a parson than he does of a painter-fellow—and that's precious little, I'm afraid.

"What will he think of a man who says:

"'Look here! the God of your belief isn't mine and never will be—but I love your daughter, and she loves me, and I'm the only man to make her happy!'

"He's no Jephthah; he's made of flesh and blood, although he's a parson—and loves his daughter as much as Shylock loved his.

"Tell me, Tray—thou that livest among parsons— what man, not being a parson himself, can guess how a parson would think, an average parson, confronted by such a poser as that?

"Does he, dare he, *can* he ever think straight or simply on any subject as any other man thinks, hedged in as he is by so many limitations?

"He is as shrewd, vain, worldly, self-seeking, ambitious, jealous, censorious, and all the rest, as you or I, Tray— for all his Christian profession—and just as fond of his kith and kin!

"He is considered a gentleman—which perhaps you and I are not—unless we happen to behave as such; it is a condition of his noble calling. Perhaps it's in order to become a gentleman that he's become a parson! It's about as short a royal road as any to that enviable distinction—as short almost as Her Majesty's commission, and much safer, and much less expensive—within reach of the sons of most fairly successful butchers and bakers and candlestick-makers.

"While still a boy he has bound himself irrevocably to certain beliefs, which he will be paid to preserve and preach and enforce through life, and act up to through thick and thin—at all events in the eyes of others—even his nearest and dearest—even the wife of his bosom.

"They are his bread and butter, these beliefs—and a man mustn't quarrel with his bread and butter. But a parson must quarrel with those who don't believe as he tells them !

"Yet a few years' thinking and reading and experience of life, one would suppose, might possibly just shake his faith a little (just as though, instead of being parson, he had been tinker, tailor, soldier, sailor, gentleman, apothecary, ploughboy, thief), and teach him that many of these beliefs are simply childish—and some of them very wicked indeed—and most immoral.

"It is very wicked and most immoral to believe, or affect to believe, and tell others to believe, that the unseen, unspeakable, unthinkable Immensity we're all part and parcel of, source of eternal, infinite, indestructible life and light and might, is a kind of wrathful, glorified, and self-glorifying ogre in human shape, with human passions, and most inhuman hates—who suddenly made us out of nothing, one fine day—just for a freak—and made us so badly that we fell the next—and turned us adrift the day after—damned us from the very beginning—*ab ovo*—*ab ovo usque ad malum*—ha, ha !—and ever since ! never gave us a chance !

"All-merciful Father, indeed ! Why, the Prince of Darkness was an angel in comparison (and a gentleman into the bargain).

"Just think of it, Tray—a finger in every little paltry pie—an eye and an ear at every keyhole, even that of the larder, to catch us tripping, and find out if we're praising loud enough, or grovelling low enough, or fasting hard enough—poor God-forsaken worms !

"And if we're naughty and disobedient, everlasting torment for us; torture of so hideous a kind that *we* wouldn't inflict it on the basest criminal, not for one single moment !

"Or else, if we're good and do as we are bid, an eternity of bliss so futile, so idle, and so tame that we couldn't stand it for a week, but for thinking of its one horrible alternative, and of our poor brother for ever and ever roasting away, and howling for the drop of water he never gets.

"Everlasting flame, or everlasting dishonour—nothing between!

"Isn't it ludicrous as well as pitiful—a thing to make one snigger through one's tears? Isn't it a grievous sin to believe in such things as these, and go about teaching and preaching them, and being paid for it—a sin to be heavily chastised, and a shame? What a legacy!

"They were shocking bad artists, those conceited, narrow-minded Jews, those poor old doting monks and priests and bigots of the grewsome, dark age of faith! They couldn't draw a bit—no perspective, no anatomy, no chiaro-oscuro; and it's a woeful image they managed to evolve for us out of the depths of their fathomless ignorance, in their zeal to keep us off all the forbidden fruit we're all so fond of, because we were built like that! And by whom? By our Maker, I suppose (who also made the forbidden fruit, and made it very nice—and put it so conveniently for you and me to see and smell and reach, Tray—and sometimes even pick, alas!).

"And even at that it's a failure, this precious image! Only the very foolish little birds are frightened into good behaviour. The naughty ones laugh and wink at each other, and pull out its hair and beard when nobody's looking, and build their nests out of the straw it's stuffed with (the naughty little birds in black, especially), and pick up what they want under its very nose, and thrive uncommonly well; and the good ones fly away out of sight; and some day, perhaps, find a home in some happy, useful fatherland far away where the Father isn't a bit like this. Who knows?

"And I'm one of the good little birds, Tray—at least, I hope so. And that unknown Father lives in me whether I will or no, and I love Him whether He be or not, just because I can't help it, and with the best and bravest love that can be—the perfect love that believeth no evil, and seeketh no reward, and casteth out fear. For I'm His father as much as He's mine, since I've conceived the thought of Him after my own fashion!

" And He lives in you too, Tray—you and all your
kind. Yes, good dog, you king of beasts, I see it in your
eyes. . . .

" Ah, bon Dieu Père, le Dieu des bonnes gens ! Oh !
if we only knew for *certain*, Tray ! what martyrdom
would we not endure, you and I, with a happy smile and
a grateful heart—for sheer *love* of such a father ! How
little should *we* care for the things of this earth !

" But the poor parson ?

" He must willy-nilly go on believing, or affecting to
believe, just as he is told, *word for word*, or else good-bye
to his wife and children's bread and butter, his own preferment, perhaps even his very gentility—that gentility
of which his Master thought so little, and he and his are
apt to think so much—with possibly the Archbishopric of
Canterbury at the end of it, the *bâton de maréchal* that
lies in every clerical knapsack.

" What a temptation ! one is but human !

" So how can he be honest without believing certain
things, to believe which (without shame) one must be as
simple as a little child ; as, by the way, he is so cleverly
told to be in these matters, and so cleverly tells us—and
so seldom is himself on any other matter whatever—his
own interests, other people's affairs, the world, the flesh,
and the devil ! And that's clever of him too. . . .

" And if he chooses to be as simple as a little child,
why shouldn't I treat him as a little child, for his own
good, and fool him to the top of his little bent for his dear
daughter's sake, that I may make her happy, and thereby
him too ?

" And if he's *not* quite so simple as all that, and makes
artful little compromises with his conscience—for a good
purpose, of course—why shouldn't I make artful little
compromises with mine, and for a better purpose still,
and try to get what I want in the way *he* does ? I want
to marry his daughter far worse than he can ever want to
live in a palace, and ride in a carriage and pair with a
mitre on the panels.

" If he *cheats*, why shouldn't I cheat too ?

" If *he* cheats, he cheats everybody all round—the
wide, wide world, and something wider and higher still

that can't be measured, something in himself. *I* only cheat *him !*

" *If* he cheats, he cheats for the sake of very worldly things indeed—tithes, honours, influence, power, authority, social consideration and respect—not to speak of bread and butter ! *I* only cheat for the love of a lady fair—and cheating for cheating, I like my cheating best.

" So, whether he cheats or not, I'll——

" Confound it ! what would old Taffy do in such a case, I wonder? . . .

" Oh, bother ! it's no good wondering what old Taffy would do.

" Taffy never wants to marry *anybody's* daughter; he doesn't even want to paint her ! He only wants to paint his beastly ragamuffins and thieves and drunkards, and be left alone.

" Besides, Taffy's as simple as a little child himself, and couldn't fool any one, and wouldn't if he could—not even a parson. But if any one tries to fool *him*, my eyes ! don't he cut up rough, and call names, and kick up a shindy, and even knock people down ! That's the worst of fellows like Taffy. They're too good for this world and too solemn. They're impossible, and lack all sense of humour. In point of fact Taffy's a *gentleman*—poor fellow ! *et puis voilà !*

" I'm not simple—worse luck ; and I can't knock people down—I only wish I could ! I can only paint them ! and not even *that* ' as they really are ! ' . . . Good old Taffy ! . . .

" Faint heart never won fair lady !

" Oh, happy, happy thought—I'll be brave and win !

" I can't knock people down, or do doughty deeds, but I'll be brave in my own little way—the only way I can. . . .

" I'll simply lie through thick and thin—I must—I will—nobody need ever be a bit the wiser ! I can do more good by lying than by telling the truth, and make more deserving people happy, including myself and the sweetest girl alive—the end shall justify the means : that's my excuse, my only excuse ! and this lie of mine is on so stupendous a scale that it will have to last me for life.

It's my only one, but its name is *Lion !* and I'll never tell another as long as I live.

"And now that I know what temptation really is, I'll never think any harm of any parson any more . . . never, never, never ! "

So the little man went on, as if he knew all about it, had found it all out for himself, and nobody else had ever found it out before ! and I am not responsible for his ways of thinking (which are not necessarily my own).

It must be remembered, in extenuation, that he was very young, and not very wise : no philosopher, no scholar —just a painter of lovely pictures ; only that and nothing more. Also, that he was reading Mr. Darwin's immortal book for the third time, and it was a little too strong for him; also, that all this happened in the early sixties, long ere Religion had made up her mind to meet Science half-way, and hobnob and kiss and be friends. Alas ! before such a lying down of the lion and the lamb can ever come to pass, Religion will have to perform a larger share of the journey than half, I fear !

Then, still carried away by the flood of his own eloquence (for he had never had such an innings as this, nor such a listener), he again apostrophised the dog Tray, who had been growing somewhat inattentive (like the reader, perhaps), in language more beautiful than ever :

"Oh, to be like you, Tray—and secrete love and good-will from morn till night, from night till morning—like saliva, without effort ! with never a moment's cessation of flow, even in disgrace and humiliation ! How much better to love than to be loved—to love as you do, my Tray—so warmly, so easily, so unremittingly—to forgive all wrongs and neglect and injustice so quickly and so well—and forget a kindness never ! Lucky dog that you are !

" ' Oh ! could I feel as I have felt, or be as I have been,
  Or weep as I could once have wept, o'er many a vanished
    scene,
  As springs in deserts found seem sweet, all brackish tho'
    they be,
  So 'midst this withered waste of life those tears would flow
    to me ! '

"What do you think of those lines, Tray? I *love* them, because my mother taught them to me when I was about your age—six years old, or seven! and before the bard who wrote them had fallen; like Lucifer, son of the morning! Have you ever heard of Lord Byron, Tray? He too, like Ulysses, loved a dog, and many people think that's about the best there is to be said of him nowadays! Poor Humpty Dumpty! Such a swell as he once was! Not all the king's horses, nor all the——"

Here Tray jumped up suddenly and bolted—he saw some one else he was fond of, and ran to meet him. It was the vicar, coming out of his vicarage.

A very nice-looking vicar—fresh, clean, alert, well tanned by sun and wind and weather—a youngish vicar still; tall, stout, gentlemanlike, shrewd, kindly, worldly, a trifle pompous, and authoritative more than a trifle; not much given to abstract speculation, and thinking fifty times more of any sporting and orthodox young country squire, well-inched and well-acred (and well-whiskered), than of all the painters in Christendom.

"'When Greeks joined Greeks, then was the tug of war,'" thought Little Billee; and he felt a little uncomfortable. Alice's father had never loomed so big and impressive before, or so distressingly nice to look at.

"Welcome, my Apelles, to your ain countree, which is growing quite proud of you, I declare! Young Lord Archie Waring was saying only last night that he wished he had half your talent! He's *crazed* about painting, you know, and actually wants to be a painter himself! The poor dear old marquis is quite sore about it!"

With this happy exordium the parson stopped and shook hands; and they both stood for a while, looking seaward. The parson said the usual things about the sea —its blueness, its grayness, its greenness, its beauty, its sadness, its treachery.

"' Who shall put forth on thee,
Unfathomable sea!'"

"Who indeed!" answered Little Billee, quite agreeing. "I vote *we* don't, at all events." So they turned inland. The parson said the usual things about the land (from

the country-gentleman's point of view), and the talk began
to flow quite pleasantly, with quoting of the usual poets,
and capping of quotations in the usual way—for they
had known each other many years, both here and in
London, Indeed, the vicar had once been Little Billee's
tutor.

And thus, amicably, they entered a small wooded hollow,
Then the vicar, turning of a sudden his full blue gaze on
the painter, asked, sternly—

" What book's that you've got in your hand, Willie ? "

" A—a—it's the *Origin of Species*, by Charles Darwin,
I'm very f-f-fond of it. I'm reading it for the third time,
. . . It's very g-g-good, It *accounts* for things, you
know."

Then, after a pause, and still more sternly—

" What place of worship do you most attend in London
—especially of an evening, William ? "

Then stammered Little Billee, all self-control forsaking
him—

" I d-d-don't attend any place of worship at all—
morning, afternoon, or evening. I've long given up going
to church altogether, I can only be frank with you; I'll
tell you why. . . ."

And as they walked along the talk drifted on to very
momentous subjects indeeed, and led, unfortunately, to a
serious falling out—for which probably both were to blame
—and closed in a distressful way at the other end of the
little wooded hollow—a way most sudden and unexpected,
and quite grievous to relate. When they emerged into
the open, the parson was quite white, and the painter
crimson.

" Sir," said the parson, squaring himself up to more
than his full height and breadth and dignity, his face big
with righteous wrath, his voice full of strong menace—
" sir, you're—you're a—you're a *thief*, sir, a *thief !* You're
trying to *rob me of my Saviour !* Never you dare to
darken *my* door-step again ! "

" Sir," said Little Billee, with a bow, " if it comes to
calling names, you're—you're a—no ; you're Alice's father ;
and whatever else you are besides, I'm another for trying
to be honest with a parson ; so good-morning to you."

"' YOU'RE A *THIEF*, SIR !'"

And each walked off in an opposite direction, stiff as pokers; and Tray stood between, looking first at one receding figure, then at the other, disconsolate.

And thus Little Billee found out that he could no more lie than he could fly. And so he did not marry sweet Alice after all, and no doubt it was ordered for her good and his. But there was tribulation for many days in the house of Bagot, and for many months in one tender, pure, and pious bosom.

And the best and the worst of it all is that, not very many years after, the good vicar—more fortunate than most clergymen who dabble in stocks and shares—grew suddenly very rich through a lucky speculation in Irish beer, and suddenly, also, took to thinking seriously about things (as a man of business should)—more seriously than he had ever thought before. So at least the story goes in North Devon, and it is not so new as to be incredible. Little doubts grew into big ones—big doubts resolved themselves into downright negations. He quarrelled with his bishop; he quarrelled with his dean; he even quarrelled with his "poor dear old marquis," who died before there was time to make it up again. And finally he felt it his duty, in conscience, to secede from a Church which had become too narrow to hold him, and took himself and his belongings to London, where at least he could breathe. But there he fell into a great disquiet, for the long habit of feeling himself always *en évidence*—of being looked up to and listened to without contradiction; of exercising influence and authority in spiritual matters (and even temporal); of impressing women, especially, with his commanding presence, his fine sonorous voice, his lofty brow, so serious and smooth, his soft, big, waving hands, which soon lost their country tan—all this had grown as a second nature to him, the breath of his nostrils, a necessity of his life. So he rose to be the most popular Positivist preacher of his day, and pretty broad at that.

But his dear daughter Alice, she stuck to the old faith, and married a venerable High-Church archdeacon, who very cleverly clutched at and caught her and saved her for himself just as she stood shivering on the very brink of Rome; and they were neither happy nor unhappy together—*un ménage bourgeois, ni beau ni laid, ni bon ni mauvais.* And thus, alas ! the bond of religious sympathy, that counts for so much in united families, no longer existed between father and daughter, and the heart's division divided them. *Ce que c'est que de nous !* ▪ ▪ ▪ The pity of it !

And so no more of sweet Alice with hair so brown.

PART SIXTH

" Vraiment, la reine auprès d'elle était laide
Quand, vers le soir,
Elle passait sur le pont de Tolède
En corset noir !
Un chapelet du temps de Charlemagne
Ornait son cou. . . .
Le vent qui vient à travers la montagne
Me rendra fou !

Dansez, chantez, villageois ! la nuit tombe. ; ; ◼
Sabine, un jour,
A tout donné—sa beauté de colombe,
Et son amour—
Pour un anneau du Comte de Saldagne,
Pour un bijou. . . .
Le vent qui vient à travers la montagne
M'a rendu fou ! "

BEHOLD our three musketeers of the brush once more
reunited in Paris, famous, after long years.

In emulation of the good Dumas, we will call it " cinq
ans après." It was a little more.

Taffy stands for Porthos and Athos rolled into one,
since he is big and good-natured, and strong enough to
" assommer un homme d'un coup de poing," and also
stately and solemn, of aristocratic and romantic appearance, and not too fat—not too much ongbongpwang, as
the Laird called it—and also he does not dislike a bottle
of wine, or even two, and looks as if he had a history.

The Laird, of course, is D'Artagnan, since he sells his
pictures well, and by the time we are writing of has
already become an Associate of the Royal Academy; like
Quentin Durward, this D'Artagnan was a Scotsman :

" Ah, wasna he a Roguey, this piper of Dundee ! "

And Little Billee, the dainty friend of duchesses, must
stand for Aramis, I fear ! It will not do to push the
simile too far; besides, unlike the good Dumas, one has
a conscience. One does not play ducks and drakes with

historical facts, or tamper with historical personages. And
if Athos, Porthos, and Co. are not historical by this time,
I should like to know who are !

Well, so are Taffy, the Laird, and Little Billee—*tout
ce qu'il y a de plus historique !*

Our three friends, well groomed, frock-coated, shirt-
collared within an inch of their lives, duly scarfed and
scarf-pinned, chimney-pot-hatted, and most beautifully
trousered, and balmorally booted, or neatly spatted (or
whatever was most correct at the time), are breakfasting
together on coffee, rolls, and butter at a little round table
in the huge courtyard of an immense caravansérai, paved
with asphalt, and covered in at the top with a glazed roof
that admits the sun and keeps out the rain—and the air.

A magnificent old man as big as Taffy, in black cloth
coat and breeches and black silk stockings, and a large
metal chain round his neck and chest, looks down like
Jove from a broad flight of marble steps—as though to
welcome the coming guests, who arrive in cabs and railway
omnibuses through a huge archway on the boulevard ; or
to speed those who part through a lesser archway opening
on to a side street.

" Bon voyage, messieurs et dames ! "

At countless other little tables other voyagers are breakfasting or ordering breakfast ; or, having breakfasted, are
smoking and chatting and looking about. It is a babel
of tongues—the cheerfullest, busiest, merriest scene in the
world, apparently the costly place of rendezvous for all
wealthy Europe and America ; an atmosphere of bank-
notes and gold.

Already Taffy has recognised (and been recognised by)
half a dozen old fellow-Crimeans, of unmistakable military
aspect like himself ; and three canny Scotsmen have discreetly greeted the Laird ; and as for Little Billee, he is
constantly jumping up from his breakfast and running to
this table or that, drawn by some irresistible British smile
of surprised and delighted female recognition : " What,
you here ? How nice ! Come over to hear La Svengali,
I suppose ? "

At the top of the marble steps in a long terrace, with
seats and people sitting, from which tall glazed doors,

"AN ATMOSPHERE OF BANK-NOTES AND GOLD"

elaborately carved and gilded, give access to luxurious
drawing-rooms, dining-rooms, reading-rooms, lavatories,
postal and telegraph offices; and all round and about are
huge square green boxes, out of which grow tropical and
exotic evergreens all the year round—with beautiful names
that I have forgotten. And leaning against these boxes
are placards announcing what theatrical or musical enter-
tainments will take place in Paris that day or night; and
the biggest of these placards (and the most fantastically
decorated) informs the cosmopolite world that Madame
Svengali intends to make her first appearance in Paris
that very evening, at nine punctually, in the Cirque des
Bashibazoucks, Rue St. Honoré!

Our friends had only arrived the previous night, but
they had managed to secure stalls a week beforehand.
No places were any longer to be got for love or money.
Many people had come to Paris on purpose to hear La
Svengali—many famous musicians from England and
everywhere else—but they would have to wait many days.

The fame of her was like a rolling snow-ball that had
been rolling all over Europe for the last two years—
wherever there was snow to be picked up in the shape of
golden ducats.

Their breakfast over, Taffy, the Laird, and Little Billee,
cigar in mouth, arm-in-arm, the huge Taffy in the middle
(*comme autrefois*), crossed the sunshiny boulevard into the
shade, and went down the Rue de la Paix, through the
Place Vendôme and the Rue Castiglione to the Rue de
Rivoli—quite leisurely, and with a tender midriff-warming
sensation of freedom and delight at almost every step.

Arrived at the corner pastrycook's, they finished the
stumps of their cigars as they looked at the well-remembered show in the window; then they went in and had,
Taffy a Madeleine, the Laird a Baba, and Little Billee a
Savarin—and each, I regret to say, a liqueur-glass of
rhum de la Jamaïque.

After this they sauntered through the Tuileries Gardens,
and by the quay to their favourite Pont des Arts, and
looked up and down the river—*comme autrefois!*

It is an enchanting prospect at any time and under
any circumstances; but on a beautiful morning in mid-

October, when you haven't seen it for five years, and are still young ! and almost every stock and stone that meets your eye, every sound, every scent, has some sweet and subtle reminder for you——

Let the reader have no fear. I will not attempt to describe it. I shouldn't know where to begin (nor when to leave off !).

Not but what many changes had been wrought; many old landmarks were missing. And among them, as they found out a few minutes later, and much to their chagrin, the good old Morgue !

They inquired of a *gardien de la paix*, who told them that a new Morgue—" une bien jolie Morgue, ma foi ! "— and much more commodious and comfortable than the old one, had been built beyond Notre Dame, a little to the right.

" Messieurs devraient voir ça—on y est très bien ! "

But Notre Dame herself was still there, and La Sainte Chapelle and Le Pont Neuf, and the equestrian statue of Henri IV. *C'est toujours ça !*

And as they gazed and gazed, each framed unto himself, mentally, a little picture of the Thames they had just left—and thought of Waterloo Bridge, and St. Paul's, and London—but felt no home-sickness whatever, no desire to go back in a hurry !

And looking down the river westward there was but little change.

On the left-hand side the terraces and garden of the Hôtel de la Rochemartel (the sculptured entrance of which was in the Rue de Lille) still overtopped the neighbouring houses and shaded the quay with tall trees, whose lightly-falling leaves yellowed the pavement for at least a hundred yards of frontage—or backage, rather; for this was but the rear of that stately palace.

" I wonder if l'Zouzou has come into his dukedom yet ? " said Taffy.

And Taffy the realist, Taffy the modern of moderns, also said many beautiful things about old historical French dukedoms; which, in spite of their plentifulness, were so much more picturesque than English ones, and constituted a far more poetical and romantic link with the past;

" A LITTLE PICTURE OF THE THAMES "

partly on account of their beautiful, high-sounding names

" Amaury de Brissac de Roncesvaulx de la Rochemartel-Boisségur ! what a generous mouthful ! Why, the very sound of it is redolent of the twelfth century ! Not even Howard of Norfolk can beat that ! "

For Taffy was getting sick of "this ghastly thin-faced time of ours," as he sadly called it (quoting from a strange and very beautiful poem called "Faustine," which had just appeared in the *Spectator*—and which our three enthusiasts already knew by heart), and beginning to love all things that were old and regal and rotten and forgotten and of bad repute, and to long to paint them just as they really were.

"Ah ! they managed these things better in France, especially in the twelfth century, and even the thirteenth ! " said the Laird. " Still, Howard of Norfolk isn't bad at a pinch—*fote de myoo !* " he continued, winking at Little Billee. And they promised themselves that they would leave cards on Zouzou, and if he wasn't a duke, invite him to dinner; and also Dodor, if they could manage to find him.

Then along the quay and up the Rue de Seine, and by well-remembered little mystic ways to the old studio in the Place St. Anatole des Arts.

Here they found many changes. A row of new houses

on the north side, by Baron Haussmann—the well-named
—a boulevard was being constructed right through the
place. But the old house had been respected; and looking up, they saw the big north window of their good old
abode blindless and blank and black, but for a white
placard in the middle of it with the words: "À louer,
Un atelier, et une chambre à coucher."

They entered the courtyard through the little door in
the porte cochère, and beheld Madame Vinard standing
on the step of her loge, her arms akimbo, giving orders
to her husband—who was sawing logs for firewood, as
usual at that time of the year—and telling him he was
the most helpless log of the lot.

She gave them one look, threw up her arms, and rushed
at them, saying, "Ah, mon Dieu! les trois Angliches!"

And they could not have complained of any lack of
warmth in her greeting, or in Monsieur Vinard's.

"Ah! mais quel bonheur de vous revoir! Et comme
vous avez bonne mine, tous! Et Monsieur Litrebili,
donc! il a grandi!" etc., etc., "Mais vous allez boire
la goutte avant tout—vite, Vinard! Le ratafia de cassis
que Monsieur Durien nous a envoyé la semaine dernière!"

And they were taken into the loge and made free of it—
welcomed like prodigal sons; a fresh bottle of black-
currant brandy was tapped, and did duty for the fatted
calf. It was an ovation, and made quite a stir in the
Quartier.

Le Retour des trois Angliches—cinq ans après!

She told them all the news: about Bouchardy; Papelard; Jules Guinot, who was now in the Ministère de la
Guerre; Barizel, who had given up the arts and gone
into his father's business (umbrellas); Durien, who had
married six months ago, and had a superb atelier in the
Rue Taitbout, and was coining money; about her own
family—Aglaë, who was going to be married to the son of
the charbonnier at the corner of the Rue de la Canicule—
"un bon mariage; bien solide!" Niniche, who was
studying the piano at the Conservatoire, and had won the
silver medal; Isidore, who, alas! had gone to the bad—
"perdu par les femmes! un si joli garçon, vous concevez!
ça ne lui a pas porté bonheur, par exemple!" And yet

she was proud! and said his father would never have
had the pluck!

"À dix-huit ans, pensez donc!"

"And that good Monsieur Carrel; he is dead, you
know! Ah, messieurs savaient ça? Yes, he died at
Dieppe, his natal town, during the winter, from the
consequences of an indigestion—que voulez-vous! He
always had the stomach so feeble! . . . Ah, the beautiful
interment, messieurs! Five thousand people, in spite of
the rain! Car il pleuvait averse! And M. le Maire and
his adjunct walking behind the hearse, and the gendarmerie
and the douaniers, and a battalion of the douzième
chasseurs-à-pied, with their music, and all the sapper-
pumpers, en grande tenue with their beautiful brass
helmets! All the town was there, following: so there
was nobody left to see the procession go by! q'c'était
beau! Mon Dieu, q'c'était beau! c'que j'ai pleuré, d'voir
ça! n'est-ce-pas, Vinard?"

"Dame, oui, ma biche! j'crois bien! It might have
been Monsieur le Maire himself that one was interring in
person!"

"Ah, ça! voyons, Vinard; thou'rt not going to compare the Maire of Dieppe to a painter like Monsieur
Carrel?"

"Certainly not, ma biche! But still, M. Carrel was a
great man all the same, in his way. Besides, I wasn't
there—nor thou either, as to that!"

"Mon Dieu! comme il est idiot, ce Vinard—of a
stupidity to cut with a knife! Why, thou might'st almost
be a Mayor thyself, sacred imbecile that thou art!"

And an animated discussion arose between husband
and wife as to the respective merits of a country mayor
on one side and a famous painter and a member of the
Institute on the other, during which *les trois Angliches*
were left out in the cold. When Madame Vinard had
sufficiently routed her husband, which did not take very
long, she turned to them again, and told them that she
had started a *magasin de bric-à-brac*, "vous verrez ça!"

Yes, the studio had been to let for three months.
Would they like to see it? Here were the keys. They
would, of course, prefer to see it by themselves, alone;

"' AH ! THE BEAUTIFUL INTERMENT, MESSIEURS ! '"

"je comprends ça ! et vous verrez ce que vous verrez !"
Then they must come and drink once more again the
drop, and inspect her *magasin de bric-à-brac.*

So they went up, all three, and let themselves into the
old place where they had been so happy—and one of
them for a while so miserable !

It was changed indeed.

Bare of all furniture, for one thing ; shabby and unswept,
with a pathetic air of dilapidation, spoliation, desecration,
and a musty, shut-up smell; the window so dirty you
could hardly see the new houses opposite; the floor a
disgrace !

All over the walls were caricatures in charcoal and
white chalk, with more or less incomprehensible legends ;
very vulgar and trivial and coarse, some of them, and
pointless for *trois Angliches.*

But among these (touching to relate) they found, under
a square of plate-glass that had been fixed on the wall by
means of an oak frame, Little Billee's old black-and-
white-and-red chalk sketch of Trilby's left foot, as fresh
as if it had been done only yesterday ! Over it was
written : "Souvenir de la Grande Trilby, par W. B.
(Litrebili)." And beneath, carefully engrossed on im-
perishable parchment, and pasted on the glass, the
following stanzas :—

> " Pauvre Trilby—la belle et bonne et chère !
> Je suis son pied. Devine qui voudra
> Quel tendre ami, la chérissant naguère,
> Encadra d'elle (et d'un amour sincère)
> Ce souvenir charmant qu'un caprice inspira—
> Qu'un souffle emportera !

> " J'étais jumeau : qu'est devenu mon frère ?
> Hélas ! Hélas ! L'Amour nous égara.
> L'Éternité nous unira, j'espère ;
> Et nous ferons comme autrefois la paire
> Au fond d'un lit bien chaste où nul ne troublera
> Trilby—qui dormira.

> " Ô tendre ami, sans nous qu'allez-vous faire ?
> La porte est close où Trilby demeura.
> Le Paradis est loin . . . et sur la terre
> (Qui nous fut douce et lui sera légère)
> Pour trouver nos pareils, si bien qu'on cherchera—
> Beau chercher l'on aura ! "

SOUVENIR
DE LA
GRANDE TRILBY
W.R.(L...)

" PAUVRE TRILBY "

Taffy drew a long breath into his manly bosom, and kept it there as he read this characteristic French doggerel (for so he chose to call this touching little symphony in *ère* and *ra*). His huge frame thrilled with tenderness and pity and fond remembrance, and he said to himself (letting out his breath): " Dear, dear Trilby ! Ah ! if you had only cared for *me*, *I* wouldn't have let you give me up— not for any one on earth. *You* were the mate for *me !* "

And that, as the reader has guessed long ago, was big Taffy's " history."

The Laird was also deeply touched, and could not speak. Had he been in love with Trilby, too? Had he ever been in love with any one?

He couldn't say. But he thought of Trilby's sweetness and unselfishness, her gaiety, her innocent kissings and caressings, her drollery and frolicsome grace, her way of filling whatever place she was in with her presence, the charming sight and the genial sound of her; and felt that no girl, no woman, no lady he had ever seen yet was a match for this poor waif and stray, this long-legged, cancan-dancing, Quartier Latin grisette, blanchisseuse de fin, " and Heaven knows what besides ! "

" Hang it all ! " he mentally ejaculated, " I wish to goodness I'd married her *myself !* "

Little Billee said nothing either. He felt unhappier than he had ever once felt for five long years—to think that he could gaze on such a memento as this, a thing so strongly personal to himself, with dry eyes and a quiet pulse ! and he unemotionally, dispassionately, wished himself dead and buried for at least the thousand-and-first time !

All three possessed casts of Trilby's hands and feet, and photographs of herself. But nothing so charmingly suggestive of Trilby as this little masterpiece of a true artist, this happy fluke of a happy moment. It was Trilbyness itself, as the Laird thought, and should not be suffered to perish.

They took the keys back to Madame Vinard in silence.

She said : " Vous avez vu—n'est-ce pas, messieurs ?— le pied de Trilby ! c'est bien gentil ! C'est Monsieur

Durien qui a fait mettre le verre, quand vous êtes partis;
et Monsieur Guinot qui a composé *l'épitaphe.* Pauvre
Trilby! qu'est-ce qu'elle est devenue! comme elle était
bonne fille, hein? et si belle! et comme elle était vive
elle était vive elle était vive! Et comme elle vous aimait
tous bien—et surtout Monsieur Litrebili—n'est-ce pas?"

Then she insisted on giving them each another liqueur-
glass of Durien's ratafia de cassis, and took them to see
her collection of *bric-à-brac* across the yard, a gorgeous
show, and explained everything about it—how she had
begun in quite a small way, but was making it a big
business.

"Voyez cette pendule! It is of the time of Louis
Onze, who gave it with his own hands to Madame de
Pompadour (!). I bought it at a sale in——"

"Combiang?" said the Laird.

"C'est cent-cinquante francs, monsieur—c'est bien bon
marché—une véritable occasion, et——"

"Je prong!" said the Laird, meaning "I take it!"

Then she showed them a beautiful brocade gown "which
she had picked up a bargain at——"

"Combiang?" said the Laird.

"Ah, ça, c'est trois cents francs, monsieur. Mais——"

"Je prong!" said the Laird.

"Et voici les souliers qui vont avec, et que——"

"Je pr——"

But here Taffy took the Laird by the arm and dragged
him by force out of this too seductive siren's cave.

The Laird told her where to send his purchases, and
with many expressions of love and good-will on both
sides, they tore themselves away from Monsieur et Madame
Vinard.

The Laird, however, rushed back for a minute, and
hurriedly whispered to Madame Vinard: "Oh—er—le
piay de Trilby—sur le mure, vous savvy—avec le verre et
toot le reste—coopy le mure—comprenny? ... Combiang?"

"Ah, monsieur!" said Madame Vinard—"c'est un peu
difficile, vous savez—couper un mur comme ça! On par-
lera au propriétaire si vous voulez, et ça pourrait peut-
être s'arranger, si c'est en bois! seulement il fau——"

" Je prong ! " said the Laird, and waved his hand in
farewell.

They went up the Rue Vieille des Trois Mauvais Ladres,
and found that about twenty yards of a high wall had
been pulled down—just at the bend where the Laird had
seen the last of Trilby, as she turned round and kissed

" ' JE PRONG ! ' "

her hand to him—and they beheld, within, a quaint and
ancient long-neglected garden; a gray old garden, with
tall, warty, black-boled trees, and damp, green, mossy
paths that lost themselves under the brown and yellow
leaves and mould and muck which had drifted into heaps
here and there, the accumulation of years—a queer old
faded pleasance, with wasted bowers and dilapidated
carved stone benches and weather-beaten discoloured

marble statues—noseless, armless, earless fauns and hama-
dryads! And at the end of it, in a tumble-down state
of utter ruin, a still inhabited little house, with shabby
blinds and window-curtains, and broken window-panes
mended with brown paper—a Pavillon de Flore, that
must have been quite beautiful a hundred years ago—the
once mysterious love-resort of long-buried abbés with
light hearts, and well-forgotten lords and ladies gay—
red-heeled, patched, powdered, frivolous, and shameless,
but, oh! how charming to the imagination of the nine-
teenth century! And right through the ragged lawn
(where lay, upset in the long dewy grass, a broken doll's
perambulator by a tattered Polichinelle) went a desecrat-
ing track made by cart-wheels and horses' hoofs; and
this, no doubt, was to be a new street—perhaps, as Taffy
suggested, "La Rue *Neuve* des Trois Mauvais Ladres!"
(The *new* street of the three bad lepers!)

"Ah, Taffy!" sententiously opined the Laird, with his
usual wink at Little Billee—"I've no doubt the *old* lepers
were the best, bad as they were!"

"I'm quite *sure* of it!" said Taffy, with sad and
sober conviction and a long-drawn sigh. "I only wish
I had a chance of painting one—just as he really
was!"

How often they had speculated on what lay hidden
behind that lofty old brick wall! and now this melancholy
little peep into the once festive past, the touching sight of
this odd old poverty-stricken abode of Heaven knows
what present grief and desolation, which a few strokes
of the pickaxe had laid bare, seemed to chime in with
their own gray mood that had been so bright and
sunny an hour ago; and they went on their way quite
dejectedly, for a stroll through the Luxembourg Gallery
and Gardens.

The same people seemed to be still copying the same
pictures in the long, quiet, genial room, so pleasantly smell-
ing of oil-paint—Rosa Bonheur's "Labourage Nivernais,"
Hébert's "Malaria," Couture's "Decadent Romans."

And in the formal dusty gardens were the same piou-
pious and zouzous still walking with the same nounous,
or sitting by their sides on benches by formal ponds with

gold and silver fish in them—and just the same old couples petting the same toutous and loulous ! [1]

Then they thought they would go and lunch at le père Trin's—the Restaurant de la Couronne, in the Rue du Luxembourg—for the sake of auld lang syne ! But when they got there, the well-remembered fumes of that humble refectory, which had once seemed not unappetising, turned their stomachs. So they contented themselves with warmly greeting le père Trin, who was quite overjoyed to see them again, and anxious to turn the whole establishment topsy-turvy that he might entertain such guests as they deserved.

Then the Laird suggested an omelet at the Café de l'Odéon. But Taffy said, in his masterful way, " Damn the Café de l'Odéon ! "

And hailing a little open fly, they drove to Ledoyen's, or some such place, in the Champs Élysées, where they feasted as became three prosperous Britons out for a holiday in Paris—three irresponsible musketeers, lords of themselves and Lutetia, *beati possidentes !*—and afterwards had themselves driven in an open carriage and pair through the Bois de Boulogne to the fête de St. Cloud (or what still remained of it, for it lasts six weeks), the scene of so many of Dodor's and Zouzou's exploits in past years, and found it more amusing than the Luxembourg Gardens ; the lively and irrepressible spirit of Dodor seemed to pervade it still.

But it doesn't want the presence of a Dodor to make the blue-bloused sons of the Gallic people (and its neatly-shod, white-capped daughters) delightful to watch as they take their pleasure. And the Laird (thinking perhaps of Hampstead Heath on an Easter Monday) must not be blamed for once more quoting his favourite phrase—the pretty little phrase with which the most humorous and least exemplary of British parsons began his famous journey to France.

[1] *Glossary.*—Pioupiou (*alias* pousse-caillou, *alias* tourlourou)—a private soldier of the line. Zouzou—a Zouave. Nounou—a wet-nurse with a pretty ribboned cap and long streamers. Toutou—a nondescript French lapdog, of no breed known to Englishmen (a regular little beast !). Loulou—a Pomeranian dog—not much better.

When they came back to the hotel to dress and dine, the Laird found he wanted a pair of white gloves for the concert—" Oon pair de gong blong," as he called it—and they walked along the boulevards till they came to a haberdasher's shop of very good and prosperous appearance, and, going in, were received graciously by the " patron," a portly little bourgeois, who waved them to a tall and aristocratic and very well-dressed young commis behind the counter, saying, " Une paire de gants blancs pour monsieur."

And what was the surprise of our three friends in recognising Dodor !

The gay Dodor, Dodor *l'irrésistible,* quite unembarrassed by his position, was exuberant in his delight at seeing them again, and introduced them to the patron and his wife and daughter, Monsieur, Madame, and Mademoiselle Passefil. And it soon became pretty evident that, in spite of his humble employment in that house, he was a great favourite in that family, and especially with mademoiselle.

Indeed, Monsieur Passefil invited our three heroes to stay and dine then and there; but they compromised matters by asking Dodor to come and dine with *them* at the hotel, and he accepted with alacrity.

Thanks to Dodor, the dinner was a very lively one, and they soon forgot the regretful impressions of the day.

They learned that he hadn't got a penny in the world, and had left the army, and had for two years kept the books at le père Passefil's and served his customers, and won his good opinion and his wife's, and especially his daughter's; and that soon he was to be not only his employer's partner, but his son-in-law; and that, in spite of his impecuniosity, he had managed to impress them with the fact that in marrying a Rigolot de Lafarce she was making a very splendid match indeed !

His brother-in-law, the Honourable Jack Reeve, had long cut him for a bad lot. But his sister, after a while, had made up her mind that to marry Mlle. Passefil wasn't the worst he could do; at all events, it would keep him out of England, and *that* was a comfort ! And passing through Paris, she had actually called on the Passefil family, and they had fallen prostrate before such splen-

"'OON PAIR DE GONG BLONG'"

dour; and no wonder, for Mrs. Jack Reeve was one of the most beautiful, elegant, and fashionable women in London, the smartest of the smart.

" And how about l'Zouzou? " asked Little Billee.

" Ah, old Gontran! I don't see much of him. We no longer quite move in the same circles, you know; not that he's proud, or me either! but he's a sub-lieutenant in the Guides—an officer! Besides, his brother's dead, and he's the Duc de la Rochemartel, and a special pet of the Empress; he makes her laugh more than anybody! He's looking out for the biggest heiress he can find, and he's pretty safe to catch her, with such a name as that! In fact, they say he's caught her already—Miss Lavinia Hunks, of Chicago. Twenty million dollars!—at least, so the *Figaro* says! "

Then he gave them news of other old friends; and they did not part till it was time for them to go to the Cirque des Bashibazoucks, and after they had arranged to dine with his future family on the following day.

In the Rue St. Honoré was a long double file of cabs and carriages slowly moving along to the portals of that huge hall, Le Cirque des Bashibazoucks. Is it there still, I wonder? I don't mind betting not! Just at this period of the Second Empire there was a mania for demolition and remolition (if there is such a word), and I have no doubt my Parisian readers would search the Rue St. Honoré for the Salle des Bashibazoucks in vain!

Our friends were shown to their stalls, and looked round in surprise. This was before the days of the Albert Hall, and they had never been in such a big place of the kind before, or one so regal in aspect, so gorgeously imperial with white and gold and crimson velvet, so dazzling with light, so crammed with people from floor to roof, and cramming itself still.

A platform carpeted with crimson cloth had been erected in front of the gates where the horses had once used to come in, and their fair riders, and the two jolly English clowns; and the beautiful nobleman with the long frock-coat and brass buttons, and soft high boots, and four-in-hand whip—*la chambrière.*

In front of this was a lower stand for the orchestra. The circus itself was filled with stalls—*stalles d'orchestre*. A pair of crimson curtains hid the entrance to the platform at the back, and by each of these stood a small page, ready to draw it aside and admit the diva.

The entrance to the orchestra was by a small door under the platform, and some thirty or forty chairs and music-stands, grouped around the conductor's *estrade*, were waiting for the band.

Little Billee looked round, and recognised many country-men and countrywomen of his own—many great musical celebrities especially, whom he had often met in London. Tiers upon tiers of people rose up all round in a widening circle, and lost themselves in a dazy mist of light at the top—it was like a picture by Martin! In the imperial box were the English ambassador and his family, with an august British personage sitting in the middle, in front, his broad blue ribbon across his breast and his opera-glass to his royal eyes.

Little Billee had never felt so excited, so exhilarated by such a show before, nor so full of eager anticipation. He looked at his programme, and saw that the Hungarian band (the first that had yet appeared in Western Europe, I believe) would play an overture of gypsy dances. Then Madame Svengali would sing " un air connu, sans accom-pagnement" and afterwards other airs, including the " Nussbaum " of Schumann (for the first time in Paris, it seemed). Then a rest of ten minutes ; then more *csárdás ;* then the diva would sing " Malbrouck s'en va-t'en guerre," of all things in the world ! and finish up with " un impromptu de Chopin, sans paroles."

Truly a somewhat incongruous bill of fare.

Close on the stroke of nine the musicians came in and took their seats. They were dressed in the foreign hussar uniform that has now become so familiar. The first violin had scarcely sat down before our friends recognised in him their old friend Gecko.

Just as the clock struck, Svengali, in irreproachable evening dress, tall and stout and quite splendid in appear-ance, notwithstanding his long black mane (which had been curled), took his place at his desk. Our friends would have known him at a glance, in spite of the wonderful alteration time and prosperity had wrought in his outward man.

He bowed right and left to the thunderous applause that greeted him, gave his three little bâton-taps, and the lovely music began at once. We have grown accustomed to strains of this kind during the last twenty years, but they were new then, and their strange seduction was a surprise as well as an enchantment.

Besides, no such band as Svengali's had ever been heard; and in listening to this overture the immense crowd almost forgot that was a mere preparation for a great musical event, and tried to encore it. But Svengali merely turned round and bowed—there were to be no encores that night.

GECKO

Then a moment of silence and breathless suspense—curiosity on tiptoe!

Then the two little page-boys each drew a silken rope, and the curtains parted and looped themselves up on each side symmetrically; and a tall female figure appeared, clad in what seemed like a classical dress of cloth of gold, embroidered with garnets and beetles' wings; her snowy arms and shoulders bare, a gold coronet of stars on her head, her thick light brown hair tied behind and flowing all down her back to nearly her knees, like those ladies in hair-dressers' shops who sit with their backs to the plate-glass window to advertise the merits of some particular hair-wash.

She walked slowly down to the front, her hands hanging at her sides in quite a simple fashion, and made a slight inclination of her head and body towards the imperial box, and then to right and left. Her lips and cheeks were rouged; her dark level eye-brows nearly met at the bridge of her short high nose. Through her parted lips you could see her large glistening white teeth; her gray eyes looked straight at Svengali.

Her face was thin, and had a rather haggard expression, in spite of its artificial freshness; but its contour was divine, and its character so tender, so humble, so touchingly simple and sweet, that one melted at the sight of her. No such magnificent or seductive apparition has ever been seen before or since on any stage or platform— not even Miss Ellen Terry as the priestess of Artemis in the late laureate's play, *The Cup.*

The house rose at her as she came down to the front; and she bowed again to right and left, and put her hand to her heart quite simply and with a most winning natural gesture, an adorable *gaucherie*—like a graceful and unconscious school-girl, quite innocent of stage deportment.

It was Trilby !

Trilby the tone-deaf, who couldn't sing one single note in tune ! Trilby, who couldn't tell a C from an F ! !

What was going to happen ?

Our three friends were almost turned to stone in the immensity of their surprise.

Yet the big Taffy was trembling all over; the Laird's jaw had all but fallen on to his chest; Little Billee was staring, staring his eyes almost out of his head. There was something, to them, so strange and uncanny about it all; so oppressive, so anxious, so momentous !

The applause had at last subsided. Trilby stood with her hands behind her, one foot (the left one) on a little stool that had been left there on purpose, her lips parted, her eyes on Svengali's, ready to begin.

He gave his three beats, and the band struck a chord. Then, at another beat from him, but in her direction, she began, without the slightest appearance of effort, without any accompaniment whatever, he still beating time— conducting her, in fact, just as if she had been an orchestra herself:

> " Au clair de la lune,
> Mon ami Pierrot!
> Prête-moi ta plume
> Pour écrire un mot.

Ma chandelle est morte . . .
    Je n'ai plus de feu !
    Ouvre-moi ta porte
    Pour l'amour de Dieu ! "

This was the absurd old nursery rhyme with which La
Svengali chose to make her *début* before the most critical
audience in the world ! She sang it three times over—
the same verse. There is but one.

The first time she sang it without any expression whatever—not the slightest. Just the words and the tune;
in the middle of her voice, and not loud at all; just as a
child sings who is thinking of something else; or just as a
young French mother sings who is darning socks by a
cradle, and rocking her baby to sleep with her foot.

But her voice was so immense in its softness, richness,
freshness, that it seemed to be pouring itself out from all
round; its intonation absolutely, mathematically pure;
one felt it to be not only faultless, but infallible; and the
seduction, the novelty of it, the strangely sympathetic
quality ! How can one describe the quality of a peach
or a nectarine to those who have only known apples?

Until La Svengali appeared, the world had only known
apples—Catalanis, Jenny Linds, Grisis, Albonis, Pattis !
The best apples that can be, for sure—but still only apples !

If she had spread a pair of large white wings and gracefully fluttered up to the roof and perched upon the chandelier, she could not have produced a greater sensation.
The like of that voice has never been heard, nor ever will
be again. A woman archangel might sing like that, or
some enchanted princess out of a fairy tale.

Little Billee had already dropped his face into his hands
and hid his eyes in his pocket-handkerchief; a big tear had
fallen on to Taffy's left whisker; the Laird was trying
hard to keep his tears back.

She sang the verse a second time, with but little added
expression and no louder; but with a sort of breathy
widening of her voice that made it like a broad heavenly
smile of universal motherhood turned into sound. One
felt all the genial gaiety and grace of impishness of Pierrot
and Columbine idealised into frolicsome beauty and holy
innocence, as though they were performing for the saints

"AU CLAIR DE LA LUNE"

in Paradise—a baby Columbine, with a cherub for clown !
The dream of it all came over you for a second or two—
a revelation of some impossible golden age—priceless—
never to be forgotten ! How on earth did she do it?

Little Billee had lost all control over himself, and
was shaking with his suppressed sobs—Little Billee, who
hadn't shed a single tear for five long years ! Half the
people in the house were in tears, but tears of sheer
delight, of delicate inner laughter.

Then she came back to earth, and saddened and veiled and darkened her voice as she sang the verse for the third time; and it was a great and sombre tragedy, too deep for any more tears; and somehow or other poor Columbine, forlorn and betrayed and dying, out in the cold at midnight—sinking down to hell, perhaps—was making her last frantic appeal! It was no longer Pierrot and Columbine—it was Marguerite—it was Faust! It was the most terrible and pathetic of all possible human

tragedies, but expressed with no dramatic or histrionic exaggeration of any sort; by mere tone, slight, subtle changes in the quality of the sound—too quick and elusive to be taken count of, but to be felt with, oh, what poignant sympathy!

When the song was over, the applause did not come immediately, and she waited with her kind wide smile, as if she were well accustomed to wait like this; and then the storm began, and grew and spread and rattled and echoed—voice, hands, feet, sticks, umbrellas!—and down came the bouquets, which the little page-boys picked up; and Trilby bowed to front and right and left in her simple *débonnaire* fashion. It was her usual triumph. It had never failed, w h a t e v e r the audience, whatever the country, whatever the song.

" OUVRE-MOI TA PORTE
POUR L'AMOUR DE DIEU ! "

Little Billee didn't applaud. He sat with his head in his hands, his shoulders still heaving. He believed himself to be fast asleep and in a dream, and was trying his utmost not to wake; for a great happiness was his. It was one of those nights to be marked with a white stone !

As the first bars of the song came pouring out of her parted lips (whose shape he so well remembered), and her dove-like eyes looked straight over Svengali's head, straight in his own direction—nay, *at* him—something melted in his brain, and all his long-lost power of loving came back with a rush.

It was like the sudden curing of a deafness that has been lasting for years. The doctor blows through your nose into your Eustachian tube with a little india-rubber machine; some obstacle gives way, there is a snap in your head, and straightway you hear better than you had ever heard in all your life, almost too well; and all your life is once more changed for you !

At length he sat up again, in the middle of La Svengali's singing of the " Nussbaum," and saw her; and saw the Laird sitting by him, and Taffy, their eyes riveted on Trilby, and knew for certain that it was *no* dream this time, and his joy was almost a pain !

She sang the " Nussbaum " (to its heavenly accompaniment) as simply as she had sung the previous song. Every separate note was a highly-finished gem of sound, linked to the next by a magic bond. You did not require to be a lover of music to fall beneath the spell of such a voice as that; the mere melodic phrase had all but ceased to matter. Her phrasing, consummate as it was, was as simple as a child's.

It was as if she said : " See ! what does the composer count for ? Here is about as beautiful a song as was ever written, with beautiful words to match, and the words have been made French for you by one of your smartest poets ! But what do the words signify, any more than the tune, or even the language ? The ' Nussbaum ' is neither better nor worse than ' Mon ami Pierrot ' when I am the singer; for I am *Svengali ;* and you shall hear nothing, see nothing, think of nothing, but *Svengali, Svengali, Svengali !* "

It was the apotheosis of voice and virtuosity ! It was "il bel canto" come back to earth after a hundred years —the bel canto of Vivarelli, let us say, who sang the same song every night to the same King of Spain for a quarter of a century, and was rewarded with a dukedom, and wealth beyond the dreams of avarice.

And, indeed, here was this immense audience, made up of the most cynically critical people in the world, and the most anti-German, assisting with rapt ears and streaming eyes at the imagined spectacle of a simple German damsel, a Mädchen, a Fräulein, just *verlobte*—a future Hausfrau— sitting under a walnut-tree in some suburban garden—à Berlin !—and around her, her family and her friends, probably drinking beer and smoking long porcelain pipes, and talking politics or business, and cracking innocent elaborate old German jokes; with bated breath, lest they should disturb her maiden dream of love ! And all as though it were a scene in Elysium, and the Fräulein a nymph of many-fountained Ida, and her people Olympian gods and goddesses.

And such, indeed, they were when Trilby sang of them !

After this, when the long, frantic applause had subsided, she made a gracious bow to the royal British opera-glass (which had never left her face), and sang " Ben Bolt " in English !

And then Little Billee remembered there was such a person as Svengali in the world, and recalled his little flexible flageolet !

" That is how I teach Gecko; that is how I teach la bedite Honorine ; that is how I teach il bel canto. . . . It was lost, il bel canto—and I found it in a dream—I, Svengali ! "

And his old cosmic vision of the beauty and sadness of things, the very heart of them, and their pathetic evanescence, came back with a tenfold clearness—that heavenly glimpse beyond the veil ! And with it a crushing sense of his own infinitesimal significance by the side of this glorious pair of artists, one of whom had been his friend and the other his love—a love who had offered to be his humble mistress and slave, not feeling herself good enough to be his wife !

It made him sick and faint to remember, and filled him with hot shame, and then and there his love for Trilby became as that of a dog for its master !

She sang once more—" Chanson de Printemps," by Gounod (who was present, and seemed very hysterical), and the first part of the concert was over, and people had time to draw breath and talk over this new wonder, this revelation of what the human voice could achieve; and an immense hum filled the hall—astonishment, enthusiasm, ecstatic delight !

But our three friends found little to say—for what *they* felt there were as yet no words !

Taffy and the Laird looked at Little Billee, who seemed to be looking inward at some transcendent dream of his own; with red eyes, and his face all pale and drawn, and his nose very pink, and rather thicker than usual; and the dream appeared to be out of the common blissful, though his eyes were swimming still, for his smile was almost idiotic in its rapture !

The second part of the concert was still shorter than the first, and created, if possible, a wilder enthusiasm.

Trilby only sang twice.

Her first song was " Malbrouck s'en va-t'en guerre."

She began it quite lightly and merrily, like a jolly march; in the middle of her voice, which had not as yet revealed any exceptional compass or range. People laughed quite frankly at the first verse :—

> " Malbrouck s'en va-t'en guerre—
> *Mironton, mironton, mirontaine !*
> Malbrouck s'en va-t'en guerre. . . .
> Ne sais quand reviendra !
> Ne sais quand reviendra !
> Ne sais quand reviendra ! "

The *mironton, mirontaine* was the very essence of high martial resolve and heroic self-confidence; one would have led a forlorn hope after hearing it once !

> " Il reviendra-z à Pâques—
> *Mirorton, mironton, mirontaine !*
> Il reviendra-z à Pâques. . . .
> Ou . . . à là Trinité ! "

People still laughed, though the *mironton, mirontaine,*

betrayed an uncomfortable sense of the dawning of doubts and fears—vague forebodings !

" La Trinité se passe—
  Mironton, mironton, mirontaine !
  La Trinité se passe. . . .
  Malbrouck ne revient pas ! "

" MALBROUCK S'EN VA-T'EN GUERRE "

And here, especially in the *mironton, mirontaine,* a note of anxiety revealed itself—so poignant, so acutely natural and human, that it became a personal anxiety of one's own, causing the heart to beat, and one's breath was short.

" Madame à sa tour monte—
  Mironton, mironton, mirontaine !
  Madame à sa tour monte,
  Si haut qu'elle peut monter ! "

Oh ! How one's heart went with her ! Anne ! Sister Anne ! Do you see anything?

" Elle voit de loin son page—
  Mironton, mironton, mirontaine !
  Elle voit de loin son page,
  Tout de noir habillé ! ''

One is almost sick with the sense of impending calamity
—it is all but unbearable !

" Mon page—mon beau page !—
  Mironton, mironton, mirontaine !
  Mon page—mon beau page !
  Quelle nouvelles apportez ? ''

And here Little Billee begins to weep again, and so does
everybody else ! The *mironton, mirontaine,* is an agonised
wail of suspense—poor bereaved duchess !—poor Sarah
Jennings ! Did it all announce itself to you just like
that ?

All this while the accompaniment had been quite simple
—just a few obvious ordinary chords.

But now, quite suddenly, without a single modulation
or note of warning, down goes the tune a full major third,
from E to C—into the graver depths of Trilby's great
contralto—so solemn and ominous that there is no more
weeping, but the flesh creeps ; the accompaniment slows
and elaborates itself ; the march becomes a funeral march,
with muted strings, and quite slowly :

" Aux nouvelles que j'apporte—
  Mironton, mironton, mirontaine !
  Aux nouvelles que j'apporte,
  Vos beaux yeux vont pleurer ! ''

Richer and richer grows the accompaniment. The
mironton, mirontaine, becomes a dirge !

" Quittez vos habits roses—
  Mironton, mironton, mirontaine !
  Quittez vos habits roses,
  Et vos satins brochés ! ''

Here the ding-donging of a big bell seems to mingle
with the score ; . . . and very slowly, and so impressively

"AUX NOUVELLES QUE J'APPORTE,
VOS BEAUX YEUX VONT PLEURER!"

that the news will ring for ever in the ears and hearts of
those who hear it from La Svengali's lips :

"Le Sieur Malbrouck est mort—
Mironton, mironton, mirontaine !
Le Sieur—Malbrouck—est—mort!
Est mort—et enterré!"

And thus it ends quite abruptly!

And this heartrending tragedy, this great historical
epic in two dozen lines, at which some five or six thousand
gay French people are sniffling and mopping their eyes
like so many Niobes, is just a common old French comic
song—a mere nursery ditty, like "Little Bo-peep"—to the
tune,

"We won't go home till morning,
Till daylight doth appear."

And after a second or two of silence (oppressive and impressive as that which occurs at a burial when the handful of earth is being dropped on the coffin lid) the audience bursts once more into madness; and La Svengali, who accepts no encores, has to bow for nearly five minutes, standing amid a sea of flowers. . . .

Then comes her great and final performance. The orchestra swiftly plays the first four bars of the bass in Chopin's Impromptu (A flat); and suddenly, without words, as a light nymph catching the whirl of a double skipping-rope, La Svengali breaks in, and vocalises that astounding piece of music that so few pianists can even play; but no pianist has ever played it like this; no piano has ever given out such notes as these !

Every single phrase is a string of perfect gems, of purest ray serene, strung together on a loose golden thread ! The higher and shriller she sings, the sweeter it is ; higher and shriller than any woman had ever sung before.

Waves of sweet and tender laughter, the very heart and essence of innocent, high-spirited girlhood, alive to all that is simple and joyous and elementary in nature—the freshness of the morning, the ripple of the stream, the click of the mill, the lisp of the wind in the trees, the song of the lark in the cloudless sky—the sun and the dew, the scent of early flowers and summer woods and meadows—the sight of birds and bees and butterflies and frolicsome young animals at play—all the sights and scents and sounds that are the birthright of happy children, happy savages in favoured climes—things within the remembrance and the reach of most of us ! All this, the memory and the feel of it, are in Trilby's voice as she warbles that long, smooth, lilting, dancing laugh, that shower of linked sweetness, that wondrous song without words ; and those who hear feel it all, and remember it with her. It is irresistible ; it forces itself on you ; no words, no pictures, could ever do the like ! So that the tears that are shed out of all these many French eyes are tears of pure, unmixed delight in happy reminiscence ! (Chopin, it is true, may have meant something quite different—a hot-house, perhaps, with orchids and arum lilies and tuberoses and hydrangeas—but all this is neither here nor there, as the Laird would say in French.)

Then comes the slow movement, the sudden adagio, with its capricious ornaments—the waking of the virgin heart, the stirring of the sap, the dawn of love; its doubts and fears and questionings; and the mellow, powerful, deep chest notes are like the pealing of great golden bells, with a light little pearl shower tinkling round—drops from the upper fringe of her grand voice as she shakes it. . . .

Then back again the quick part, childhood once more, *da capo*, only quicker! hurry, hurry! but distinct as ever. Loud and shrill and sweet beyond compare—drowning the orchestra; of a piercing quality quite ineffable; a joy there is no telling; a clear, purling, crystal stream that gurgles and foams and bubbles along over sunlit stones; a wonder, a world's delight!

And there is not a sign of effort, of difficulty overcome. All through, Trilby smiles her broad, angelic smile; her lips well parted, her big white teeth glistening as she gently jerks her head from side to side in time to Svengali's bâton, as if to shake the willing notes out quicker and higher and shriller. . . .

And in a minute or two it is all over, like the lovely bouquet of fireworks at the end of the show, and she lets what remains of it die out and away like the afterglow of fading Bengal fires—her voice receding into the distance——coming back to you like an echo from all round, from anywhere you please—quite soft—hardly more than a breath; but *such* a breath! Then one last chromatically ascending rocket, *pianissimo*, up to E in alt, and then darkness and silence!

And after a little pause the many-headed rises as one and waves its hats and sticks and handkerchiefs, and stamps and shouts . . . " Vive La Svengali! Vive La Svengali!"

Svengali steps on to the platform by his wife's side and kisses her hand; and they both bow themselves backward through the curtains, which fall, to rise again and again and again on this astounding pair!

Such was La Svengali's *début* in Paris.

It had lasted little over an hour, one quarter of which, at least, had been spent in plaudits and courtesies!

UN IMPROMPTU DE CHOPIN

The writer is no musician, alas ! (as, no doubt, his musical readers have found out by this) save in his thraldom to music of not too severe a kind, and laments the clumsiness and inadequacy of this wild (though somewhat ambitious) attempt to recall an impression received more than thirty years ago; to revive the ever-blessed memory of that unforgettable first night at the Cirque des Bashibazoucks.

Would that I could transcribe here Berlioz's famous series of twelve articles, entitled " La Svengali," which were republished from *La Lyre Éolienne,* and are now out of print !

Or Théophile Gautier's elaborate rhapsody, " Madame Svengali—*Ange ou Femme ?* " in which he proves that one need not have a musical ear (he hadn't) to be enslaved by such a voice as hers, any more than the eye for beauty (this he *had*) to fall the victim of " her celestial form and face." It is enough, he says, to be simply human ! I forget in which journal this eloquent tribute appeared; it is not to be found in his collected works.

Or the intemperate diatribe by Herr Blagner (as I will christen him) on the tyranny of the prima donna called " Svengalismus "; in which he attempts to show that mere virtuosity carried to such a pitch is mere viciosity—base acrobatismus of the vocal chords, a hysteric appeal to morbid Gallic " sentimentalismus "; and that this monstrous development of a phenomenal larynx, this degrading cultivation and practice of the abnormalismus of a mere physical peculiarity, are death and destruction to all true music; since they place Mozart and Beethoven, and even *himself,* on a level with Bellini, Donizetti, Offenbach—any Italian tune-tinkler, any ballad-monger of the hated Paris pavement ! and can make the highest music of all (even *his own*) go down with the common French herd at the very first hearing, just as if it were some idiotic refrain of the *café chantant !*

So much for Blagnerismus *v.* Svengalismus.

But I fear there is no space within the limits of this humble tale for these masterpieces of technical musical criticism.

Besides, there are other reasons.

Our three heroes walked back to the boulevards, the only silent ones amid the throng that poured through the Rue St. Honoré, as the Cirque des Bashibazoucks emptied itself of its over-excited audience.

They went arm-in-arm, as usual; but this time Little Billee was in the middle. He wished to feel on each side of him the warm and genial contact of his two beloved old friends. It seemed as if they had suddenly been restored to him, after five long years of separation; his heart was overflowing with affection for them, too full to speak just yet! Overflowing, indeed, with the love of love, the love of life, the love of death—the love of all that is, and ever was, and ever will be! just as in his old way.

He could have hugged them both in the open street, before the whole world; and the delight of it was that this was no dream; about that there was no mistake. He was himself again at last, after five years, and wide awake; and he owed it all to Trilby!

And what did he feel for Trilby? He couldn't tell yet. It was too vast as yet to be measured; and, alas! it was weighted with such a burden of sorrow and regret that he might well put off the thought of it a little while longer, and gather in what bliss he might: like the man whose hearing has been restored after long years, he would revel in the mere physical delight of hearing for a space, and not go out of his way as yet to listen for the bad news that was already in the air, and would come to roost quite soon enough.

Taffy and the Laird were silent also; Trilby's voice was still in their ears and hearts, her image in their eyes, and utter bewilderment still oppressed them and kept them dumb.

It was a warm and balmy night, almost like midsummer; and they stopped at the first café they met on the Boulevard de la Madeleine (*comme autrefois*), and ordered bocks of beer, and sat at a little table on the pavement, the only one unoccupied; for the café was already crowded, the hum of lively talk was great, and "La Svengali" was in every mouth.

The Laird was the first to speak. He emptied his bock at a draught, and called for another, and lit a cigar, and said, "I don't believe it was Trilby, after all!" It was

the first time her name had been mentioned between them
that evening—and for five years !

"Good heavens !" said Taffy. "Can you doubt it?"

"Oh yes ! that was Trilby," said Little Billee.

Then the Laird proceeded to explain that, putting aside
the impossibility of Trilby's ever being taught to sing in
tune, and her well-remembered loathing for Svengali, he
had narrowly scanned her face through his opera-glass, and
found that in spite of a likeness quite marvellous there were
well-marked differences. Her face was narrower and longer,
her eyes larger, and their expression not the same; then
she seemed taller and stouter, and her shoulders broader
and more drooping, and so forth.

But the others wouldn't hear of it, and voted him cracked,
and declared they even recognised the peculiar twang of her
old speaking voice in the voice she now sang with, especially
when she sang low down. And they all three fell to discussing the wonders of her performance like everybody else
all round; Little Billee leading, with an eloquence and a
seeming of technical musical knowledge that quite impressed them, and made them feel happy and at ease;
for they were anxious for his sake about the effect this
sudden and so unexpected sight of her would have upon
him after all that had passed.

He seemed transcendently happy and elate—incompre-
hensibly so, in fact—and looked at them both with quite a
new light in his eyes, as if all the music he had heard had
trebled not only his joy in being alive, but his pleasure at
being with them. Evidently he had quite outgrown his
old passion for her, and that was a comfort indeed !

But Little Billee knew better.

He knew that his old passion for her had all come back,
and was so overwhelming and immense that he could not
feel it just yet, nor yet the hideous pangs of a jealousy so
consuming that it would burn up his life. He gave himself
another twenty-four hours.

But he had not to wait so long. He woke up after a
short, uneasy sleep that very night, to find that the flood
was over him; and he realised how hopelessly, desperately,
wickedly, insanely he loved this woman, who might have
been his, but was now the wife of another man; a greater

than he, and one to whom she owed it that she was more
glorious than any other woman on earth—a queen among
queens—a goddess ! for what was any earthly throne com-
pared to that she established in the hearts and souls of all
who came within the sight and hearing of her; beautiful
as she was besides—beautiful, beautiful ! And what must
be her love for the man who had taught her and trained her,

" AND THE REMEMBRANCE OF THEM—HAND IN HAND "

and revealed her towering genius to herself and to the world
—a man resplendent also, handsome and tall and commanding— a great artist from the crown of his head to the
sole of his foot !

And the remembrance of them—hand in hand, master
and pupil, husband and wife—smiling and bowing in the
face of all that splendid tumult they had called forth and
could quell, stung and tortured and maddened him so that
he could not lie still, but got up and raged and rampaged
up and down his hot, narrow, stuffy bedroom, and longed
for his old familiar brain-disease to come back and narcotise

his trouble, and be his friend, and stay with him till he died !

Where was he to fly for relief from such new memories as these, which would never cease; and the old memories, and all the glamour and grace of them that had been so suddenly called out of the grave? And how could he escape, now that he felt the sight of her face and the sound of her voice would be a craving—a daily want—like that of some poor starving outcast for warmth and meat and drink?

And little innocent, pathetic, ineffable, well-remembered sweetness of her changing face kept painting themselves on his retina; and incomparable tones of this new thing, her voice, her infinite voice, went ringing in his head, till he all but shrieked aloud in his agony.

And then the poisoned and delirious sweetness of those mad kisses,

> " by hopeless fancy feigned
> On lips that are for others " !

And then the grewsome physical jealousy, that miserable inheritance of all artistic sons of Adam, that plague and torment of the dramatic, plastic imagination, which can idealise so well, and yet realise, alas ! so keenly. After three or four hours spent like this, he could stand it no longer; madness was lying his way. So he hurried on a garment, and went and knocked at Taffy's door.

" Good God ! what's the matter with you ? " exclaimed the good Taffy, as Little Billee tumbled into his room, calling out :

" Oh, Taffy, Taffy, I've g-g-gone mad, I think ! " And then, shivering all over, and stammering incoherently, he tried to tell his friend what was the matter with him, with great simplicity.

Taffy, in much alarm, slipped on his trousers and made Little Billee get into his bed, and sat by his side holding his hand. He was greatly perplexed, fearing the recurrence of another attack like that of five years back. He didn't dare leave him for an instant to wake the Laird and send for a doctor.

Suddenly Little Billee buried his face in the pillow and began to sob, and some instinct told Taffy this was the best thing that could happen. The boy had always been a highly-strung, emotional, over-excitable, over-sensitive, and quite uncontrolled mammy's-darling, a cry-baby sort of chap, who had never been to school. It was all a part of his genius, and also a part of his charm. It would do him good once more to have a good blub after five years ! After a while Little Billee grew quieter, and then suddenly he said : " What a miserable ass you must think me, what an unmanly duffer ! "

" Why, my friend ? "

" Why, for going on in this idiotic way. I really couldn't help it. I went mad, I tell you. I've been walking up and down my room all night, till everything seemed to go round."

" So have I."

" You ? What for ? "

" The very same reason."

" *What !* "

" I was just as fond of Trilby as you were. Only she happened to prefer *you.*"

" *What !* " cried Little Billee again. " *You* were fond of Trilby ? "

" I believe you, my boy ! "

" In *love* with her ? "

" I believe you, my boy ! "

" She never knew it, then ! "

" Oh yes, she did."

" She never told me, then ! "

" Didn't she ? That's like her. *I* told *her*, at all events. I asked her to marry me."

" Well—I *am* damned ! When ? "

" That day we took her to Meudon, with Jeannot, and dined at the garde champêtre's, and she danced the cancan with Sandy."

" Well—I *am*—— And she *refused* you ? "

" Apparently so."

" Well, I—— Why on earth did she refuse you ? "

" Oh, I suppose she'd already begun to fancy *you,* my friend. *Il y en a toujours un autre !* "

" Fancy *me*—prefer *me*—to *you* ? "

" Well, yes. It *does* seem odd—eh, old fellow ? But

there's no accounting for tastes, you know. She's built on such an ample scale herself, I suppose, that she likes little 'uns—contrast, you see. She's very maternal, I think. Besides, you're a smart little chap; and you ain't half bad; and you've got brains and talent, and lots of cheek, and all that. I'm rather a *ponderous* kind of party."

" Well—I *am* damned ! "

" *C'est comme ça !* I took it lying down you see."

" ' I BELIEVE YOU, MY BOY ! ' "

" Does the Laird know ? "

" No; and I don't want him to—nor anybody else."

" Taffy, what a regular downright old trump you are ! "

" Glad you think so; anyhow, we're both in the same boat, and we've got to make the best of it. She's another man's wife, and probably she's very fond of him. I'm sure she ought to be, cad as he is, after all he's done for her. So there's an end of it."

" Ah ! there'll never be an end of it for *me*—never—

never—oh, never, my God ! She would have married me but for my mother's meddling, and that stupid old ass, my uncle. What a wife ! Think of all she must have in her heart and brain, only to *sing* like that ! And, O Lord ! how beautiful she is—a goddess ! Oh, the brow and cheek and chin, and the way her head's put on ! did you *ever* see anything like it ? Oh, if only I hadn't written and told my mother I was going to marry her ! why, we should have been man and wife for five years by this time—living at Barbizon—painting away like mad ! Oh, what a heavenly life ! Oh, curse all officious meddling with other people's affairs ! Oh ! oh ! . . . ."

" There you go again ! What's the good ? And where do *I* come in, my friend ? *I* should have been no better off, old fellow—worse than ever, I think."

Then there was a long silence.

At length Little Billee said :

" Taffy, I can't tell you what a trump you are. All I've ever thought of you—and God knows that's enough—will be nothing to what I shall always think of you after this."

" All right, old chap ! "

" And now I think *I'm* all right again, for a time—and I shall cut back to bed. Good night ! Thanks more than I can ever express ! " And Little Billee, restored to his balance, cut back to his own bed just as the day was breaking.

PART SEVENTH

" The moon made thy lips pale, beloved,
The wind made thy bosom chill;
The night did shed
On thy dear head
Its frozen dew, and thou didst lie
Where the bitter breath of the naked sky
Might visit thee at will."

NEXT morning our three friends lay late abed, and breakfasted in their rooms.

They had all three passed " white nights "—even the
Laird, who had tossed about and pressed a sleepless pillow
till dawn, so excited had he been by the wonder of Trilby's
reincarnation, so perplexed by his own doubts as to
whether it was really Trilby or not.

And certain haunting tones of her voice, that voice so
cruelly sweet (which clove the stillness with a clang so
utterly new, so strangely heart-piercing and seductive,
that the desire to hear it once more became nostalgic—
almost an ache !), certain bits and bars and phrases of the
music she had sung, unspeakable felicities and facilities of
execution; sudden exotic warmths, fragrances, tender-
nesses, graces, depths, and breadths; quick changes from
grave to gay, from rough to smooth, from great metallic
brazen clangours to soft golden suavities; all the varied
modes of sound we try so vainly to borrow from vocal
nature by means of wind and reed and string—all this
new " Trilbyness " kept echoing in his brain all night (for
he was of a nature deeply musical), and sleep had been
impossible to him.

" As when we dwell upon a word we know,
Repeating, till the word we know so well
Becomes a wonder, and we know not why,"

so dwelt the Laird upon the poor old tune " Ben Bolt,"
which kept singing itself over and over again in his tired
consciousness, and maddened him with novel, strange, un-

hackneyed, unsuspected beauties such as he had never dreamed of in any earthly music.

It had become a wonder, and he knew not why !

They spent what was left of the morning at the Louvre, and tried to interest themselves in the " Marriage of Cana," and the " Woman at the Well," and Vandyck's man with the glove, and the little Princess of Velasquez, and Lisa Gioconda's smile : it was of no use trying. There was no sight worth looking at in all Paris but Trilby in her golden raiment; no other princess in the world; no smile but hers, when through her parted lips came bubbling Chopin's Impromptu. They had not long to stay in Paris, and they must drink of that bubbling fountain once more—*coûte que coûte !* They went to the Salle des Bashibazoucks, and found that all seats all over the house had been taken for days and weeks; and the " queue " at the door had already begun ! and they had to give up all hopes of slaking this particular thirst.

Then they went and lunched perfunctorily, and talked desultorily over lunch, and read criticisms of La Svengali's *début* in the morning papers—a chorus of journalistic acclamation gone mad, a frenzied eulogy in every key— but nothing was good enough for them ! Brand-new words were wanted—another language !

Then they wanted a long walk, and could think of no-where to go in all Paris—that immense Paris, where they had promised themselves to see so much that the week they were to spend there had seemed too short !

Looking in a paper, they saw it announced that the band of the Imperial Guides would play that afternoon in the Pré Catelan, Bois de Boulogne, and thought they might as well walk there as anywhere else, and walk back again in time to dine with the Passefils—a prandial function which did not promise to be very amusing; but still it was something to kill the evening with, since they couldn't go and hear Trilby again.

Outside the Pré Catelan they found a crowd of cabs and carriages, saddle-horses and grooms. One might have thought one's self in the height of the Paris season. They went in, and strolled about here and there, and listened to the band, which was famous (it has performed in London at the Crystal Palace), and they looked about and studied life, or tried to.

Suddenly they saw, sitting with three ladies (one of whom, the eldest, was in black), a very smart young officer, a Guide, all red and green and gold, and recognised their old friend Zouzou. They bowed, and he knew them at once, and jumped up and came to them and greeted them warmly, especially his old friend Taffy, whom he took to his mother—the lady in black—and introduced to the other ladies, the younger of whom (strangely unlike the rest of her countrywomen) was so lamentably, so pathetically plain that it would be brutal to attempt the cheap and easy task of describing her. It was Miss Lavinia Hunks, the famous American millionairess, and her mother. Then the good Zouzou came back and talked to the Laird and Little Billee.

Zouzou, in some subtle and indescribable way, had become very ducal indeed.

He looked extremely distinguished, for one thing, in his beautiful Guides' uniform, and was most gracefully and winningly polite. He inquired warmly after Mrs. and Miss Bagot, and begged Little Billee would recall him to their amiable remembrance when he saw them again. He expressed most sympathetically his delight to see Little Billee looking so strong and so well (Little Billee looked like a pallid little washed-out ghost, after his white night).

They talked of Dodor. He said how attached he was to Dodor, and always should be; but Dodor, it seemed, had made a great mistake in leaving the army and going into a retail business (*petit commerce*). He had done for himself—*dégringolé!* He should have stuck to the *dragons* —with a little patience and good conduct he would have " won his epaulet "—and then one might have arranged for him a good little marriage—*un parti convenable*—for he was " très joli garçon, Dodor ! bonne tournure—et très gentiment né ! C'est très ancien, les Rigolot—dans le Poitou, je crois—Lafarce, et tout ça ; tout à fait bien ! "

It was difficult to realise that this polished and discreet and somewhat patronising young man of the world was the jolly dog who had gone after Little Billee's hat on all

fours in the Rue Vieille des Trois Mauvais Ladres and
brought it back in his mouth—the Caryhatide !

Little Billee little knew that Monsieur le Duc de la
Rochemartel-Boisségur had quite recently delighted a very
small and select and most august imperial supper-party at
Compiègne with this very story, not blinking a single detail
of his own share in it—and had given a most touching and
sympathetic description of " le joli petit peintre anglais
qui s'appelait Litrebili, et ne pouvait pas se tenir sur ses
jambes—et qui pleurait d'amour fraternel dans les bras
de mon copain Dodor ! "

" Ah ! Monsieur Gontran, ce que je donnerais pour avoir
vu ça ! " had said the greatest lady in France ; " un de
mes zouaves—à quatre pattes—dans la rue—un chapeau
dans la bouche—oh—c'est impayable ! "

Zouzou kept these blackguard bohemian reminiscences
for the imperial circle alone—to which it was suspected that
he was secretly rallying himself. Among all outsiders—
especially within the narrow precincts of the cream of the
noble Faubourg (which remained aloof from the Tuileries)
—he was a very proper and gentlemanlike person indeed,
as his brother had been—and, in his mother's fond belief,
" très bien pensant, très bien vu, à Frohsdorf et à Rome."

On lui aurait donné le bon Dieu sans confession—as
Madame Vinard had said of Little Billee—they would have
shriven him at sight, and admitted him to the holy
communion on trust !

He did not present Little Billee and the Laird to his
mother, nor to Mrs. and Miss Hunks ; that honour was
reserved for " the Man of Blood " alone ; nor did he ask
where they were staying, nor invite them to call on him.
But in parting he expressed the immense pleasure it had
given him to meet them again, and the hope he had of some
day shaking their hands in London.

As the friends walked back to Paris together, it trans-
pired that " the Man of Blood " had been invited by
Madame Duchesse Mère (Maman Duchesse, as Zouzou
called her) to dine with her next day, and meet the Hunkses
at a furnished apartment she had taken in the Place
Vendôme ; for they had let (to the Hunkses) the Hôtel de
la Rochemartel in the Rue de Lille ; they had also been

"MAMAN DUCHESSE"

obliged to let their place in the country, le château de
Boisségur (to Monsieur Despoires, or " des Poires," as he
chose to spell himself on his visiting cards—the famous
soap manufacturer—" Un très brave homme, à ce qu'on
dit ! " and whose only son, by the way, soon after married
Mademoiselle Jeanne-Adélaïde d'Amaury-Brissac de
Roncesvaulx de Boisségur de la Rochemartel).

"Il ne fait pas gras chez nous à présent—je vous assure!"
Madame Duchesse Mère had pathetically said to Taffy—
but had given him to understand that things would be very
much better for her son in the event of his marriage with
Miss Hunks.

" Good heavens ? " said Little Billee, on hearing this;
" that grotesque little bogy in blue ?   Why, she's deformed
—she squints—she's a dwarf, and looks like an idiot !
Millions or no millions, the man who marries her is a felon !
As long as there are stones to break and a road to break
them on, the able-bodied man who marries a woman like
that for anything but pity and kindness—and even then—
dishonours himself, insults his ancestry, and inflicts on his
descendants a wrong that nothing will ever redeem—he
nips them in the bud—he blasts them for ever !   He ought
to be cut by his fellow-men—sent to Coventry—to jail—
to penal servitude for life !   He ought to have a separate
hell to nimself when he dies—he ought to——"

" Shut up, you little blaspheming ruffian ! " said the
Laird. " Where do *you* expect to go to, yourself, with
such frightful sentiments?   And what would become of
your beautiful old twelfth-century dukedoms, with a
hundred yards of back frontage opposite the Louvre, on
a beautiful historic river, and a dozen beautiful historic
names, and no money—if *you* had your way? " and the
Laird wunk his historic wink.

" Twelfth-century dukedoms be damned ! " said Taffy,
au grand sérieux, as usual. " Little Billee's quite right,
and Zouzou makes me sick !   Besides, what does she
marry *him* for—not for his beauty either, I guess !   She's
his fellow-criminal, his deliberate accomplice, *particeps
delicti*, accessory before the act and after !   She has no
right to marry at all !   tar and feathers and a rail for both
of them—and for Maman Duchesse too—and I suppose

that's why I refused her invitation to dinner! and now
let's go and dine with Dodor— . . . anyhow Dodor's
young woman doesn't marry him for a dukedom—or
even his ' de '—*mais bien pour ses beaux yeux !* and if the
Rigolots of the future turn out less nice to look at than
their sire, and not quite so amusing, they will probably be
a great improvement on him in many other ways.   There's
room enough—and to spare ! "

" 'Ear ! 'ear ! " said Little Billee (who always grew
flippant when Taffy got on his high horse).   " Your 'ealth
and song, sir—them's my sentiments to a T !   What shall
we 'ave the pleasure of drinkin', after that wery nice
'armony ? "

After which they walked on in silence, each, no doubt,
musing on the general contrariness of things, and imagin-
ing what splendid little Wynnes, or Bagots, or M'Allisters
might have been ushered into a decadent world for its
regeneration if fate had so willed it that a certain magnificent and singularly gifted grisette, etc. etc. etc. . . .

Mrs. and Miss Hunks passed them as they walked
along, in a beautiful blue barouche with C-springs—*un
" huit-ressorts "* ; Maman Duchesse passed them in a hired
fly ; Zouzou passed them on horseback ; " tout Paris "
passed them ; but they were none the wiser, and agreed
that the show was not a patch on that in Hyde Park
during the London season.

When they reached the Place de la Concorde it was
that lovely hour of a fine autumn day in beautiful bright
cities when all the lamps are lit in the shops and streets
and under the trees, and it is still daylight—a quickly
fleeting joy ; and as a special treat on this particular
occasion the sun set, and up rose the yellow moon over
eastern Paris, and floated above the chimney-pots of the
Tuileries.

They stopped to gaze at the homeward procession of
cabs and carriages, as they used to do in the old
times.   Tout Paris was still passing ; tout Paris is very
long.

They stood among a little crowd of sightseers like
themselves, Little Billee right in front—in the road.

Presently a magnificent open carriage came by—more

magnificent than even the Hunkses', with liveries and
harness quite vulgarly resplendent—almost Napoleonic.

Lolling back in it lay Monsieur et Madame Svengali—
he with his broad-brimmed felt sombrero over his long
black curls, wrapped in costly furs, smoking his big cigar
of the Havana.

By his side La Svengali—also in sables—with a large
black velvet hat on, her light brown hair done up in a
huge knot on the nape of
her neck. She was rouged
and pearl-powdered, and
her eyes were blackened

THE CUT DIRECT

beneath, and thus made to look twice their size; but in
spite of all such disfigurements she was a most splendid
vision, and caused quite a little sensation in the crowd
as she came slowly by.

Little Billee's heart was in his mouth. He caught
Svengali's eye, and saw him speak to her. She turned
her head and looked at him standing there—they both
did. Little Billee bowed. She stared at him with a cold
stare of disdain, and cut him dead—so did Svengali.

And as they passed he heard them both snigger—she
with a little high-pitched flippant snigger worthy of a
London barmaid.

Little Billee was utterly crushed, and everything seemed
turning round.

The Laird and Taffy had seen it all without losing a
detail. The Svengalis had not even looked their way.
The Laird said:

"It's not Trilby—I swear! She could *never* have done
that—it's not *in* her! and it's another face altogether—
I'm sure of it!"

Taffy was also staggered and in doubt. They caught
hold of Little Billee, each by an arm, and walked him off
to the boulevards. He was quite demoralised, and wanted
not to dine at Passefil's. He wanted to go straight home
at once. He longed for his mother as he used to long for
her when he was in trouble as a small boy and she was
away from home—longed for her desperately—to hug her
and hold her and fondle her, and be fondled, for his own
sake and hers; all his old love for her had come back in
full—with what arrears! all his old love for his sister,
for his old home.

When they went back to the hotel to dress (for Dodor
had begged them to put on their best evening war-paint,
so as to impress his future mother-in-law), Little Billee
became fractious and intractable. And it was only on
Taffy's promising that he would go all the way to Devonshire with him on the morrow, and stay with him there,
that he could be got to dress and dine.

The huge Taffy lived entirely by his affections, and he
hadn't many to live by—the Laird, Trilby, and Little
Billee.

Trilby was unattainable, the Laird was quite strong
and independent enough to get on by himself, and Taffy
had concentrated all his faculties of protection and affection on Little Billee, and was equal to any burden or
responsibility all this instinctive young fathering might
involve.

In the first place, Little Billee had always been able to
do quite easily, and better than any one else in the world,
the very things Taffy most longed to do himself and

couldn't, and this inspired the good Taffy with a chronic reverence and wonder he could not have expressed in words.

Then Little Billee was physically small and weak, and incapable of self-control. Then he was generous, amiable, affectionate, transparent as crystal, without an atom of either egotism or conceit : and had a gift of amusing you and interesting you by his talk (and its complete sincerity) that never palled ; and even his silence was charming—one felt so sure of him—so there was hardly any sacrifice, little or big, that big Taffy was not ready and glad to make for Little Billee. On the other hand, there lay deep down under Taffy's surface irascibility and earnestness about trifles (and beneath his harmless vanity of the strong man), a long-suffering patience, a real humility, a robustness of judgment, a sincerity and all-roundness, a completeness of sympathy, that made him very good to trust and safe to lean upon. Then his powerful, impressive aspect, his great stature, the gladiator-like poise of his small round head on his big neck and shoulders, his huge deltoids and deep chest and slender loins, his clean-cut ankles and wrists, all the long and bold and highly-finished athletic shapes of him, that easy grace of strength that made all his movements a pleasure to watch, and any garment look well when he wore it—all this was a perpetual feast to the quick, prehensile, æsthetic eye. And then he had such a solemn, earnest, lovable way of bending pokers round his neck, and breaking them on his arm, and jumping his own height (or near it), and lifting up arm-chairs by one leg with one hand, and what not else !

So that there was hardly any sacrifice, little or big, that Little Billee would not accept from big Taffy as a mere matter of course—a fitting and proper tribute rendered by bodily strength to genius.

Par nobile fratrum—well met and well mated for fast and long-enduring friendship.

. . . . . .

The family banquet at Monsieur Passefil's would have been dull but for the irrepressible Dodor, and still more for the Laird of Cockpen, who rose to the occasion, and surpassed himself in geniality, drollery, and eccentricity of French grammar and accent. Monsieur Passefil was also a droll in his way, and had the quickly familiar, jocose facetiousness that seems to belong to the successful middle-aged bourgeois all over the world, when he's not pompous instead (he can even be both sometimes).

Madame Passefil was not jocose. She was much impressed by the aristocratic splendour of Taffy, the romantic melancholy and refinement of Little Billee, and their quiet and dignified politeness. She always spoke of Dodor as Monsieur de Lafarce, though the rest of the family (and one or two friends who had been invited) always called him Monsieur Théodore, and he was officially known as Monsieur Rigolot.

Whenever Madame Passefil addressed him or spoke of him in this aristocratic manner (which happened very often), Dodor would wink at his friends, with his tongue in his cheek. It seemed to amuse him beyond measure.

" PETIT ENFANT, J'AIMAIS D'UN AMOUR TENDRE
MA MÈRE ET DIEU—SAINTES AFFECTIONS !
PUIS MON AMOUR AUX FLEURS SE FIT ENTENDRE,
PUIS AUX OISEAUX, ET PUIS AUX PAPILLONS !

Mademoiselle Ernestine was evidently too much in love to say anything, and seldom took her eyes off Monsieur Théodore, whom she had never seen in evening dress before. It must be owned that he looked very nice—more ducal than even Zouzou—and to be Madame de Lafarce *en perspective*, and the future owner of such a brilliant husband as Dodor, was enough to turn a stronger little bourgeois head than Mademoiselle Ernestine's.

She was not beautiful, but healthy, well grown, well brought up, and presumably of a sweet, kind, and amiable disposition—an *ingénue* fresh from her convent—innocent as a child, no doubt; and it was felt that Dodor had done better for himself (and for his race) than Monsieur le Duc. Little Dodors need have no fear.

After dinner the ladies and gentlemen left the dining-room together, and sat in a pretty salon overlooking the boulevard, where cigarettes were allowed, and there was music. Mademoiselle Ernestine laboriously played " Les Cloches du Monastère " (by Monsieur Lefébure-Wély, if I'm not mistaken). It's the most bourgeois piece of music I know.

Then Dodor, with his sweet high voice, so strangely pathetic and true, sang goody-goody little French songs of innocence (of which he seemed to have an endless *répertoire*) to his future wife's conscientious accompaniment—to the immense delight, also, of all his future family, who were almost in tears—and to the great amusement of the Laird, at whom he winked in the most pathetic parts, putting his forefinger to the side of his nose, like Noah Claypole in *Oliver Twist*.

The wonder of the hour, La Svengali, was discussed, of course; it was unavoidable. But our friends did not think it necessary to reveal that she was " la grande Trilby." That would soon transpire by itself.

And, indeed, before the month was a week older the papers were full of nothing else.

Madame Svengali—" la grande Trilby,"—was the only daughter of the honourable and reverend Sir Lord O'Ferrall.

She had run away from the primeval forests and lonely marshes of le Dublin, to lead a free-and-easy life among the artists of the Quartier Latin of Paris—*une vie de bohème !*

She was the Venus Anadyomene from top to toe.

She was *blanche comme neige, avec un volcan dans le cœur.*

Casts of her alabaster feet could be had at Brucciani's, in the Rue de la Souricière St. Denis. (He made a fortune.)

Monsieur Ingres had painted her left foot on the wall of a studio in the Place St. Anatole des Arts; and an eccentric Scotch milord (le Comte de Pencock) had bought the house containing the flat containing the studio containing the wall on which it was painted, had had the house pulled down, and the wall framed and glazed and sent to his castle of Édimbourg.

(This, unfortunately, was in excess of the truth. It was found impossible to execute the Laird's wish, on account of the material the wall was made of. So the Lord Count of Pencock—such was Madame Vinard's version of Sandy's nickname—had to forgo his purchase.)

Next morning our friends were in readiness to leave Paris; even the Laird had had enough of it, and longed to get back to his work again—a " Hari-Kari in Yokohama." (He had never been to Japan; but no more had any one else in those early days.)

They had just finished breakfast, and were sitting in the courtyard of the hotel, which was crowded, as usual.

Little Billee went into the hotel post-office to despatch a note to his mother. Sitting sideways there at a small table and reading letters was Svengali—of all people in the world. But for these two and a couple of clerks the room was empty.

Svengali looked up; they were quite close together.

Little Billee, in his nervousness, began to shake, and half put out his hand, and drew it back again, seeing the look of hate on Svengali's face.

Svengali jumped up, put his letters together, and passing by Little Billee on his way to the door, called him " verfluchter Schweinhund," and deliberately spat in his face.

Little Billee was paralysed for a second or two; then

he ran after Svengali, and caught him just at the top of
the marble stairs, and kicked him, and knocked off his
hat, and made him drop all his letters. Svengali turned
round and struck him over the mouth and made it bleed,
and Little Billee hit out like a fury, but with no effect:
he couldn't reach high enough, for Svengali was well over
six feet.

There was a crowd round them in a minute, including
the beautiful old man in the court suit and gold chain, who
called out:

"Vite! vite! un commissaire de police!"—a cry that
was echoed all over the place.

Taffy saw the row, and shouted, "Bravo, little 'un!"
and jumping up from his table, jostled his way through
the crowd; and Little Billee, bleeding and gasping and
perspiring and stammering said:

"He spat in my face, Taffy—damn him! I'd never
even spoken to him—not a word, I swear!"

Svengali had not reckoned on Taffy's being there; he
recognised him at once, and turned white.

Taffy, who had dogskin gloves on, put out his right
hand, and deftly seized Svengali's nose between his fore
and middle fingers and nearly pulled it off, and swung his
head two or three times backward and forward by it, and
then from side to side, Svengali holding on to his wrist;
and then, letting him go, gave him a sounding open-handed
smack on his right cheek—and a smack on the face from
Taffy (even in play) was no joke, I'm told; it made one
smell brimstone, and see and hear things that didn't exist.

Svengali gasped worse than Little Billee, and couldn't
speak for a while. Then he said:

"Lâche—grand lâche! che fous enferrai mes témoins!"

"At your orders!" said Taffy, in beautiful French, and
drew out his card-case, and gave him his card in quite
the orthodox French manner, adding: "I shall be here
till to-morrow at twelve—but that is my London address,
in case I don't hear from you before I leave. I'm sorry,
but you really mustn't spit, you know—it's not done. I
will come to you whenever you send for me—even if I
have to come from the end of the world."

"Très bien! très bien!" said a military-looking old

"' VITE | VITE | UN COMMISSAIRE DE POLICE | '"

gentleman close by, who gave Taffy *his* card, in case he
might be of any service—and who seemed quite delighted
at the row—and indeed it was really pleasant to note with
what a smooth, flowing, rhythmical spontaneity the good
Taffy could always improvise these swift little acts of
summary retributive justice : no hurry or scurry or flurry
whatever—not an inharmonious gesture, not an infelicitous
line—the very poetry of violence, and almost its only
excuse !

Whatever it was worth, this was Taffy's special gift,
and it never failed him at a pinch.

When the commissaire de police arrived, all was over.
Svengali had gone away in a cab, and Taffy put himself
at the disposition of the commissaire.

They went into the post-office and discussed it all with
the old military gentleman, and the majordome in velvet,
and the two clerks who had seen the original insult. And
all that was required of Taffy and his friends for the present
was " their names, prenames, titles, qualities, age, address,
nationality, occupation," etc.

" C'est une affaire qui s'arrangera autrement, et autre
part ! " had said the military gentleman—monsieur le
général Comte de la Tour-aux-Loups.

So it blew over quite simply, and all that day a fierce
unholy joy burned in Taffy's choleric blue eye.

Not, indeed, that he had any wish to injure Trilby's
husband, or meant to do him any grievous bodily harm,
whatever happened. But he was glad to have given
Svengali a lesson in manners.

That Svengali should injure *him* never entered into his
calculations for a moment. Besides, he didn't believe
Svengali would show ₌fight; and in this he was not
mistaken.

But he had, for hours, the feel of that long, thick,
shapely Hebrew nose being kneaded between his gloved
knuckles, and a pleasing sense of the effectiveness of
the tweak he had given it. So he went about chewing
the cud of that heavenly remembrance all day, till
reflection brought remorse, and he felt sorry; for he was
really the mildest-mannered man that ever broke a
head !

Only the sight of Little Billee's blood (which had been made to flow by such an unequal antagonist) had roused the old Adam.

No message came from Svengali to ask for the names and addresses of Taffy's seconds; so Dodor and Zouzou (not to mention Mister the general Count of the Tooraloorals, as the Laird called him) were left undisturbed; and our three musketeers went back to London clean of blood, whole of limb, and heartily sick of Paris.

Little Billee stayed with his mother and sister in Devonshire till Christmas, Taffy staying at the village inn.

It was Taffy who told Mrs. Bagot about La Svengali's all but certain identity with Trilby, after Little Billee had gone to bed, tired and worn out, the night of their arrival.

"Good heavens!" said poor Mrs. Bagot. "Why, that's the new singing woman who's coming over here! There's an article about her in to-day's *Times*. It says she's a wonder, and that there's no one like her! Surely, that can't be the Miss O'Ferrall I saw in Paris!"

"It seems impossible—but I'm almost certain it is—and Willy has no doubts in the matter. On the other hand, M'Allister declares it isn't."

"Oh, what trouble! So *that's* why poor Willy looks so ill and miserable! It's all come back again. Could she sing at all then, when you knew her in Paris?"

"Not a note—her attempts at singing were quite grotesque."

"Is she still very beautiful?"

"Oh yes; there's no doubt about that; more than ever!"

"And her singing—is that so very wonderful? I remember that she had a beautiful voice in speaking."

"Wonderful? Ah, yes; I never heard or dreamed the like of it. Grisi, Alboni, Patti—not one of them to be mentioned in the same breath!"

"Good heavens! Why, she must be simply irresistible! I wonder you're not in love with her yourself. How dreadful these sirens are, wrecking the peace of families!"

"You mustn't forget that she gave way at once at a

"I SUPPOSE YOU DO ALL THIS KIND OF THING FOR MERE
AMUSEMENT, MR. WYNNE?"

word from you, Mrs. Bagot; and she was very fond of
Willy. She wasn't a siren then."

"Oh yes—oh yes! that's true—she behaved very well
—she did her duty—I can't deny that! You must try
and forgive me, Mr. Wynne—although I can't forgive
her!—that dreadful illness of poor Willy's—that bitter
time in Paris——"

And Mrs. Bagot began to cry, and Taffy forgave. "Oh,
Mr. Wynne, let us still hope that there's some mistake—
that it's only somebody like her! Why, she's coming to
sing in London after Christmas! My poor boy's infatuation
will only increase. What *shall* I do?"

" Well—she's another man's wife, you see. So Willy's infatuation is bound to burn itself out as soon as he fully recognises that important fact. Besides, she cut him dead in the Champs Élysées—and her husband and Willy had a row next day at the hotel, and cuffed and kicked each other—that's rather a bar to any future intimacy, I think."

" Oh, Mr. Wynne ! my son cuffing and kicking a man whose wife he's in love with ! Good heavens ! "

" Oh, it was all right—the man had grossly insulted him ; and Willy behaved like a brick, and got the best of it in the end, and nothing came of it. I saw it all."

" Oh, Mr. Wynne—and you didn't interfere ? "

" Oh yes, I interfered—everybody interfered ! It was all right, I assure you. No bones were broken on either side, and there was no nonsense about calling out, or swords or pistols, and all that."

" Thank Heaven ! "

In a week or two Little Billee grew more like himself again, and painted endless studies of rocks and cliffs and sea—and Taffy painted with him, and was very content. The vicar and Little Billee patched up their feud. The vicar also took an immense fancy to Taffy, whose cousin, Sir Oscar Wynne, he had known at college, and lost no opportunity of being hospitable and civil to him. And his daughter was away in Algiers.

And all " the nobility and gentry " of the neighbour-hood, including " the poor dear marquis " (one of whose sons was in Taffy's old regiment), were civil and hospitable also to the two painters—and Taffy got as much sport as he wanted, and became immensely popular. And they had, on the whole, a very good time till Christmas, and a very pleasant Christmas, if not an exuberantly merry one.

After Christmas Little Billee insisted on going back to London—to paint a picture for the Royal Academy ; and Taffy went with him ; and there was dulness in the house of Bagot—and many misgivings in the maternal heart of its mistress.

And people of all kinds, high and low, from the family at the Court to the fishermen on the little pier and their wives and children, missed the two genial painters, who

were the friends of everybody, and made such beautiful
sketches of their beautiful coast.

.   .   .   .   .   .

La Svengali has arrived in London. Her name is in
every mouth. Her photograph is in the shop-windows.
She is to sing at J——'s monster concerts next week. She
was to have sung sooner, but it seems some hitch has
occurred—a quarrel between Monsieur Svengali and his
first violin, who is a very important person.

A crowd of people as usual, only bigger, is assembled
in front of the windows of the Stereoscopic Company in
Regent Street, gazing at presentments of Madame Svengali
in all sizes and costumes. She is very beautiful—there is
no doubt of that; and the expression of her face is sweet
and kind and sad, and of such a distinction that one feels
an imperial crown would become her even better than her
modest little coronet of golden stars. One of the photographs represents her in classical dress, with her left foot
on a little stool, in something of the attitude of the Venus
of Milo, except that her hands are clasped behind her back;
and the foot is bare but for a Greek sandal, and so smooth
and delicate and charming, and with so rhythmical a set
and curl of the five slender toes (the big one slightly tip-
tilted and well apart from its longer and slighter and more
aquiline neighbour), that this presentment of her sells
quicker than all the rest.

And a little man who, with two bigger men, has just
forced his way in front says to one of his friends : " Look,
Sandy, look—*the foot ! Now* have you got any doubts ? "

" Oh yes—those are Trilby's toes, sure enough ! " says
Sandy. And they all go in and purchase largely.

As far as I have been able to discover, the row between
Svengali and his first violin had occurred at a rehearsal in
Drury Lane Theatre.

Svengali, it seems, had never been quite the same since
the 15th of October previous, and that was the day he had
got his face slapped and his nose tweaked by Taffy in
Paris. He had become short-tempered and irritable,
especially with his wife (if she *was* his wife). Svengali, it
seems, had reasons for passionately hating Little Billee.

He had not seen him for five years—not since the Christmas festivity in the Place St. Anatole, when they had sparred together after supper, and Svengali's nose had got in the way on this occasion, and had been made to bleed; but that was not why he hated Little Billee.

When he caught sight of him standing on the curb in the Place de la Concorde and watching the procession of "tout Paris," he knew him directly, and all his hate flared up; he cut him dead, and made his wife do the same.

Next morning he saw him again in the hotel post-office, looking small and weak and flurried, and apparently alone; and being an Oriental Israelite Hebrew Jew, he had not been able to resist the temptation of spitting in his face, since he must not throttle him to death.

The minute he had done this he had regretted the folly of it. Little Billee had run after him, and kicked and struck him, and he had returned the blow and drawn blood; and then, suddenly and quite unexpected, had come upon the scene that apparition so loathed and dreaded of old— the pig-headed Yorkshireman—the huge British philistine, the irresponsible bull, the junker, the ex-Crimean, Front-de-Bœuf, who had always reminded him of the brutal and contemptuous sword-clanking, spur-jingling aristocrats of his own country—ruffians that treated Jews like dogs. Callous as he was to the woes of others, the self-indulgent and highly-strung musician was extra sensitive about himself—a very bundle of nerves—and especially sensitive to pain and rough usage, and by no means physically brave. The stern, choleric, invincible blue eye of the hated northern Gentile had cowed him at once. And that violent tweaking of his nose, that heavy open-handed blow on his face, had so shaken and demoralised him that he had never recovered from it.

He was thinking about it always—night and day—and constantly dreaming at night that he was being tweaked and slapped over again by a colossal nightmare Taffy, and waking up in agonies of terror, rage, and shame. All healthy sleep had forsaken him.

Moreover, he was much older than he looked—nearly fifty—and far from sound. His life had been a long, hard struggle.

He had for his wife, slave, and pupil a fierce, jealous kind of affection that was a source of endless torment to him; for indelibly graven in her heart, which he wished to occupy alone, was the never-fading image of the little English painter, and of this she made no secret.

Gecko no longer cared for the master. All Gecko's doglike devotion was concentrated on the slave and pupil, whom he worshipped with a fierce but pure and unselfish passion. The only living soul that Svengali could trust was the old Jewess who lived with them—his relative—but even she had come to love the pupil as much as the master.

On the occasion of this rehearsal at Drury Lane he (Svengali) was conducting and Madame Svengali was singing. He interrupted her several times, angrily and most unjustly, and told her she was singing out of tune, " like a verfluchter tomcat," which was quite untrue. She was singing beautifully, " Home, Sweet Home."

Finally he struck her two or three smart blows on her knuckles with his little bâton, and she fell on her knees, weeping and crying out :

" Oh ! oh ! Svengali ! ne me battez pas, mon ami—je fais tout ce que je peux ! "

On which little Gecko had suddenly jumped up and struck Svengali on the neck near the collar-bone, and then it was seen that he had a little bloody knife in his hand, and blood flowed from Svengali's neck, and at the sight of it Svengali had fainted ; and Madame Svengali had taken his head on her lap, looking dazed and stupefied, as in a waking dream.

Gecko had been disarmed, but as Svengali recovered from his faint and was taken home, the police had not been sent for, and the affair was hushed up, and a public scandal avoided. But La Svengali's first appearance, to Monsieur J——'s despair, had to be put off for a week. For Svengali would not allow her to sing without him ; nor, indeed, would he be parted from her for a minute, or trust her out of his sight.

The wound was a slight one. The doctor who attended Svengali described the wife as being quite imbecile, no doubt from grief and anxiety. But she never left her husband's bedside for a moment, and had the obedience and devotion of a dog.

THE FIRST VIOLIN LOSES HIS TEMPER

When the night came round for the postponed *début*,
Svengali was allowed by the doctor to go to the theatre,
but he was absolutely forbidden to conduct. His grief and
anxiety at this were uncontrollable; he raved like a mad-
man; and Monsieur J—— was almost as bad.

Monsieur J—— had been conducting the Svengali band
at rehearsals during the week, in the absence of its master
—an easy task. It had been so thoroughly drilled and
knew its business so well that it could almost conduct
itself, and it had played all the music it had to play (much
of which consisted of accompaniments to La Svengali's
songs) many times before. Her *répertoire* was immense,
and Svengali had written these orchestral scores with
great care and felicity.

On the famous night it was arranged that Svengali
should sit in a box alone, exactly opposite his wife's place
on the platform, where she could see him well; and a code
of simple signals was arranged between him and Monsieur
J—— and the band, so that virtually he might conduct,
himself, from his box, should any hesitation or hitch occur.
This arrangement was rehearsed the day before (a Sunday)
and had turned out quite successfully, and La Svengali
had sung in perfection in the empty theatre.

When Monday evening arrived everything seemed to
be going smoothly; the house was soon crammed to
suffocation, all but the middle box on the grand tier. It
was not a promenade concert, and the pit was turned into
guinea stalls (the promenade concerts were to begin a
week later).

Right in the middle of these stalls sat the Laird and
Taffy and Little Billee.

The band came in by degrees and tuned their instru-
ments.

Eyes were constantly being turned to the empty box,
and people wondered what royal personages would appear.

Monsieur J—— took his place amid immense applause,
and bowed in his inimitable way, looking often at the
empty box.

Then he tapped and waved his bâton, and the band
played its Hungarian dance music with immense success;
when this was over there was a pause, and soon some signs

of impatience from the gallery. Monsieur J—— had disappeared.

Taffy stood up, his back to the orchestra, looking round.

Some one came into the empty box, and stood for a moment in front, gazing at the house. A tall man, deathly pale, with long black hair and a beard.

It was Svengali.

He caught sight of Taffy and met his eyes, and Taffy said : "Good God ! Look ! look ! "

Then Little Billee and the Laird got up and looked,

" HAST THOU FOUND ME, O MINE ENEMY ? "

And Svengali for a moment glared at them. And the expression of his face was so terrible with wonder, rage, and fear that they were quite appalled—and then he sat down, still glaring at Taffy, the whites of his eyes showing at the top, and his teeth bared in a spasmodic grin of hate.

Then thunders of applause filled the house, and turning round and seating themselves, Taffy and Little Billee and the Laird saw Trilby being led by J—— down the platform, between the players, to the front, her face smiling rather vacantly, her eyes anxiously intent on Svengali in his box,

She made her bows to right and left just as she had done in Paris.

The band struck up the opening bars of " Ben Bolt," with which she was announced to make her *début.*

She still stared—but she didn't sing—and they played the little symphony three times.

One could hear Monsieur J—— in a hoarse, anxious whisper saying,

" Mais chantez donc, madame—pour l'amour de Dieu, commencez donc—commencez ! "

She turned round with an extraordinary expression of face, and said,

" Chanter? pourquoi donc voulez-vous que je chante, moi? chanter quoi, alors? "

" Mais ' Ben Bolt,' parbleu—chantez ! "

" Ah—' Ben Bolt ! ' oui—je connais ça ! "

Then the band began again.

And she tried, but failed to begin herself. She turned round and said,

" Comment diable voulez-vous que je chante avec tout ce train qu'ils font, ces diables de musiciens ! "

" Mais, mon Dieu, madame—qu'est-ce que vous avez donc? " cried Monsieur J——.

" J'ai que j'aime mieux chanter sans toute cette satanée musique, parbleu ! J'aime mieux chanter toute seule ! "

" Sans musique, alors—mais chantez—chantez ! "

The band was stopped—the house was in a state of indescribable wonder and suspense.

She looked all round, and down at herself, and fingered her dress. Then she looked up to the chandelier with a tender, sentimental smile and began—

" Oh, don't you remember sweet Alice, Ben Bolt?
    Sweet Alice with hair so brown,
  Who wept with delight when you gave her a smile—— "

She had not got further than this when the whole house was in an uproar—shouts from the gallery—shouts of laughter, hoots, hisses, cat-calls, cock-crows.

She stopped and glared like a brave lioness, and called out—

" Qu'est-ce que vous avez donc, tous ! tas de vieilles

"'OH, DON'T YOU REMEMBER SWEET ALICE, BEN BOLT?'"

pommes cuites que vous êtes ! Est-ce qu'on a peur de
vous ? " and then, suddenly—

"Why, you're all English, aren't you?—what's all the
row about?—what have you brought me here for?—what
have *I* done, I should like to know?"

And in asking these questions the depth and splendour
of her voice were so extraordinary—its tone so pathetically
feminine, yet so full of hurt and indignant command, that
the tumult was stilled for a moment.

It was the voice of some being from another world—
some insulted daughter of a race more puissant and nobler
than ours; a voice that seemed as if it could never utter
a false note.

Then came a voice from the gods in answer—

"Oh, ye're Henglish, har yer? Why don't yer sing as
yer *hought* to sing—yer've got *voice* enough, any'ow ! why
don't yer sing in *tune ?* "

"Sing in *tune !* " cried Trilby. "I didn't want to sing
at all—I only sang because I was asked to sing—that
gentleman asked me—that French gentleman with the
white waistcoat ! I won't sing another note ! "

"Oh, yer won't, won't yer ! then let us 'ave our money
back, or we'll know what for ! "

And again the din broke out, and the uproar was
frightful.

Monsieur J—— screamed out across the theatre:
"Svengali ! Svengali ! qu'est-ce qu'elle a donc, votre
femme? . . . Elle est devenue folle ! "

Indeed she had tried to sing "Ben Bolt," but had sung
it in her old way—as she used to sing it in the Quartier
Latin—the most lamentably grotesque performance ever
heard out of a human throat !

"Svengali ! Svengali ! " shrieked poor Monsieur J——,
gesticulating towards the box where Svengali was sitting,
quite impassible, gazing at Monsieur J——, and smiling
a ghastly, sardonic smile, a *rictus* of hate and triumphant
revenge—as if he were saying—

"I've got the laugh of you *all*, this time ! "

Taffy, the Laird, Little Billee, the whole house, were
now staring at Svengali, and his wife was forgotten.

She stood vacantly looking at everybody and everything—the chandelier, Monsieur J——, Svengali in his box, the people in the stalls, in the gallery—and smiling as if the noisy scene amused and excited her.

"Svengali! Svengali! Svengali!"

The whole house took up the cry, derisively. Monsieur J—— led Madame Svengali away; she seemed quite passive. That terrible figure of Svengali still sat, immovable, watching his wife's retreat—still smiling his ghastly smile. All eyes were now turned on him once more.

Monsieur J—— was then seen to enter his box with a policeman and two or three other men, one of them in evening dress. He quickly drew the curtains to; then, a minute or two after, he reappeared on the platform, bowing and scraping to the audience, as pale as death, and called for silence, the gentleman in evening dress by his side; and this person explained that a very dreadful thing had happened—that Monsieur Svengali had suddenly died in that box—of apoplexy or heart disease; that his wife had seen it from her place on the stage, and had apparently gone out of her senses, which accounted for her extraordinary behaviour.

He added that the money would be returned at the doors, and begged the audience to disperse quietly.

Taffy, with his two friends behind him, forced his way to a stage door he knew. The Laird had no longer any doubts on the score of Trilby's identity—*this* Trilby, at all events.

Taffy knocked and thumped till the door was opened, and gave his card to the man who opened it, stating that he and his friends were old friends of Madame Svengali, and must see her at once.

The man tried to slam the door in his face, but Taffy pushed through, and shut it on the crowd outside, and insisted on being taken to Monsieur J—— immediately; and was so authoritative and big, and looked such a swell, that the man was cowed, and led him.

They passed an open door, through which they had a glimpse of a prostrate form on a table—a man partially undressed, and some men bending over him, doctors probably.

That was the last they saw of Svengali.

" THE LAST THEY SAW OF SVENGALI "

Then they were taken to another door, and Monsieur
J—— came out, and Taffy explained who they were, and
they were admitted.

La Svengali was there, sitting in an armchair by the
fire, while several of the band stood round gesticulating,
and talking German or Polish or Yiddish. Gecko, on his
knees, was alternately chafing her hands and feet. She
seemed quite dazed.

But at the sight of Taffy she jumped up and rushed at
him, saying : " Oh, Taffy dear—oh, Taffy ! what's it all
about ? Where on earth am I ? What an age since we
met ! "

Then she caught sight of the Laird, and kissed him; and
then she recognised Little Billee.

She looked at him for a long while in great surprise, and
then shook hands with him.

" How pale you are ! and so changed—you've got a
moustache ! What's the matter ? Why are you all
dressed in black, with white cravats, as if you were going
to a funeral ? Where's Svengali ? I should like to go
home ! "

" Where—what do you call—home, I mean—where is
it ? " asked Taffy.

" C'est à l'Hôtel de Normandie, dans le Haymarket.
On va vous y conduire, madame ! " said Monsieur
J——.

" Oui—c'est ça ! " said Trilby—" Hôtel de Normandie
—mais Svengali—où est-ce qu'il est ? "

" Hélas ! madame—il est très malade ! "

" Malade ? Qu'est-ce qu'il a ? How funny you look,
with your moustache, Little Billee ! dear, *dear* Little
Billee ! so pale, so very pale ! Are you ill too ? Oh, I
hope not ! How *glad* I am to see you again—you can't
tell ! though I promised your mother I wouldn't—never,
never ! Where are we now, dear Little Billee ? "

Monsieur J—— seemed to have lost his head. He was
constantly running in and out of the room, distracted.
The bandsmen began to talk and try to explain, in incomprehensible French, to Taffy. Gecko seemed to have disappeared. It was a bewildering business—noises from
outside, the tramp and bustle and shouts of the departing

crowd, people running in and out and asking for Monsieur J——, policemen, firemen, and what not !

Then Little Billee, who had been exerting the most heroic self-control, suggested that Trilby should come to his house in Fitzroy Square, first of all, and be taken out of all this—and the idea struck Taffy as a happy one—and it was proposed to Monsieur J——, who saw that our three friends were old friends of Madame Svengali's, and people to be trusted; and he was only too glad to be relieved of her, and gave his consent.

Little Billee and Taffy drove to Fitzroy Square to prepare Little Billee's landlady, who was much put out at first at having such a novel and unexpected charge imposed on her. It was all explained to her that it must be so. That Madame Svengali, the greatest singer in Europe and an old friend of her tenant's, had suddenly gone out of her mind from grief at the tragic death of her husband, and that for this night at least the unhappy lady must sleep under that roof—indeed, in Little Billee's own bed, and that he would sleep at a hotel; and that a nurse would be provided at once—it might be only for that one night; and that the lady was as quiet as a lamb, and would probably recover her faculties after a night's rest. A doctor was sent for from close by, and soon Trilby appeared, with the Laird, and her appearance and her magnificent sables impressed Mrs. Godwin, the landlady—brought her figuratively on her knees. Then Taffy, the Laird, and Little Billee departed again and dispersed—to procure a nurse for the night, to find Gecko, to fetch some of Trilby's belongings from the Hôtel de Normandie, and her maid.

The maid (the old German Jewess and Svengali's relative), distracted by the news of her master's death, had gone to the theatre. Gecko was in the hands of the police. Things had got to a terrible pass. But our three friends did their best. and were up most of the night.

So much for La Svengali's *début* in London.

The present scribe was not present on that memorable occasion, and has written this inadequate and most incomplete description partly from hearsay and private information, partly from the reports in the contemporary newspapers.

Should any surviving eye-witness of that lamentable fiasco read these pages, and see any gross inaccuracy in this bald account of it, the P. S. will feel deeply obliged to the same for any corrections or additions, and these will be duly acted upon and gratefully acknowledged in all subsequent editions; which will be numerous, no doubt, on account of the great interest still felt in "La Svengali," even by those who never saw or heard her (and they are many), and also because the present scribe is better qualified (by his opportunities) for the compiling of this brief biographical sketch than any person now living, with the exception, of course, of "Taffy" and "the Laird," to whose kindness, even more than to his own personal recollections, he owes whatever it may contain of serious historical value.

Next morning they all three went to Fitzroy Square. Little Billee had slept at Taffy's rooms in Jermyn Street.

Trilby seemed quite pathetically glad to see them again. She was dressed simply and plainly—in black; her trunks had been sent from the hotel.

The hospital nurse was with her; the doctor had just left. He had said that she was suffering from some great nervous shock—a pretty safe diagnosis!

Her wits had apparently not come back, and she seemed in no way to realise her position.

"Ah! what it is to see you again, all three! It makes one feel glad to be alive! I've thought of many things, but never of this—never! Three nice clean Englishmen, all speaking English—and *such* dear old friends! Ah! j'aime tant ça—c'est le ciel! I wonder I've got a word of English left!"

Her voice was so soft and sweet and low that these ingenuous remarks sounded like a beautiful song. And she "made the soft eyes" at them all three, one after another, in her old way; and the soft eyes quickly filled with tears.

She seemed ill and weak and worn out, and insisted on keeping the Laird's hand in hers.

"What's the matter with Svengali? He must be dead!"

They all three looked at each other, perplexed.

" ' THREE NICE CLEAN ENGLISHMEN ' "

" Ah ! he's dead ! I can see it in your faces. He'd got
heart disease. I'm sorry ! oh, very sorry indeed ! He was
always very kind, poor Svengali ! "

" Yes. He's dead," said Taffy.

" And Gecko—dear little Gecko—is he dead too ? I
saw him last night—he warmed my hands and feet : where
were we ? "

" No. Gecko's not dead. But he's had to be locked up
for a little while. He struck Svengali, you know. You
saw it all."

" I ? No ! I never saw it. But I *dreamt* something
like it ! Gecko with a knife, and people holding him, and
Svengali bleeding on the ground. That was just before
Svengali's illness. He'd cut himself in the neck, you
know—with a rusty nail, he told me. I wonder how ?
. . . But it was wrong of Gecko to strike him. They were
such friends. Why did he ? "

"Well—it was because Svengali struck you with his conductor's wand when you were rehearsing. Struck you on the fingers and made you cry! don't you remember?"

"Struck *me! rehearsing?*—made me *cry!* what *are* you talking about, dear Taffy? Svengali never *struck* me! He was kindness itself—always! and what should *I* rehearse?"

"Well, the songs you were to sing at the theatre in the evening."

"Sing at the theatre! *I* never sang at any theatre—except last night, if that big place was a theatre! and they didn't seem to like it! I'll take precious good care never to sing in a theatre again! How they howled! and there was Svengali in the box opposite, laughing at me. Why was I taken there? and why did that funny little Frenchman in the white waistcoat ask me to sing? I know very well I can't sing well enough to sing in a place like that! What a fool I was! It all seems like a bad dream! What was it all about? *Was* it a dream, I wonder!"

"Well—but don't you remember singing at Paris, in the Salle des Bashibazoucks—and at Vienna—St. Petersburg—lots of places?"

"What nonsense, dear—you're thinking of some one else! *I* never sang anywhere! I've been to Vienna and St. Petersburg—but I never *sang* there—good heavens!"

Then there was a pause, and our three friends looked at her helplessly.

Little Billee said: "Tell me, Trilby—what made you cut me dead when I bowed to you in the Place de la Concorde, and you were riding with Svengali in that swell carriage?"

"*I* never rode in a swell carriage with Svengali! Omnibuses were more in *our* line! You're dreaming, dear Little Billee—you're taking me for somebody else; and as for my cutting *you*—why, I'd sooner cut myself—into little pieces!"

"*Where* were you staying with Svengali in Paris?"

"I really forget. *Were* we in Paris? Oh yes, of course. Hôtel Bertrand, Place Notre Dame des Victoires."

"How long have you been going about with Svengali?"

"Oh, months, years—I forget. I was very ill. He cured me."

"Ill! What was the matter?"

"Oh! I was mad with grief, and pain in my eyes, and wanted to kill myself, when I lost my dear little Jeannot, at Vibraye. I fancied I hadn't been careful enough with him. I was crazed! Don't you remember writing to me there, Taffy—through Angèle Boisse? Such a sweet letter you wrote! I know it by heart! And you too, Sandy"; and she kissed him. "I wonder where they are, your letters? I've got nothing of my own in the world— not even your dear letters —nor Little Billee's—such lots of them!

"Well, Svengali used to write to me too—and then he got my address from Angèle. . . .

"When Jeannot died, I felt I must kill myself or get away from Vibraye— get away from the people there; so when he was buried I cut my hair short and got a workman's cap and blouse and trousers and walked all the way to Paris

"PŒNA PEDE CLAUDO"

without saying anything to anybody. I didn't want anybody to know; I wanted to escape from Svengali, who wrote that he was coming there to fetch me. I wanted to hide in Paris. When I got there at last it was two o'clock in the morning, and I was in dreadful pain— and I'd lost all my money—thirty francs—through a hole in my trousers' pocket. Besides, I had a row with a carter in the Halle. He thought I was a man, and hit

me and gave me a black eye, just because I patted his
horse and fed it with a carrot I'd been trying to eat myself.
He was tipsy, I think. Well, I looked over the bridge at
the river—just by the Morgue—and wanted to jump in.
But the Morgue sickened me, so I hadn't the pluck.
Svengali used to be always talking about the Morgue, and
my going there some day. He used to say he'd come and
look at me there, and the idea made me so sick I couldn't.
I got bewildered and quite stupid.

"Then I went to Angèle's, in the Rue des Cloîtres Ste.
Pétronille, and waited about ; but I hadn't the courage to
ring, so I went to the Place St. Anatole des Arts, and
looked up at the old studio window, and thought how
comfortable it was in there, with the big settee near the
stove, and all that, and felt inclined to ring up Madame
Vinard ; and then I remembered Little Billee was ill there,
and his mother and sister were with him. Angèle had
written me, you know. Poor Little Billee ! There he
was, very ill !

"So I walked about the place, and up and down the
Rue des Trois Mauvais Ladres. Then I went down the
Rue de Seine to the river again, and again I hadn't the
pluck to jump in. Besides, there was a *sergent-de-ville*
who followed and watched me. And the fun of it was that
I knew him quite well, and he didn't know me a bit. It
was Célestin Beaumollet, who got so tipsy on Christmas
night. Don't you remember ? The tall one, who was
pitted with the small-pox.

"Then I walked about till near daylight. Then I could
stand it no longer, and went to Svengali's, in the Rue
Tireliard, but he'd moved to the Rue des Saints Pères ;
and I went there and found him. I didn't want to a bit,
but I couldn't help myself. It was fate, I suppose ! He
was very kind, and cured me almost directly, and got me
coffee and bread and butter—the best I ever tasted—and
a warm bath from Bidet Frères, in the Rue Savonarole. It
was heavenly ! And I slept for two days and two nights !
And then he told me how fond he was of me, and how he
would always cure me, and take care of me, and marry me,
if I would go away with him. He said he would devote his
whole life to me, and took a small room for me, next to his.

" I stayed with him there a week, never going out or seeing any one, mostly asleep. I'd caught a chill.

" He played in two concerts and made a lot of money; and then we went away to Germany together; and no one was a bit the wiser."

" And *did* he marry you? "

" Well—no. He couldn't, poor fellow! He'd already got a wife living, and three children, which he declared were not his. They live in Elberfeld in Prussia; she keeps a small sweet-stuff shop there. He behaved very badly to them. But it was not through me! He'd deserted them long before; but he used to send them plenty of money when he'd got any; I made him, for I was very sorry for her. He was always talking about her, and what she said and what she did, and imitating her saying her prayers and eating pickled cucumber with one hand and drinking schnapps with the other, so as not to lose any time; till he made me die of laughing. He could be very funny, Svengali, though he *was* German, poor dear! And then Gecko joined us, and Marta."

" Who's Marta? "

" His aunt. She cooked for us, and all that. She's coming here presently; she sent word from the hotel; she's very fond of him. Poor Marta! Poor Gecko! What *will* they ever do without Svengali? "

" THE OLD STUDIO "

" Then what did he do to live ? "

" Oh ! he played at concerts, I suppose—and all that."

" Did you ever hear him ? "

" Yes. Sometimes Marta took me; at the beginning, you know. He was always very much applauded. He plays beautifully. Everybody said so."

" Did he never try and teach you to sing ? "

" Oh, maïe aïe ! not he ! Why, he always laughed when I tried to sing; and so did Marta; and so did Gecko ! It made them roar ! I used to sing ' Ben Bolt.' They used to make me, just for fun—and go into fits. *I* didn't mind a scrap. I'd had no training, you know ! "

" Was there anybody else he knew—any other woman ? "

" Not that *I* know of ! He always made out he was so fond of me that he couldn't even *look* at another woman. Poor Svengali ! " (Here her eyes filled with tears again.) " He was always very kind ! But I never could be fond of him in the way he wished—never ! It made me sick even to think of ! Once I used to hate him—in Paris— in the studio; don't you remember?

" He hardly ever left me; and then Marta looked after me—for I've always been weak and ill, and often so languid that I could hardly walk across the room. It was that three days' walk from Vibraye to Paris. I never got over it.

" I used to try and do all I could—be a daughter to him, as I couldn't be anything else—mend his things, and all that, and cook him little French dishes. I fancy he was very poor at one time; we were always moving from place to place. But I always had the best of every-thing. He insisted on that—even if he had to go without himself. It made him quite unhappy when I wouldn't eat, so I used to force myself.

" Then, as soon as I felt uneasy about things, or had any pain, he would say, ' Dors, ma mignonne ! ' and I would sleep at once—for hours, I think—and wake up oh, so tired ! and find him kneeling by me, always so anxious and kind—and Marta and Gecko ! and sometimes we had the doctor, and I was ill in bed.

" Gecko used to dine and breakfast with us—you've no idea what an angel he is, poor little Gecko ! But what a

dreadful thing to strike Svengali ! *Why* did he ? Svengali
taught him all he knows ! "

" And you knew no one else—no other woman ? "

" No one that I can remember—except Marta—not a
soul ! "

" And that beautiful dress you had on last night ? "

" It isn't mine. It's on the bed upstairs, and so's
the fur cloak. They belong to Marta. She's got lots
of them, lovely things—silk, satin, velvet—and lots of
beautiful jewels. Marta deals in them, and makes lots of
money.

" I've often tried them on; I'm very easy to fit," she
said, " being so tall and thin. And poor Svengali would
kneel down and cry, and kiss my hands and feet, and tell
me I was his goddess and empress, and all that, which I
hate. And Marta used to cry, too. And then he would
say—

" ' Et maintenant dors, ma mignonne ! '

" And when I woke up I was so tired that I went to
sleep again on my own account.

" But he was very patient. Oh, dear me ! I've always
been a poor, helpless, useless log and burden to him !

" Once I actually walked in my sleep—and woke up in
the market-place at Prague—and found an immense crowd,
and poor Svengali bleeding from the forehead, in a faint
on the ground. He'd been knocked down by a horse and
cart, he told me. He'd got his guitar with him. I suppose he and Gecko had been playing somewhere, for Gecko
had his fiddle. If Gecko hadn't been there, I don't know
what we should have done. You never saw such queer
people as they were—such crowds—you'd think they'd
never seen an Englishwoman before. The noise they
made, and the things they gave me . . . some of them
went down on their knees, and kissed my hands and the
skirts of my gown.

" He was ill in bed for a week after that, and I nursed
him, and he was very grateful. Poor Svengali ! God
knows *I* felt grateful to *him* for many things ! Tell me
how he died ! I hope he hadn't much pain."

They told her it was quite sudden, from heart disease.

" Ah ! I knew he had that; he wasn't a healthy man;

" ' ET MAINTENANT DORS, MA MIGNONNE ! ' "

he used to smoke too much. Marta used always to be very anxious."

Just then Marta came in.

Marta was a fat elderly Jewess of rather a grotesque and ignoble type. She seemed overcome with grief—all but prostrate.

Trilby hugged and kissed her, and took off her bonnet and shawl, and made her sit down in a big arm-chair, and got her a foot-stool.

She couldn't speak a word of anything but Polish and a little German. Trilby had also picked up a little German, and with this and by means of signs, and no doubt through a long intimacy with each other's ways, they understood each other very well. She seemed a very good old creature, and very fond of Trilby, but in mortal terror of the three Englishmen.

Lunch was brought up for the two women and the nurse, and our friends left them, promising to come again that day.

They were utterly bewildered; and the Laird would have it that there was another Madame Svengali somewhere, the real one, and that Trilby was a fraud—self-deceived and self-deceiving—quite unconsciously so, of course.

Truth looked out of her eyes, as it always had done—truth was in every line of her face.

The truth only—nothing but the truth could ever be told in that " voice of velvet," which rang as true when she spoke as that of any thrush or nightingale, however rebellious it might be now (and for ever perhaps) to artificial melodic laws and limitations and restraints. The long training it had been subjected to had made it " a wonder, a world's delight," and though she might never sing another note, her mere speech would always be more golden than any silence, whatever she might say.

Except on the one particular point of her singing, she had seemed absolutely sane—so, at least, thought Taffy, the Laird, and Little Billee. And each thought to himself, besides, that this last incarnation of Trilbyness was quite the sweetest, most touching, most endearing of all.

They had not failed to note how rapidly she had aged,

now that they had seen her without her rouge and pearl-powder; she looked thirty at least—she was only twenty-three.

Her hands were almost transparent in their waxen whiteness; delicate little frosty wrinkles had gathered round her eyes; there were gray streaks in her hair; all strength and straightness and elasticity seemed to have gone out of her with the memory of her endless triumphs (if she really *was* La Svengali), and of her many wanderings from city to city all over Europe.

It was evident enough that the sudden stroke which had destroyed her power of singing had left her physically a wreck.

But she was one of those rarely-gifted beings who cannot look or speak or even stir without waking up (and satisfying) some vague longing that lies dormant in the hearts of most of us, men and women alike; grace, charm, magnetism—whatever the nameless seduction should be called that she possessed to such an unusual degree—she had lost none of it when she lost her high spirits, her buoyant health and energy, her wits !

Tuneless and insane, she was more of a siren than ever—a quite unconscious siren—without any guile, who appealed to the heart all the more directly and irresistibly that she could no longer stir the passions.

All this was keenly felt by all three—each in his different way—by Taffy and Little Billee especially.

All her past life was forgiven—her sins of omission and commission ! And whatever might be her fate—recovery, madness, disease, or death—the care of her till she died or recovered should be the principal business of their lives.

Both had loved her. All three, perhaps. One had been loved by her as passionately, as purely, as unselfishly, as any man could wish to be loved, and in some extraordinary manner had recovered, after many years, at the mere sudden sight and sound of her, his lost share in our common inheritance—the power to love, and all its joy and sorrow; without which he had found life not worth living, though he had possessed every other gift and blessing in such abundance.

" Oh, Circe, poor Circe, dear Circe, divine enchantress

that you were ! " he said to himself, in his excitable way.
" A mere look from your eyes, a mere note of your heavenly
voice, has turned a poor, miserable, callous brute back
into a man again ! and I will never forget it—never !
And now that a still worse trouble than mine has befallen
you, you shall always be first in my thoughts till the end ! "
And Taffy felt pretty much the same, though he was
not by way of talking to himself so eloquently about
things as Little Billee.

As they lunched, they read the accounts of the previous
evening's events in different papers, three or four of which
(including the *Times*) had already got leaders about the
famous but unhappy singer who had been so suddenly
widowed and struck down in the midst of her glory. All
these accounts were more or less correct. In one paper it
was mentioned that Madame Svengali was under the roof
and care of Mr. William Bagot, the painter, in Fitzroy
Square.

The inquest on Svengali was to take place that afternoon,
and also Gecko's examination at the Bow Street Police
Court, for his assault.

Taffy was allowed to see Gecko, who was remanded till
the result of the *post-mortem* should be made public. But
beyond inquiring most anxiously and minutely after
Trilby, and betraying the most passionate concern for her,
he would say nothing, and seemed indifferent as to his
own fate.

When they went to Fitzroy Square, late in the afternoon, they found that many people, musical, literary,
fashionable, and otherwise (and many foreigners), had
called to inquire after Madame Svengali, but no one had
been admitted to see her. Mrs. Godwin was much elated
by the importance of her new lodger.

Trilby had been writing to Angèle Boisse, at her old
address in the Rue des Cloîtres Ste. Pétronille, in the hope
that this letter would find her still there. She was anxious
to go back and be a *blanchisseuse de fin* with her friend.
It was a kind of nostalgia for Paris, the Quartier Latin,
her clean old trade.

This project our three heroes did not think it necessary

to discuss with her just yet; she seemed quite unfit for work of any kind.

The doctor, who had seen her again, had been puzzled by her strange physical weakness, and wished for a consultation with some special authority; Little Billee, who was intimate with most of the great physicians, wrote about her to Sir Oliver Calthorpe.

"TAFFY WAS ALLOWED TO SEE GECKO"

She seemed to find a deep happiness in being with her three old friends, and talked and listened with all her old eagerness and geniality, and much of her old gaiety, in spite of her strange and sorrowful position. But for this it was impossible to realise that her brain was affected in the slightest degree, except when some reference was made to her singing, and this seemed to annoy and irritate her, as though she were being made fun of. The whole of her marvellous musical career, and everything connected with it, had been clean wiped out of her recollection.

She was very anxious to get into other quarters, that
Little Billee should suffer no inconvenience, and they
promised to take rooms for her and Marta on the morrow.

They told her cautiously all about Svengali and Gecko;
she was deeply concerned, but betrayed no such poignant
anguish as might have been expected. The thought of
Gecko troubled her most, and she showed much anxiety
as to what might befall him.

A FAIR BLANCHISSEUSE DE FIN

Next day she moved with Marta to some lodgings in
Charlotte Street, where everything was made as comfortable for them as possible.

Sir Oliver saw her with Dr. Thorne (the doctor who was
attending her) and Dr. Jakes Talboys.

Sir Oliver took the greatest interest in her case, both
for her sake and his friend Little Billee's. Also his own,
for he was charmed with her. He saw her three times in

the course of the week, but could not say for certain what was the matter with her, beyond taking the very gravest view of her condition. For all he could advise or prescribe, her weakness and physical prostration increased rapidly, through no cause he could discover. Her insanity was not enough to account for it. She lost weight daily; she seemed to be wasting and fading away from sheer general atrophy.

Two or three times he took her and Marta for a drive.

On one of these occasions, as they went down Charlotte Street, she saw a shop with transparent French blinds in the window, and through them some Frenchwomen, with neat white caps, ironing. It was a French *blanchisserie de fin*, and the sight of it interested and excited her so much that she must needs insist on being put down and on going into it.

" Je voudrais bien parler à la patronne, si ça ne la dérange pas," she said.

The *patronne*, a genial Parisian, was much astonished to hear a great French lady, in costly garments, evidently a person of fashion and importance, applying to her rather humbly for employment in the business, and showing a thorough knowledge of the work (and of the Parisian work-woman's colloquial dialect). Marta managed to catch the *patronne's* eye, and tapped her own forehead significantly, and Sir Oliver nodded. So the good woman humoured the great lady's fancy, and promised her abundance of employment whenever she should want it.

Employment ! Poor Trilby was hardly strong enough to walk back to the carriage ; and this was her last outing.

But this little adventure had filled her with hope and good spirits—for she had as yet received no answer from Angèle Boisse (who was in Marseilles), and had begun to realise how dreary the Quartier Latin would be without Jeannot, without Angèle, without the *trois Angliches* in the Place St. Anatole des Arts.

She was not allowed to see any of the strangers who came and made kind inquiries. This her doctors had strictly forbidden. Any reference to music or singing irritated her beyond measure. She would say to Marta, in bad German—

"Tell them, Marta—what nonsense it is! They are taking me for another—they are mad. They are trying to make a fool of me!"

And Marta would betray great uneasiness—almost terror—when she was appealed to in this way.

PART EIGHTH

"La vie est vaine :
  Un peu d'amour,
  Un peu de haine. . . .
    Et puis—bonjour !

"La vie est brève :
  Un peu d'espoir,
  Un peu de rève. . . .
    Et puis—bonsoir."

SVENGALI had died from heart disease. The cut he had received from Gecko had not apparently (as far as the verdict of a coroner's inquest could be trusted) had any effect in aggravating his malady or hastening his death.

But Gecko was sent for trial at the Old Bailey, and sentenced to hard labour for six months (a sentence which, if I remember aright, gave rise to much comment at the time). Taffy saw him again, but with no better result than before. He chose to preserve an obstinate silence on his relations with the Svengalis and their relations with each other.

When he was told how hopelessly ill and insane Madame Svengali was, he shed a few tears, and said : " Ah, pauvrette, pauvrette—ah ! monsieur—je l'aimais tant, je l'aimais tant ! il n'y en a pas beaucoup comme elle, Dieu de misère ! C'est un ange du Paradis ! "

And not another word was to be got out of him.

It took some time to settle Svengali's affairs after his death. No will was found. His old mother came over from Germany, and two of his sisters, but no wife. The comic wife and the three children, and the sweet-stuff shop in Elberfeld, had been humorous inventions of his own—a kind of Mrs. Harris !

He left three thousand pounds, every penny of which (and of far larger sums that he had spent) had been earned by " La Svengali," but nothing came to Trilby of this; nothing but the clothes and jewels he had given her, and

316

in this respect he had been lavish enough; and there were
countless costly gifts from emperors, kings, great people
of all kinds. Trilby was under the impression that all
these belonged to Marta. Marta behaved admirably;
she seemed bound hand and foot to Trilby by a kind of
slavish adoration, as that of a plain old mother for a
brilliant and beautiful but dying child.

It soon became evident that, whatever her disease might
be, Trilby had but a very short time to live.

She was soon too weak even to be taken out in a Bath
chair, and remained all day in her large sitting-room with
Marta; and there, to her great and only joy, she received
her three old friends every afternoon, and gave them coffee,
and made them smoke cigarettes of caporal as of old; and
their hearts were daily harrowed as they watched her rapid
decline.

Day by day she grew more beautiful in their eyes, in
spite of her increasing pallor and emaciation—her skin was
so pure and white and delicate, and the bones of her face
so admirable!

Her eyes recovered all their old humorous brightness
when *les trois Angliches* were with her, and the expression
of her face was so wistful and tender for all her playfulness,
so full of eager clinging to existence and to them, that
they felt the memory of it would haunt them for ever,
and be the sweetest and saddest memory of their lives.

Her quick, though feeble gestures, full of reminiscences
of the vigorous and lively girl they had known a few years
back, sent waves of pity through them and pure brotherly
love; and the incomparable tones and changes and modu-
lations of her voice, as she chatted and laughed, bewitched
them almost as much as when she had sung the " Nussbaum " of Schumann in the Salle des Bashibazoucks.

Sometimes Lorrimer came, and Antony, and the Greek.
It was like a genial little court of bohemia. And Lorrimer,
Antony, the Laird, and Little Billee made those beautiful
chalk and pencil studies of her head which are now so
well known—all so singularly like her, and so singularly
unlike each other! *Trilby vue à travers quatre tempéra-
ments!*

These afternoons were probably the happiest poor Trilby

A THRONE IN BOHEMIA

had ever spent in her life—with these dear people round
her, speaking the language she loved; talking of old times
and jolly Paris days, she never thought of the morrow.

But later—at night, in the small hours—she would
wake up with a start from some dream full of tender and
blissful recollections, and suddenly realise her own mischance, and feel the icy hand of that which was to come
before many morrows were over; and taste the bitterness
of death so keenly that she longed to scream out loud,
and get up, and walk up and down, and wring her hands
at the dreadful thought of parting for ever !

But she lay motionless and mum as a poor little frightened mouse in a trap, for fear of waking up the good old
tired Marta, who was snoring at her side.

And in an hour or two the bitterness would pass away,
the creeps and the horrors; and the stoical spirit of
resignation would steal over her—the balm, the blessed
calm ! and all her old bravery would come back.

And then she would sink into sleep again, and dream
more blissfully than ever, till the good Marta woke her
with a motherly kiss and a fragrant cup of coffee; and
she would find, feeble as she was, and doomed as she felt
herself to be, that joy cometh of a morning; and life was
still sweet for her, with yet a whole day to look forward to.

One day she was deeply moved at receiving a visit from
Mrs. Bagot, who, at Little Billee's earnest desire, had come
all the way from Devonshire to see her.

As the graceful little lady came in, pale and trembling
all over, Trilby rose from her chair to receive her, and
rather timidly put out her hand, and smiled in a frightened
manner. Neither could speak for a second. Mrs. Bagot
stood stock-still by the door gazing (with all her heart in
her eyes) at the so terribly altered Trilby—the girl she
had once so dreaded.

Trilby, who seemed also bereft of motion, and whose
face and lips were ashen, exclaimed, " I'm afraid I haven't
quite kept my promise to you, after all ! but things have
turned out so differently ! anyhow, you needn't have any
fear of me *now*."

At the mere sound of that voice, Mrs. Bagot, who was

as impulsive, emotional, and unregulated as her son,
rushed forward, crying, " Oh, my poor girl, my poor girl ! "
and caught her in her arms, and kissed and caressed her,
and burst into a flood of tears, and forced her back into
her chair, hugging her as if she were a long-lost child.

" I love you now as much as I always admired you—
pray believe it ! "

" ' OH, MY POOR GIRL ! MY POOR GIRL ! ' "

" Oh, how kind of you to say that ! " said Trilby, her
own eyes filling. " I'm not at all the dangerous or designing person you thought. I knew quite well I wasn't a
proper person to marry your son all the time ; and told
him so again and again. It was very stupid of me to say
yes at last. I was miserable directly after, I assure you.
Somehow I couldn't help myself—I was driven."

" Oh, don't talk of that ! don't talk of that ! You've
never been to blame in any way—I've long known it—
I've been full of remorse ! You've been in my thoughts

always, night and day. Forgive a poor jealous mother.
As if *any* man could help loving you—or any woman
either. Forgive me ! "

" Oh, Mrs. Bagot—forgive *you !* What a funny idea !
But, anyhow, you have forgiven *me*, and that's all I care
for now. I was very fond of your son—as fond as could
be. I am now, but in quite a different sort of way, you
know—the sort of way *you* must be, I fancy ! There was
never another like him that I ever met—anywhere ! You
must be so proud of him; who wouldn't? *Nobody's* good
enough for him. I would have been only too glad to be
his servant, his humble servant ! I used to tell him so—
but he wouldn't hear of it—he was much too kind ! He
always thought of others before himself. And, oh ! how
rich and famous he's become ! I've heard all about it,
and it did me good. It does me more good to think of
than anything else; far more than if I were to be ever so
rich and famous myself, I can tell you ! "

This from La Svengali, whose overpowering fame, so
utterly forgotten by herself, was still ringing all over
Europe; whose lamentable illness and approaching death
were being mourned and discussed and commented upon
in every capital of the civilised world, as one distressing
bulletin appeared after another. She might have been a
royal personage !

Mrs. Bagot knew, of course, the strange form her insanity
had taken, and made no allusion to the flood of thoughts
that rushed through her own brain as she listened to this
towering goddess of song, this poor mad queen of the
nightingales, humbly gloating over her son's success. . . .

Poor Mrs. Bagot had just come from Little Billee's, in
Fitzroy Square, close by. There she had seen Taffy, in a
corner of Little Billee's studio, laboriously answering endless letters and telegrams from all parts of Europe—for the
good Taffy had constituted himself Trilby's secretary and
homme d'affaires—unknown to her, of course. And this
was no sinecure (though he liked it): putting aside the
numerous people he had to see and be interviewed by
there were kind inquiries and messages of condolence and
sympathy from nearly all the crowned heads of Europe,
through their chamberlains; applications for help from

unsuccessful musical strugglers all over the world to the
pre-eminently successful one; beautiful letters from great
and famous people, musical or otherwise; disinterested
offers of service; interested proposals for engagements
when the present trouble should be over; beggings for an
interview from famous *impresarios*, to obtain which no
distance would be thought too great, etc. etc. etc. It was
endless, in English, French, German, Italian—in languages
quite incomprehensible (many letters had to remain
unanswered)—Taffy took an almost malicious pleasure in
explaining all this to Mrs. Bagot.

Then there was a constant rolling of carriages up to the
door, and a thundering of Little Billee's knocker : Lord
and Lady Palmerston wish to know—the Lord Chief
Justice wishes to know—the Dean of Westminster wishes
to know—the Marchioness of Westminster wishes to
know—everybody wishes to know if there is any better
news of Madame Svengali !

These were small things, truly; but Mrs. Bagot was a
small person from a small village in Devonshire, and one
whose heart and eye had hitherto been filled by no larger
image than that of Little Billee; and Little Billee's fame,
as she now discovered for the first time, did not quite fill
the entire universe.

And she mustn't be too much blamed if all these obvious
signs of a world-wide colossal celebrity impressed and even
awed her a little.

Madame Svengali ! Why, this was the beautiful girl
whom she remembered so well, whom she had so grandly
discarded with a word, and who had accepted her *congé*
so meekly in a minute; whom, indeed, she had been
cursing in her heart for years, because—because what?

Poor Mrs. Bagot felt herself turn hot and red all over,
and humbled herself to the very dust, and almost forgot
that she had been in the right, after all, and that " la
grande Trilby " was certainly no fit match for her son !

So she went quite humbly to see Trilby, and found a
poor pathetic mad creature still more humble than herself,
who still apologised for—for what?

A poor, pathetic, mad creature who had clean forgotten
that she was the greatest singer in all the world—one of

the greatest artists that had ever lived; but who remembered with shame and contrition that she had once taken the liberty of yielding (after endless pressure and repeated disinterested refusals of her own, and out of sheer irresistible affection) to the passionate pleadings of a little obscure art student, a mere boy—no better off than herself—just as penniless and insignificant a nobody; but—the son of Mrs. Bagot!

All due sense of proportion died out of the poor lady as she remembered and realised all this!

And then Trilby's pathetic beauty, so touching, so winning, in its rapid decay; the nameless charm of look and voice and manner that was her special appanage, and which her malady and singular madness had only increased; her childlike simplicity, her transparent forgetfulness of self—all these so fascinated and entranced Mrs. Bagot, whose quick susceptibility to such impressions was just as keen as her son's, that she very soon found herself all but worshipping this fast-fading lily—for so she called her in her own mind—quite forgetting (or affecting to forget) on what very questionable soil the lily had been reared, and through what strange vicissitudes of evil and corruption it had managed to grow so tall and white and fragrant!

Oh, strange compelling power of weakness and grace and prettiness combined, and sweet, sincere unconscious natural manners! not to speak of world-wide fame!

For Mrs. Bagot was just a shrewd little conventional British country matron of the good upper middle-class type, bristling all over with provincial proprieties and respectabilities, a philistine of the philistines, in spite of her artistic instincts; one who for years had (rather unjustly) thought of Trilby as a wanton and perilous siren, an unchaste and unprincipled and most dangerous daughter of Heth, and the special enemy of her house.

And here she was—like all the rest of us monads and nomads and bohemians—just sitting at Trilby's feet. . . .
" A washerwoman! a figure model! and Heaven knows what besides!" and she had never even heard her sing!

It was truly comical to see and hear!

Mrs. Bagot did not go back to Devonshire. She

remained in Fitzroy Square, at her son's, and spent most of her time with Trilby, doing and devising all kinds of things to distract and amuse her, and lead her thoughts gently to heaven, and soften for her the coming end of all.

Trilby had a way of saying, and especially of looking, "Thank you" that made one wish to do as many things for her as one could, if only to make her say and look it again.

And she had retained much of her old, quaint, and amusing manner ot telling things, and had much to tell

still left of her wandering life, although there were so many strange lapses in her powers of memory — gaps — which, if they could only have been filled up, would have been full of such surpassing interest !

Then she was never tired of talking and hearing of Little Billee; and that was a subject of which Mrs. Bagot could never tire either !

Then there were the recollections of her childhood. One day,

"'AH, POOR MAMMA! SHE WAS EVER SO MUCH PRETTIER THAN THAT!'"

in a drawer, Mrs. Bagot came upon a faded daguerreotype of a woman in a Tam o' Shanter, with a face so sweet and beautiful and saint-like that it almost took her breath away.   It was Trilby's mother.

"Who and what was your mother, Trilby?"

"Ah, poor mamma !" said Trilby, and she looked at the portrait a long time.   "Ah, she was ever so much prettier than that !   Mamma was once a *demoiselle de comptoir*— that's a barmaid, you know—at the Montagnards Écossais, in the Rue du Paradis Poissonnière—a place where men used to drink and smoke without sitting down. That was unfortunate, wasn't it?

" Papa loved her with all his heart, although, of course, she wasn't his equal. They were married at the Embassy, in the Rue du Faubourg St.-Honoré.

" *Her* parents weren't married at all. Her mother was the daughter of a boatman on Loch Ness, near a place called Drumnadrochit; but her father was the Honourable Colonel Desmond. He was related to all sorts of great people in England and Ireland. He behaved very badly to my grandmother and to poor mamma—his own daughter ! deserted them both ! Not very *honourable* of him, *was* it? And that's all I know about him."

And then she went on to tell of the home in Paris that might have been so happy but for her father's passion for drink; of her parents' deaths, and little Jeannot, and so forth. And Mrs. Bagot was much moved and interested by these naïve revelations, which accounted in a measure for so much that seemed unaccountable in this extra-ordinary woman ; who thus turned out to be a kind of cousin (though on the wrong side of the blanket) to no less a person than the famous Duchess of Towers.

With what joy would that ever kind and gracious lady have taken poor Trilby to her bosom had she only known ! She had once been all the way from Paris to Vienna merely to hear her sing. But, unfortunately, the Svengalis had just left for St. Petersburg, and she had her long journey for nothing !

Mrs. Bagot brought her many good books, and read them to her—Dr. Cummings on the approaching end of the world, and other works of a like comforting tendency for those who are just about to leave it; the *Pilgrim's Progress*, sweet little tracts, and what not.

Trilby was so grateful that she listened with much patient attention. Only now and then a faint gleam of amusement would steal over her face, and her lips would almost form themselves to ejaculate, " Oh, maïe, aïe ! "

Then Mrs. Bagot, as a reward for such winning docility, would read her *David Copperfield*, and that was heavenly indeed !

But the best of all was for Trilby to look over John Leech's *Pictures of Life and Character*, just out. She had never seen any drawings of Leech before, except now and then in an occasional *Punch* that turned up in the studio in Paris. And they never palled upon her, and taught her more of the aspect of English life (the life she loved) than any book she had ever read. She laughed and laughed; and it was almost as sweet to listen to as if she were vocalising the quick part in Chopin's Impromptu.

One day she said, her lips trembling: "I can't make out why you're so wonderfully kind to me, Mrs. Bagot. I hope you have not forgotten who and what I am, and what my story is. I hope you haven't forgotten that I'm not a respectable woman?"

"Oh, my dear child—don't ask me. . . . I only know that you are you! . . . and I am I! and that is enough for me . . . you're my poor, gentle, patient, suffering daughter, whatever else you are—more sinned against than sinning, I feel sure! But there . . . I've misjudged you so, and been so unjust, that I would give worlds to make you some amends . . . besides, I should be just as fond of you if you'd committed a murder, I really believe —you're so strange! you're irresistible! Did you ever, in all your life, meet anybody that *wasn't* fond of you?"

Trilby's eyes moistened with tender pleasure at such a pretty compliment. Then, after a few minutes' thought, she said, with engaging candour and quite simply: "No, I can't say I ever did, that I can think of just now. But I've forgotten such lots of people!"

One day Mrs. Bagot told Trilby that her brother-in-law, Mr. Thomas Bagot, would much like to come and talk to her.

"Was that the gentleman who came with you to the studio in Paris?"

"Yes."

"Why, he's a clergyman, isn't he? What does he want to come and talk to *me* about?"

"Ah! my dear child . . ." said Mrs. Bagot, her eyes filling.

Trilby was thoughtful for a while, and then said : " I'm going to die, I suppose. Oh yes ! oh yes ! There's no mistake about that ! "

" Dear Trilby, we are all in the hands of an Almighty Merciful God ! " And the tears rolled down Mrs. Bagot's cheeks.

After a long pause, during which she gazed out of the window, Trilby said, in an abstracted kind of way, as though she were talking to herself : " Après tout, c'est pas déjà si raide, de claquer ! J'en ai tant vus, qui ont passé par la ! Au bout du fossé la culbute, ma foi ! "

" What are you saying to yourself in French, Trilby ? Your French is so difficult to understand ! "

" Oh, I beg your pardon ! I was thinking it's not so difficult to die, after all ! I've seen such lots of people do it. I've nursed them, you know—papa and mamma and Jeannot, and Angèle Boisse's mother-in-law, and a poor *casseur de pierres*, Colin Maigret, who lived in the Impasse des Taupes St. Germain. He'd been run over by an omnibus in the Rue Vaugirard, and had to have both his legs cut off just above the knee. They none of them seemed to mind dying a bit. They weren't a bit afraid ! *I'm* not !

" Poor people don't think much of death. Rich people shouldn't either. They should be taught when they're quite young to laugh at it and despise it, like the Chinese. The Chinese die of laughing just as their heads are being cut off, and cheat the executioner ! It's all in the day's work, and we're all in the same boat—so who's afraid ! "

" Dying is not all, my poor child ! Are you prepared to meet your Maker face to face ? Have you ever thought about God, and the possible wrath to come if you should die unrepentant ? "

" Oh, but I sha'n't ! I've been repenting all my life ! Besides, there'll be no wrath for any of us—not even the worst ! *Il y aura amnistie générale !* Papa told me so, and he'd been a clergyman, like Mr. Thomas Bagot. I often think about God. I'm very fond of Him. One *must* have something perfect to look up to and be fond of—even if it's only an idea ! even if it's too good to be true !

"Though some people don't even believe He exists!
Le père Martin didn't—but, of course, *he* was only a
chiffonnier, and doesn't count.

"One day, though, Durien, the sculptor, who's very
clever, and a very good fellow indeed, said :

"'Vois-tu, Trilby—I'm very much afraid He doesn't
really exist, le bon Dieu! most unfortunately for *me*, for
I *adore* Him! I never do a piece of work without thinking how nice it would be if I could only please *Him*
with it!'

"And I've often thought, myself, how heavenly it must
be to be able to paint, or sculpt, or make music, or write
beautiful poetry, for that very reason!

"Why, once on a very hot afternoon we were sitting, a
lot of us, in the court-yard outside la mère Martin's shop,
drinking coffee with an old Invalide called Bastide Lendormi, one of the Vieille Garde, who'd only got one leg
and one arm and one eye, and everybody was very fond
of him. Well, a model called Mimi la Salope came out
of the Mont-de-piété opposite, and Père Martin called out
to her to come and sit down, and gave her a cup of coffee,
and asked her to sing.

"She sang a song of Béranger's, about Napoleon the
Great, in which it says—

"'Parlez-nous de lui, grandmère!
Grandmère, parlez-nous de lui!'

I suppose she sang it very well, for it made old Bastide
Lendormi cry; and when Père Martin *blagué'd* him about
it, he said—

"'C'est égal, voyez-vous! to sing like that is *to pray!*'

"And then I thought how lovely it would be if *I* could
only sing like Mimi la Salope, and I've thought so ever
since—just to *pray!*"

"*What!* Trilby? if *you* could only sing like—— Oh,
but never mind, I forgot! Tell me, Trilby—do you ever
pray to Him, as other people pray?"

"Pray to Him? Well, no—not often—not in words
and on my knees and with my hands together, you know!
Thinking's praying, very often—don't you think so? And
so's being sorry and ashamed when one's done a mean

thing, and glad when one's resisted a temptation, and grateful when it's a fine day and one's enjoying one's self without hurting any one else! What is it but praying when you try and bear up after losing all you cared to live for? And very good praying too! There can be prayers without words just as well as songs, I suppose; and Svengali used to say that songs without words are the best!

"'TO SING LIKE THAT IS *TO PRAY!*'"

"And then it seems mean to be always asking for things. Besides, you don't get them any the faster that way, and that shows!

"La mère Martin used to be always praying. And Père Martin used always to laugh at her; yet he always seemed to get the things *he* wanted oftenest!

"*I* prayed once, very hard indeed! I prayed for Jeannot not to die!"

"Well—but how do you *repent*, Trilby, if you do not

humble yourself, and pray for forgiveness on your knees ? "

" Oh, well—I don't exactly know ! Look here, Mrs. Bagot, I'll tell you the lowest and meanest thing I ever did. . . ."

(Mrs. Bagot felt a little nervous.)

" I'd promised to take Jeannot on Palm-Sunday to St. Philippe du Roule, to hear l'abbé Bergamot. But Durien (that's the sculptor, you know) asked me to go with him to St. Germain, where there was a fair, or something ; and with Mathieu, who was a student in law ; and a certain Victorine Letellier, who—who was Mathieu's mistress, in fact—a lace-mender in the Rue Ste. Maritorne la Pocharde. And so I went on Sunday morning to tell Jeannot that I couldn't take him.

" He cried so dreadfully that I thought I'd give up the others and take him to St. Philippe, as I'd promised. But then Durien and Mathieu and Victorine drove up and waited outside, and so I *didn't* take him, and went with them, and I didn't enjoy anything all day, and was miserable.

" They were in an open carriage with two horses ; it was Mathieu's treat, and Jeannot might have ridden on the box by the coachman without being in anybody's way. But I was afraid they didn't want him, as they didn't say anything, and so I didn't dare ask—and Jeannot saw us drive away, and I *couldn't* look back ! And the worst of it is that when we were half-way to St. Germain, Durien said, ' What a pity you didn't bring Jeannot ! ' and they were all sorry I hadn't.

" It was six or seven years ago, and I really believe I've thought of it every day, and sometimes in the middle of the night !

" Ah ! and when Jeannot was dying ! and when he was dead—the remembrance of that Palm-Sunday !

" And if *that's* not repenting, I don't know what is ! "

" Oh, Trilby, what nonsense ! *that's* nothing ; good heavens !—putting off a small child ! I'm thinking of far worse things—when you were in the Quartier Latin, you know—sitting to painters and sculptors. . . . Surely, so attractive as you are . . ."

"Oh yes. . . . I know what you mean—it was horrid, and I was frightfully ashamed of myself; and it wasn't amusing a bit; *nothing* was, till I met your son and Taffy and dear Sandy M'Allister ! But then it wasn't deceiving or disappointing anybody, or hurting their feelings—it was only hurting myself !

"THE REMEMBRANCE OF THAT PALM-SUNDAY !"

"Besides, all that sort of thing, in women, is punished severely enough down here, God knows ! unless one's a Russian empress like Catherine the Great, or a grande dame like lots of them, or a great genius like Madame Rachael or George Sand !

"Why, if it hadn't been for that, and sitting for the figure, I should have felt myself good enough to marry your son, *although* I was only a *blanchisseuse de fin*— you've said so yourself !

"And I should have made him a good wife—of that I feel sure. He wanted to live all his life at Barbizon, and paint, you know; and didn't care for society in the least. Anyhow, I should have been equal to such a life as that! Lots of their wives are *blanchisseuses* over there, or people of that sort; and they get on very well indeed, and nobody troubles about it!

"So I think I've been pretty well punished—richly as I've deserved to!"

"Trilby, have you ever been confirmed?"

"I forget. I fancy not!"

"Oh dear, oh dear! And do you know about our blessed Saviour, and the Atonement and the Incarnation and the Resurrection. . . ."

"Oh yes—I *used* to, at least. I used to have to learn the Catechism on Sundays—mamma made me. Whatever her faults and mistakes were, poor mamma was always very particular about *that!* It all seemed very complicated. But papa told me not to bother too much about it, but to be good. He said that God would make it all right for us somehow, in the end—all of us. And that seems sensible, *doesn't* it?

"He told me to be good, and not to mind what priests and clergymen tell us. He'd been a clergyman himself, and knew all about it, he said.

"I haven't been very good—there's not much doubt about that, I'm afraid! But God knows I've repented often enough and sore enough; I do now! But I'm rather glad to die, I think; and not a bit afraid—not a scrap! I believe in poor papa, though he *was* so unfortunate! He was the cleverest man I ever knew, and the best—except Taffy and the Laird and your dear son!

"There'll be no hell for any of us—he told me so—except what we make for ourselves and each other down here; and that's bad enough for anything. He told me that *he* was responsible for me—he often said so—and that mamma was too, and his parents for *him*, and his grandfathers and grandmothers for *them*, and so on up to Noah and ever so far beyond, and God for us all!

" He told me always to think of other people before myself; as Taffy does, and your son; and never to tell lies or be afraid, and keep away from drink, and I should be all right. But I've sometimes been all wrong, all the same; and it wasn't papa's fault, but poor mamma's and mine; and I've known it, and been miserable at the time, and after ! and I'm sure to be forgiven—perfectly certain —and so will everybody else, even the wickedest that ever lived ! Why, just give them sense enough in the next world to understand all their wickedness in this, and that'll punish them enough for anything, I think ! That's simple enough, *isn't* it ? Besides, there may be *no* next world—that's on the cards too, you know !—and that will be simpler still !

" Not all the clergymen in all the world, not even the Pope of Rome, will ever make me doubt papa, or believe in any punishment after what we've all got to go through here. *Ce serait trop bête !*

" So that if you don't want me to very much, and he won't think it unkind, I'd rather not talk to Mr. Thomas Bagot about it. I'd rather talk to Taffy if I *must*. He's very clever, Taffy, though he doesn't often say such clever things as your son does, or paint nearly so well; and I'm sure he'll think papa was right."

And as a matter of fact the good Taffy, in his opinion on this solemn subject, was found to be at one with the late Reverend Patrick Michael O'Ferrall—and so was the Laird—and so (to his mother's shocked and pained surprise) was Little Billee.

And so were Sir Oliver Calthorpe and Sir Jakes (then Mr.) Talboys and Doctor Thorne and Antony and Lorrimer and the Greek !

And so—in after-years, when grief had well pierced and torn and riddled her through and through, and time and age had healed the wounds, and nothing remained but the consciousness of great inward scars of recollection to remind her how deep and jagged and wide the wounds had once been—did Mrs. Bagot herself !

Late on one memorable Saturday afternoon, just as it was getting dusk in Charlotte Street, Trilby, in her pretty

blue dressing-gown, lay on the sofa by the fire—her head
well propped, her knees drawn up—looking very placid
and content.

She had spent the early part of the day dictating her
will to the conscientious Taffy.

It was a simple document, although she was not without many valuable trinkets to leave; quite a fortune!
Souvenirs from many men and women she had charmed
by her singing, from royalties downward.

She had been looking them over with the faithful
Marta, to whom she had always thought they belonged.
It was explained to her that they were gifts of Svengali's;
since she did not remember when and where and by
whom they were presented to her, except a few that
Svengali had given her himself, with many passionate
expressions of his love, which seems to have been deep
and constant and sincere; none the less so, perhaps, that
she could never return it!

She had left the bulk of these to the faithful Marta.

But to each of the *trois Angliches* she had bequeathed
a beautiful ring, which was to be worn by their brides if
they ever married, and the brides didn't object.

To Mrs. Bagot she left a pearl necklace, to Miss Bagot
her gold coronet of stars; and pretty (and most costly)
gifts to each of the three doctors who had attended her
and been so assiduous in their care; and who, as she was
told, would make no charge for attending on Madame
Svengali. And studs and scarf-pins to Antony, Lorrimer,
the Greek, Dodor, and Zouzou; and to Carnegie a little
German-silver vinaigrette which had once belonged to
Lord Witlow; and pretty souvenirs to the Vinards,
Angèle Boisse, Durien, and others.

And she left a magnificent gold watch and chain to
Gecko, with a most affectionate letter and a hundred
pounds—which was all she had in money of her own.

She had taken great interest in discussing with Taffy
the particular kind of trinket which would best suit the
idiosyncrasy of each particular legatee, and derived great
comfort from the business-like and sympathetic con-
scientiousness with which the good Taffy entered upon all
these minutiæ—he was so solemn and serious about it,

and took such pains. She little guessed how his dumb but deeply feeling heart was harrowed !

This document had been duly signed and witnessed and entrusted to his care; and Trilby lay tranquil and happy, and with a sense that nothing remained for her but to enjoy the fleeting hour, and make the most of each precious moment as it went by.

She was quite without pain of either mind or body, and surrounded by the people she adored—Taffy, the Laird, and Little Billee, and Mrs. Bagot, and Marta, who sat knitting in a corner with her black mittens on, and her brass spectacles.

She listened to the chat and joined in it, laughing as usual; ".love in her eyes sat playing " as she looked from one to another, for she loved them all beyond expression. " Love on her lips was straying, and warbling in her breath," whenever she spoke; and her weakened voice was still larger, fuller, softer than any other voice in the room, in the world—of another kind, from another sphere.

A cart drove up, there was a ring at the door, and presently a wooden packing-case was brought into the room.

At Trilby's request it was opened, and found to contain a large photograph, framed and glazed, of Svengali, in the military uniform of his own Hungarian band (which he had always worn until he came to Paris and London, where he conducted in ordinary evening dress), and looking straight out of the picture, straight at you. He was standing by his desk with his left hand turning over a leaf of music, and waving his bâton with his right. It was a splendid photograph, by a Viennese photographer, and a most speaking likeness; and Svengali looked truly fine—all made up of importance and authority, and his big black eyes were full of stern command.

Marta trembled as she looked. It was handed to Trilby, who exclaimed in surprise. She had never seen it. She had no photograph of him, and had never possessed one.

No message of any kind, no letter of explanation, accompanied this unexpected present, which, from the

postmarks on the case, seemed to have travelled all over
Europe to London, out of some remote province in eastern
Russia—out of the mysterious East! The poisonous
East—birthplace and home of an ill wind that blows
nobody good.

Trilby laid it against her legs as on a lectern, and lay
gazing at it with close attention for a long time, making
a casual remark now and
then, as, " He was very
handsome, I think "; or,
" That uniform becomes
him very well. Why has
he got it on, I wonder? "

The others went on talk-
ing, and Mrs. Bagot made
coffee.

Presently Mrs. Bagot took
a cup of coffee to Trilby,
and found her still staring
intently at the portrait, but
with her eyes dilated, and
quite a strange light in
them.

" Trilby, Trilby, your
coffee ! What is the matter,
Trilby? "

Trilby was smiling, with
fixed eyes, and made no
answer.

The others got up and
gathered round her in some
alarm. Marta seemed

" OUT OF THE MYSTERIOUS
EAST "

terror-stricken, and wished to snatch the photograph
away, but was prevented from doing so; one didn't know
what the consequences might be.

Taffy rang the bell, and sent a servant for Dr. Thorne,
who lived close by, in Fitzroy Square.

Presently Trilby began to speak, quite softly, in French :
" Encore une fois? bon ! je veux bien ! avec la voix
blanche alors, n'est-ce pas? et puis foncer au milieu. Et
pas trop vite en commençant ! Battez bien la mesure,

Svengali—que je puisse bien voir—car il fait déjà nuit !
c'est ça ! Allons, Gecko—donne-moi le ton ! "

Then she smiled, and seemed to beat time softly by
moving her head a little from side to side, her eyes intent
on Svengali's in the portrait, and suddenly she began to
sing Chopin's Impromptu in A flat.

She hardly seemed to breathe as the notes came pouring out, without words—mere vocalising. It was as if
breath were unnecessary for so little voice as she was
using, though there was enough of it to fill the room—to
fill the house—to drown her small audience in holy,
heavenly sweetness.

She was a consummate mistress of her art. How that
could be seen ! And also how splendid had been her
training. It all seemed as easy to her as opening and
shutting her eyes, and yet how utterly impossible to anybody else !

Between wonder, enchantment, and alarm they were
frozen to statues—all except Marta, who ran out of the
room crying, " Got im Himmel ! wieder zurück ! wieder
zurück ! "

She sang it just as she had sung it at the Salle des
Bashibazoucks, only it sounded still more ineffably
seductive, as she was using less voice—using the essence
of her voice in fact—the pure spirit, the very cream of it.

There can be little doubt that these four watchers
by that enchanted couch were listening to not only the
most divinely beautiful, but also the most astounding
feat of musical utterance ever heard out of a human
throat.

The usual effect was produced. Tears were streaming
down the cheeks of Mrs. Bagot and Little Billee. Tears
were in the Laird's eyes, a tear on one of Taffy's whiskers
—tears of sheer delight.

When she came back to the quick movement again,
after the adagio, her voice grew louder and shriller, and
sweet with a sweetness not of this earth ; and went on
increasing in volume as she quickened the time, nearing
the end ; and then came the dying away into all but
nothing—a mere melodic breath ; and then the little soft
chromatic ascending rocket, up to E in alt, the last part-

"'SVENGALI!...SVENGALI!...SVENGALI!...'"

ing caress (which Svengali had introduced as a finale, for it does not exist in the piano score).

When it was over, she said: "Ca y est-il, cette fois, Svengali? Ah! tant mieux, à la fin! c'est pas malheureux! Et maintenant, mon ami, *je suis fatiguée—bon soir!*"

Her head fell back on the pillow, and she lay fast asleep.

Mrs. Bagot took the portrait away gently. Little Billee knelt down and held Trilby's hand in his and felt for her pulse, and could not find it.

He said, "Trilby! Trilby!" and put his ear to her mouth to hear her breathe. Her breath was inaudible.

But soon she folded her hands across her breast, and uttered a little short sigh, and in a weak voice said: "*Svengali . . . Svengali . . . Svengali . . .*"

They remained in silence round her for several minutes, terror-stricken.

The doctor came; he put his hand to her heart, his ear to her lips. He turned up one of her eyelids and looked at her eye. And then, his voice quivering with strong emotion, he stood up and said, "Madame Svengali's trials and sufferings are all over!"

"Oh, good God! is she *dead?*" cried Mrs. Bagot.

"Yes, Mrs. Bagot. She has been dead several minutes —perhaps a quarter of an hour."

VINGT ANS APRÈS

Porthos-Athos, *alias* Taffy Wynne, is sitting to breakfast (opposite his wife) at a little table in the courtyard of that huge caravansérai on the Boulevard des Capucines, Paris, where he had sat more than twenty years ago with the Laird and Little Billee; where, in fact, he had pulled Svengali's nose.

Little is changed in the aspect of the place: the same cosmopolite company, with more of the American element, perhaps; the same arrivals and departures in railway omnibuses, cabs, hired carriages; and, airing his calves on the marble steps, stood just such another colossal and beautiful old man in black cloth coat and knee-breeches

and silk stockings as of yore, with probably the very
same pinchbeck chain. Where do they breed these
magnificent old Frenchmen? In Germany, perhaps,
"where all the good big waiters come from!"

And also the same fine weather. It is always fine
weather in the courtyard of the Grand Hôtel. As the
Laird would say, they manage these things better there!

Taffy wears a short beard, which is turning gray. His
kind blue eye is no longer choleric, but mild and friendly
—as frank as ever; and full of humorous patience. He
has grown stouter; he is very big indeed, in all three
dimensions, but the symmetry and the gainliness of the
athlete belong to him still in movement and repose; and
his clothes fit him beautifully, though they are not new,
and show careful beating and brushing and ironing, and
even a faint suspicion of all but imperceptible fine-drawing
here and there.

What a magnificent old man *he* will make some day,
should the Grand Hôtel ever run short of them! He
looks as if he could be trusted down to the ground—in
all things, little or big; as if his word were as good as
his bond, and even better; his wink as good as his word,
his nod as good as his wink; and, in truth, as he looks,
so he is.

The most cynical disbeliever in "the grand old name
of gentleman," and its virtues as a noun of definition,
would almost be justified in quite dogmatically asserting
at sight, and without even being introduced, that, at all
events, Taffy is a "gentleman," inside and out, up and
down—from the crown of his head (which is getting
rather bald) to the sole of his foot (by no means a small
one, or a lightly shod—*ex pede Herculem*)!

Indeed, this is always the first thing people say of
Taffy—and the last. It means, perhaps, that he may be
a trifle dull. Well, one can't be everything!

Porthos was a trifle dull—and so was Athos, I think;
and likewise his son, the faithful Viscount of Bragelonne
—*bon chien chasse de race!* And so was Wilfred of
Ivanhoe, the disinherited; and Edgar, the Lord of
Ravenswood! and so, for that matter, was Colonel New-
come, of immortal memory!

"TOUT VIENT À POINT, À QUI SAIT ATTENDRE"

Yet who does not love them—who would not wish to be like them, for better, for worse !

Taffy's wife is unlike Taffy in many ways; but fortunately for both) very like him in some. She is a little woman, very well shaped, very dark, with black, wavy hair, and very small hands and feet; a very graceful, handsome, and vivacious person; by no means dull; full, indeed, of quick perceptions and intuitions; deeply interested in all that is going on about and around her, and with always lots to say about it, but not too much.

She distinctly belongs to the rare, and ever-blessed, and most precious race of charmers.

She had fallen in love with the stalwart Taffy more than a quarter of a century ago in the Place St. Anatole des Arts, where he and she and her mother had tended

the sick couch of Little Billee—but she had never told
her love. *Tout vient à point, à qui sait attendre !*
That is a capital proverb, and sometimes even a true
one. Blanche Bagot had found it to be both !

One terrible night, never to be forgotten, Taffy lay fast
asleep in bed, at his rooms in Jermyn Street, for he was
very tired; grief tires more than anything, and brings a
deeper slumber.
That day he had followed Trilby to her last home in
Kensal Green, with Little Billee, Mrs. Bagot, the Laird,
Antony, the Greek, and Durien (who had come over from
Paris on purpose) as chief mourners; and very many
other people, noble, famous, or otherwise, English and
foreign; a splendid and most representative gathering,
as was duly chronicled in all the newspapers here and
abroad; a fitting ceremony to close the brief but splendid
career of the greatest pleasure-giver of our time.
He was awakened by a tremendous ringing at the
street-door bell, as if the house were on fire; and then
there was a hurried scrambling up in the dark, a tumbling
over stairs and kicking against banisters, and Little
Billee had burst into his room, calling out : "Oh ! Taffy,
Taffy ! I'm g-going mad—I'm g-going m-mad ! I'm
d-d-done for. . . ."
"All right, old fellow—just wait till I strike a light !"
"Oh, Taffy ! I haven't slept for four nights—not a
wink ! She d-d-died with Sv—Sv—Sv . . . damn it, I
can't get it out ! that ruffian's name on her lips ! . . . it
was just as if he were calling her from the t-t-tomb !
She recovered her senses the very minute she saw his
photograph—she was so f-fond of him she f-forgot everybody else ! She's gone straight to him, after all—in
some other life ! . . . to slave for him, and sing for him,
and help him to make better music than ever ! Oh,
T—T—oh—oh ! Taffy—oh ! oh ! oh ! catch hold !
c-c-catch. . . ." And Little Billee had all but fallen on
the floor in a fit.
And all the old miserable business of five years before
had begun over again !
There has been too much sickness in this story, so I

will tell as little as possible of poor Little Billee's long illness, his slow and only partial recovery, the paralysis of his powers as a painter, his quick decline, his early death, his manly, calm, and most beautiful surrender—the wedding of the moth with the star, of the night with the morrow!

For all but blameless as his short life had been, and so full of splendid promise and performance, nothing ever became him better than the way he left it. It was as if he were starting on some distant holy quest, like some gallant knight of old—"A Bagot to the rescue!" in another life. It shook the infallibility of a certain vicar down to its very founda-tions, and made him think more deeply about things than he had ever thought yet. It gave him pause! . . . and so

"I, PETE COELESTES. . . ."

wrung his heart that when, at the last, he stooped to kiss his poor young dead friend's pure white forehead, he dropped a bigger tear on it than Little Billee (once so given to the dropping of big tears) had ever dropped in his life.

But it is all too sad to write about.

It was by Little Billee's bedside, in Devonshire, that Taffy had grown to love Blanche Bagot, and not very many weeks after it was all over that Taffy had asked her to be his wife; and in a year they were married, and a very happy marriage it turned out—the one thing that poor Mrs. Bagot still looks upon as a compensation for all the griefs and troubles of her life.

During the first year or two Blanche had perhaps been the most ardently loving of this well-assorted pair. That beautiful look of love surprised (which makes all women's eyes look the same) came into hers whenever she looked at Taffy, and filled his heart with tender compunction, and a queer sense of his own unworthiness.

Then a boy was born to them, and that look fell on the boy, and the good Taffy caught it as it passed him by, and he felt a helpless, absurd jealousy, that was none the less painful for being so ridiculous! and then that look fell on another boy, and yet another, so that it was through these boys that she looked at their father. Then *his* eyes caught the look, and kept it for their own use; and he grew never to look at his wife without it; and as no daughter came, she retained for life the monopoly of that most sweet and expressive regard.

They are not very rich. He is a far better sportsman than he will ever be a painter; and if he doesn't sell his pictures, it is not because they are too good for the public taste: indeed, he has no illusions on that score himself, even if his wife has! He is quite the least conceited art-duffer I ever met—and I have met many far worse duffers than Taffy.

Would only that I might kill off his cousin Sir Oscar, and Sir Oscar's five sons (the Wynnes are good at sons), and his seventeen grandsons, and the fourteen cousins (and their numerous male progeny), that stand between Taffy and the baronetcy, and whatever property goes

with it; so that he might be Sir Taffy, and dear Blanche
Bagot (that was) might be called "my lady"! This
Shakespearian holocaust would scarcely cost me a pang!

It is a great temptation, when you have duly slain your
first hero, to enrich hero number two beyond the dreams
of avarice, and provide him with a title and castle and
park, as well as a handsome wife and a nice family! But
truth is inexorable—and, besides, they are just as happy
as they are.

They are well off enough, anyhow, to spend a week in
Paris at last, and even to stop at the Grand Hôtel! now
that two of their sons are at Harrow (where their father
was before them), and the third is safe at a preparatory
school at Elstree, Herts.

It is their first outing since the honeymoon, and the
Laird should have come with them.

But the good Laird of Cockpen (who is now a famous
Royal Academician) is preparing for a honeymoon of his
own. He has gone to Scotland to be married himself—
to wed a fair and clever countrywoman of just a suitable
age, for he has known her ever since she was a bright little
lassie in short frocks, and he a promising A.R.A. (the
pride of his native Dundee)—a marriage of reason, and
well-seasoned affection, and mutual esteem—and therefore
sure to turn out a happy one! and in another fortnight or
so the pair of them will very possibly be sitting to breakfast opposite each other at that very corner table in the
courtyard of the Grand Hôtel! and she will laugh at everything he says—and they will live happily ever after.

So much for hero number three—D'Artagnan? Here's
to you, Sandy M'Allister, canniest, genialest, and most
humorous of Scots? most delicate, and dainty, and fanciful
of British painters? "I trink your health, mit your
family's—may you lif long—and brosper?"

So Taffy and his wife have come for their second
honeymoon, their Indian-summer honeymoon, alone;
and are well content that it should be so. Two's always
company for such a pair—the amusing one and the
amusable!—and they are making the most of it!

They have been all over the Quartier Latin, and

revisited the well-remembered spots; and even been allowed to enter the old studio, through the kindness of the *concierge* (who is no longer Madame Vinard). It is tenanted by two American painters, who are coldly civil on being thus disturbed in the middle of their work. The studio is very spick and span, and most respectable. Trilby's foot, and the poem, and the sheet of plate-glass have been improved away, and a bookshelf put in their place. The new *concierge* (who has only been there a year) knows nothing of Trilby; and of the Vinards, only that they are rich and prosperous, and live somewhere in the south of France, and that Monsieur Vinard is mayor of his commune. *Que le bon Dieu les bénisse ! c'étaient de bien braves gens.*

Then Mr. and Mrs. Taffy have also been driven (in an open *calèche* with two horses) through the Bois de Boulogne to St. Cloud; and to Versailles, where they lunched at the Hôtel des Réservoirs—*parlez-moi de ça !* and to St. Germain, and to Meudon (where they lunched at *la loge du garde champêtre*—a new one); they have visited the Salon, the Louvre, the porcelain manufactory at Sèvres, the Gobelins, the Hôtel Cluny, the Invalides, with Napoleon's tomb; and seen half a dozen churches, including Notre Dame and the Sainte Chapelle; and dined with the Dodors at their charming villa near Asnières, and with the Zouzous at the splendid Hôtel de la Rochemartel, and with the Duriens in the Parc Monceau (Dodor's food was best and Zouzou's worst; and at Durien's the company and talk were so good that one forgot to notice the food—and that was a pity). And the young Dodors are all right—and so are the young Duriens. As for the young Zouzous, there aren't any—and *that's* a weight off one's mind !

And they've been to the Variétés and seen Madame Chaumont, and to the Français and seen Sarah Bernhardt and Coquelin and Delaunay, and to the Opéra and heard Monsieur Lassalle.

And to-day being their last day, they are going to laze and flâne about the boulevards, and buy things, and lunch anywhere, *sur le pouce,* and do the Bois once more and see *tout* Paris, and dine early at Durand's, or Bignon's (or else the Café des Ambassadeurs), and finish up the well-spent day at the "Mouches d'Espagne"—the new theatre in the Boulevard Poissonnière—to see Madame Cantharidi in "Petits Bonheurs de Contrebande," which they are told is immensely droll and quite proper—funny without being vulgar! Dodor was their informant—he had taken Madame Dodor to see it three or four times.

Madame Cantharidi, as everybody knows, is a very clever but extremely plain old woman with a cracked voice—of spotless reputation, and the irreproachable

"PETITS BONHEURS DE CONTREBANDE"

mother of a grown-up family whom she has brought up in perfection. They have never been allowed to see their mother (and grandmother) act—not even the sons. Their excellent father (who adores both them and her) has drawn the line at that!

In private life she is "quite the lady," but on the stage —well, go and see her, and you will understand how she comes to be the idol of the Parisian public. For she is the true and liberal dispenser to them of that modern *esprit gaulois* which would make the good Rabelais turn uneasily in his grave and blush there like a Benedictine Sister.

And truly she deserves the reverential love and gratitude of her *chers Parisiens!* She amused them all through

the Empire; during the *année terrible* she was their only
stay and comfort, and has been their chief delight ever
since, and is now.

When they come back from *La Revanche*, may Madame
Cantharidi be still at her post, " Les mouches d'Espagne,"
to welcome the returning heroes, and exult and crow with
them in her funny cracked old voice; or, haply, even
console them once more, as the case may be.

" Victors or vanquished, they will laugh the same ! "

Mrs. Taffy is a poor French scholar. One must know
French very well indeed (and many other things besides)
to seize the subtle points of Madame Cantharidi's play
(and by-play) !

But Madame Cantharidi has so droll a face and voice,
and such very droll, odd movements, that Mrs. Taffy goes
into fits of laughter as soon as the quaint little old lady
comes on the stage. So heartily does she laugh that a
good Parisian bourgeois turns round and remarks to his
wife : " V'là une jolie p'tite Anglaise qui n'est pas bégueule,
au moins ! Et l' gros bœuf avec les yeux bleus en boules
de loto—c'est son mari, sans doute ! il n'a pas l'air trop
content par exemple, celui-là ! "

The fact is that the good Taffy (who knows French
very well indeed) is quite scandalised, and very angry
with Dodor for sending them there; and as soon as the
first act is finished he means, without any fuss, to take his
wife away.

As he sits patiently, too indignant to laugh at what is
really funny in the piece (much of it is vulgar *without*
being funny), he finds himself watching a little white-
haired man in the orchestra, a fiddler, the shape of whose
back seems somehow familiar, as he plays an *obbligato*
accompaniment to a very broadly comic song of Madame
Cantharidi's. He plays beautifully—like a master—and
the loud applause is as much for him as for the vocalist.

Presently this fiddler turns his head so that his profile
can be seen, and Taffy recognises him.

After five minutes' thought, Taffy takes a leaf out of
his pocket-book and writes (in perfectly grammatical
French) :—

" DEAR GECKO—You have not forgotten Taffy Wynne,
I hope; and Litrebili, and Litrebili's sister, who is now
Mrs. Taffy Wynne. We leave Paris to-morrow, and would
like very much to see you once more. Will you, after the
play, come and sup with us at the Café Anglais? If so,
look up and make ' yes ' with the head, and enchant—
Your well-devoted   ,TAFFY WYNNE."

He gives this, folded, to an attendant—for " le premier
violon—celui qui a des cheveux blancs."

Presently he sees Gecko receive the note and read it
and ponder for a while.

Then Gecko looks round the theatre, and Taffy waves
his handkerchief and catches the eye of the premier violon,
who " makes ' yes ' with the head."

And then, the first act over, Mr. and Mrs. Wynne
leave the theatre; Mr. explaining why, and Mrs. very
ready to go, as she was beginning to feel strangely uncomfortable without quite realising as yet what was amiss with
the lively Madame Cantharidi.

They went to the Café Anglais and bespoke a nice
little room on the *entresol* overlooking the boulevard, and
ordered a nice little supper; salmi of something very
good, mayonnaise of lobster, and one or two other dishes
better still—and chambertin of the best. Taffy was
particular about these things on a holiday, and regardless
of expense. Porthos was very hospitable, and liked good
food and plenty of it; and Athos dearly loved good wine !

And then they went and sat at a little round table
outside the Café de la Paix on the boulevard, near the
Grand Opéra, where it is always very gay, and studied
Paris life, and nursed their appetites till supper-time.

At half-past eleven Gecko made his appearance—very
meek and humble. He looked old—ten years older than
he really was—much bowed down, and as if he had
roughed it all his life, and had found living a desperate
long, hard grind.

He kissed Mrs. Taffy's hand, and seemed half inclined
to kiss Taffy's too, and was almost tearful in his pleasure
at meeting them again, and his gratitude at being asked
to sup with them. He had soft, clinging, caressing

manners, like a nice dog's, that made you his friend at once. He was obviously genuine and sincere, and quite pathetically simple, as he always had been.

At first he could scarcely eat for nervous excitement; but Taffy's fine example and Mrs. Taffy's genial, easy-going cordiality (and a couple of glasses of chambertin) soon put him at his ease and woke up his dormant appetite, which was a very large one, poor fellow !

He was told all about Little Billee's death, and deeply moved to hear the cause which had brought it about, and then they talked of Trilby.

He pulled her watch out of his waistcoat-pocket and reverently kissed it, exclaiming : " Ah ! c'était un ange ! un ange du Paradis ! when I tell you I lived with them for five years ! Oh ! her kindness, Dio, Dio Maria ! It was ' Gecko this ! ' and ' Gecko that ! ' and ' Poor Gecko, your toothache, how it worries me ! ' and ' Gecko, how tired and pale you look—you distress me so, looking like that ! Shall I mix you a maitrank ? ' And ' Gecko, you love artichokes à la Barigoule ; they remind you of Paris—I have heard you say so. Well, I have found out where to get artichokes, and I know how to do them à la Barigoule, and you shall have them for dinner to-day and to-morrow and all the week after ! ' and we did !

" Ach ! dear kind one—what did I really care for artichokes à la Barigoule ? . . .

" And it was always like that—always—and to Svengali and old Marta just the same ! and she was never well— never ! *toujours souffrante !*

" And it was she who supported us all—in luxury and splendour sometimes ! "

" And *what* an artist ! " said Taffy.

" Ah, yes ! but all that was Svengali, you know. Svengali was the greatest artist I ever met ! Monsieur, Svengali was a demon, a magician ! I used to think him a god ! He found me playing in the streets for copper coins, and took me by the hand, and was my only friend, and taught me all I ever knew—and yet he could not play my instrument !

" And now he is dead, I have forgotten how to play it myself ! That English jail ! it demoralised me, ruined

me for ever! ach! quel enfer, nom de Dieu (pardon,
madame)! I am just good enough to play the *obbligato*
at the Mouches d'Espagne, when the old Cantharidi
sings,

   "'V'là mon mari qui r'garde!
   Prends garde—ne m'chatouille plus!'

"It does not want much of an *obbligato, hein,* a song
so noble and so beautiful as that!

"And that song, monsieur, all Paris is singing it now.
And that is the Paris that went mad when Trilby sang
the 'Nussbaum' of Schumann at the Salle des Bashibazoucks. You heard her? Well!"

And here poor Gecko tried to laugh a little sardonic
laugh in falsetto, like Svengali's, full of scorn and bitterness—and very nearly succeeded.

"But what made you strike him with—with that
knife, you know?"

"Ah, monsieur, it had been coming on for a long time.
He used to work Trilby too hard; it was killing her—it
killed her at last! And then at the end he was unkind
to her and scolded her and called her names—horrid
names—and then one day in London he struck her. He
struck her on the fingers with his bâton, and she fell
down on her knees and cried. . . .

"Monsieur, I would have defended Trilby against a
locomotive going *grande vitesse!* against my own father—
against the Emperor of Austria—against the Pope! and
I am a good Catholic, monsieur! I would have gone to
the scaffold for her, and to the devil after!"

And he piously crossed himself.

"But, Svengali—wasn't *he* very fond of her?"

"Oh yes, monsieur! *quant à ça,* passionately! But
she did not love him as he wished to be loved. She
loved Litrebili, monsieur! Litrebili, the brother of
madame. And I suppose that Svengali grew angry and
jealous at last. He changed as soon as he came to Paris.
Perhaps Paris reminded him of Litrebili—and reminded
Trilby, too!"

"But how on earth did Svengali ever manage to teach
her how to sing like that? She had no ear for music
whatever when *we* knew her!"

Gecko was silent for a while, and Taffy filled his glass, and gave him a cigar, and lit one himself.

"Monsieur, no—that is true. She had not much ear. But she had such a voice as had never been heard. Svengali knew that. He had found it out long ago. Litolff had found it out, too. One day Svengali heard Litolff tell Meyerbeer that the most beautiful female voice

"'WE TOOK HER VOICE NOTE BY NOTE'"

in Europe belonged to an English grisette who sat as a model to sculptors in the Quartier Latin, but that unfortunately she was quite tone-deaf, and couldn't sing one single note in tune. Imagine how Svengali chuckled! I see it from here!

"Well, we both taught her together—for three years—morning, noon, and night—six—eight hours a day. It used to split me the heart to see her worked like that!

We took her voice note by note—there was no end to
her notes, each more beautiful than the other—velvet and
gold, beautiful flowers, pearls, diamonds, rubies—drops of
dew and honey; peaches, oranges, and lemons ! *en veux-
tu en voilà !*—all the perfumes and spices of the Garden
of Eden ! Svengali with his little flexible flageolet, I
with my violin—that is how we taught her to make the
sounds—and then how to use them. She was a *phénomène,*
monsieur ! She could keep on one note and make it go
through all the colours in the rainbow—according to the
way Svengali looked at her. It would make you laugh
—it would make you cry—but, cry or laugh, it was the
sweetest, the most touching, the most beautiful note you
ever heard—except all her others ! and each had as
many overtones as the bells in the Carillon de Notre
Dame. She could run up and down the scales, chromatic
scales, quicker and better and smoother than Svengali on
the piano, and more in tune than any piano ! and her
shake—*ach !* twin stars, monsieur ! She was the greatest
contralto, the greatest soprano the world has ever known !
the like of her has never been ! the like of her will never
be again ! and yet she only sang in public for two
years !

" *Ach !* those breaks and runs and sudden leaps from
darkness into light and back again—from earth to
heaven ! . . . those slurs and swoops and slides à la
Paganini from one note to another, like a swallow flying !
₣ . . . or a gull ? Do you remember them ? how they
drove you mad ? Let any other singer in the world try
to imitate them—they would make you sick ! That was
Svengali . . . he was a magician !

" And how she looked, singing ! do you remember ?
her hands behind her—her dear, sweet, slender foot on a
little stool—her thick hair lying down all along her back !
And that good smile like the Madonna's, so soft and
bright and kind ! *Ach ! Bel ucel di Dio !* it was to
make you weep for love, merely to see her (*c'était à vous
faire pleurer d'amour, rien que de la voir*) ! That was
Trilby ! Nightingale and bird of paradise in one !

" *Enfin* she could do anything—utter any sound she
liked, when once Svengali had shown her how—and he

was the greatest master that ever lived ! and when once
she knew a thing, she knew it. *Et voilà !* "

" How strange," said Taffy, " that she should have
suddenly gone out of her senses that night at Drury Lane,
and so completely forgotten it all ! I suppose she saw
Svengali die in the box opposite, and that drove her
mad ! "

And then Taffy told the little fiddler about Trilby's
death-song, like a swan's, and Svengali's photograph.
But Gecko had heard it all from Marta, who was now
dead.

Gecko sat and smoked and pondered for a while, and
looked from one to the other. Then he pulled himself
together with an effort, so to speak, and said, " Monsieur,
she never went mad—not for one moment ! "

" What ? Do you mean to say she *deceived* us all ? "

" Non, monsieur ! She could never deceive anybody,
and never would. *She had forgotten—voilà tout !* "

" But hang it all, my friend, one doesn't *forget* such
a——"

" Monsieur, listen ! She is dead. And Svengali is dead
—and Marta also. And I have a good little malady that
will kill me soon, *Gott sei dank*—and without much pain.

" I will tell you a secret.

" *There were two Trilbys.* There was the Trilby you
knew, who could not sing one single note in tune. She
was an angel of paradise. She is now ! But she had no
more idea of singing than I have of winning a steeple-
chase at the croix de Berny. She could no more sing
than a fiddle can play itself ! She could never tell one
tune from another—one note from the next. Do you
remember how she tried to sing ' Ben Bolt ' that day
when she first came to the studio in the Place St. Anatole
des Arts ? It was droll, *hein ? à se boucher les oreilles !*
Well, that was Trilby, your Trilby ! that was my Trilby
too—and I loved her as one loves an only love, an only
sister, an only child—a gentle martyr on earth, a blessed
saint in heaven ! And that Trilby was enough for *me !*

" And that was the Trilby that loved your brother,
madame—oh ! but with all the love that was in her !
He did not know what he had lost, your brother ! Her

love, it was immense, like her voice, and just as full of celestial sweetness and sympathy! She told me every-thing! *ce pauvre Litrebili, ce qu'il a perdu!*

"But all at once—pr-r-r-out! presto! *augenblick!* ⸱ ⸱ ⸱ with one wave of his hand over her—with one look of his eye—with a word—Svengali could turn her into the other Trilby, *his* Trilby—and make her do whatever he liked . . . you might have run a red-hot needle into her and she would not have felt it. ⸱ ⸱ ⸱

"He had but to say ' *Dors!* ' and she suddenly became an unconscious Trilby of marble, who could produce wonderful sounds—just the sounds he wanted, and nothing else—and think his thoughts and wish his wishes—and love him at his bidding with a strange, unreal, factitious love . . . just his own love for himself turned inside out —*à l'envers*—and reflected back on him, as from a mirror ⸱ ⸱ ⸱ *un écho, un simulacre, quoi! pas autre chose!* ⸱ ⸱ ⸱ It was not worth having! I was not even jealous!

"Well, that was the Trilby he taught how to sing—and—and I helped him, God of heaven forgive me! That Trilby was just a singing-machine—an organ to play upon—an instrument of music—a Stradivarius—a flexible flageolet of flesh and blood—a voice, and nothing more—just the unconscious voice that Svengali sang with —for it takes two to sing like La Svengali, monsieur—the one who has got the voice, and the one who knows what to do with it. . . . So that when you heard her sing the ' Nussbaum,' the ' Impromptu,' you heard Sven-gali singing with her voice, just as you hear Joachim play a *chaconne* of Bach with his fiddle! . . . Herr Joachim's fiddle ⸱ ⸱ ⸱ what does it know of Sebastian Bach? and as for *chaconnes* ⸱ ⸱ ⸱ *il s'en moque pas mal, ce fameux violon!* ⸱ ⸱ ⸱

"And *our* Trilby ⸱ ⸱ ⸱ what did she know of Schumann, Chopin?—nothing at all! She mocked herself not badly of Nussbaums and Impromptus . . . they would make her yawn to demantibulate her jaws! . . . When Sven-gali's Trilby was being taught to sing . . . when Svengali's Trilby was singing—or seemed to *you* as if she were sing-ing—*our* Trilby had ceased to exist . . . *our* Trilby was fast asleep ⸱ ⸱ ⸱ in fact, *our* Trilby was *dead.* ⸱ ⸱ ⸱

"Ah, monsieur . . . that Trilby of Svengali's ! I have heard her sing to kings and queens in royal palaces ! . . . as no woman has ever sung before or since. . . . I have seen emperors and grand-dukes kiss her hand, monsieur—and their wives and daughters kiss her lips, and weep. . . .

THE NIGHTINGALE'S FIRST SONG

"I have seen the horses taken out of her sledge and the pick of the nobility drag her home to the hotel . . . with torchlights and choruses and shoutings of glory and long life to her ! . . . and serenades all night, under the window ! . . . *she* never knew ! she heard nothing—felt nothing—saw nothing ! and she bowed to them, right and left, like a queen !

"I have played the fiddle for her while she sang in the

streets, at fairs and festas and Kermessen ، . . and seen
the people go mad to hear her . . . and once, at Prague,
Svengali fell down in a fit from sheer excitement ! and
then, suddenly, *our* Trilby woke up and wondered what it
was all about . . . and we took him home and put him
to bed and left him with Marta—and Trilby and I went
together arm-in-arm all over the town to fetch a doctor
and buy things for supper—and that was the happiest
hour in all my life !

"*Ach !* what an existence ! what travels ! what
triumphs ! what adventures ! Things to fill a book—a
dozen books— Those five happy years—with those two
Trilbys ! what recollections ! . . . I think of nothing else,
night or day . . . even as I play the fiddle for old
Cantharidi. *Ach !* . . . To think how often I have
played the fiddle for La Svengali . . . to have done that
is to have lived . . . and then to come home to Trilby
. . . *our* Trilby . . . the *real* Trilby ! . . . Gott sei dank !
Ich habe *geliebt und gelebet ! geliebt und gelebet ! geliebt
und gelebet !* Cristo di Dio . . . Sweet sister in heaven . . ؛
Ô Dieu de Misère, ayez pitié de nous. . . ."

His eyes were red, and his voice was high and shrill
and tremulous and full of tears; these remembrances
were too much for him ; and perhaps also the chambertin !
He put his elbows on the table and hid his face in his
hands and wept, muttering to himself in his own language
(whatever that might have been—Polish, probably) as if
he were praying.

Taffy and his wife got up and leaned on the window-
bar and looked out on the deserted boulevards, where
an army of scavengers, noiseless and taciturn, was cleansing
the asphalt roadway. The night above was dark, but
"star-dials hinted of morn," and a fresh breeze had
sprung up, making the leaves dance and rustle on the
sycamore trees along the boulevard—a nice little breeze;
just the sort of little breeze to do Paris good. A four-
wheel cab came by at a foot pace, the driver humming
a tune; Taffy hailed him; he said, " V'là, m'sieur ! "
and drew up.

Taffy rang the bell, and asked for the bill, and paid it.

Gecko had apparently fallen asleep. Taffy gently woke
him up and told him how late it was. The poor little
man seemed dazed and rather tipsy, and looked older
than ever; sixty, seventy—any age you like. Taffy
helped him on with his great-coat, and taking him by
the arm, led him downstairs, giving him his card, and
telling him how glad he was to have seen him, and that
he would write to him from England—a promise that was
kept, one may be sure.

Gecko uncovered his fuzzy white head, and took Mrs.
Taffy's hand and kissed it, and thanked her warmly for
her " si bon et sympathique accueil."

Then Taffy all but lifted him into the cab, the jolly
cabman saying—

" Ah ! bon — connais
bien, celui là ; vous savez
—c'est lui qui joue du
violon aux Mouches
d'Espagne ! Il a soupé,
l'bourgeois ; n'est-ce pas,
m'sieur ? ' petits bonheurs

" ' ICH HABE *GELIEBT UND GELEBET !* ' "

de contrebande,' hein? ... ayez pas peur! on vous aura
soin de lui! il joue joliment bien, m'sieur; n'est-ce pas?"
Taffy shook Gecko's hand and asked,
"Où restez-vous, Gecko?"
"Quarante-huit Rue des Pousse-cailloux, au cinquième."
"How strange!" said Taffy to his wife—"how touch-
ing! why, that's where Trilby used to live—the very
number! the very floor!"
"Oui, oui," said Gecko, waking up; "c'est l'ancienne
mansarde à Trilby—j'y suis depuis douze ans—*j'y suis,
j'y reste*. . . ."
And he laughed feebly at his mild little joke.
Taffy told the address to the cabman, and gave him
five francs.
"Merci, m'sieur! C'est de l'aut'côté de l'eau—près de
la Sorbonne, s'pas? On vous aura soin du bourgeois;
soyez tranquille—ayez pas peur! quarante-huit; on y va.
Bonsoir, monsieur et dame!" And he clacked his whip
and rattled away, singing:—

> "V'là mon mari qui r'garde—
> Prends garde!
> Ne m'chatouill' plus!"

Mr. and Mrs. Wynne walked back to the hotel, which
was not far. She hung on to his big arm and crept close
to him, and shivered a little. It was quite chilly. Their
footsteps were very audible in the stillness; "pit-pat,
floppety-clop," otherwise they were both silent. They
were tired, yawny, sleepy, and very sad; and each was
thinking (and knew the other was thinking) that a week
in Paris was just enough—and how nice it would be, in
just a few hours more, to hear the rooks cawing round
their own quiet little English country home—where three
jolly boys would soon be coming for the holidays.
And there we will leave them to their useful, hum-
drum, happy domestic existence—than which there is no
better that I know of, at their time of life—and no better
time of life than theirs!

"Où peut-on être mieux qu'au sein de sa famille?"

That blessed harbour of refuge well within our reach,
and having really cut our wisdom teeth at last, and

learned the ropes, and left off hankering after the moon—
we can do with so little down here. . . .

> A little work, a little play
> To keep us going—and so, good-day!
>
> A little warmth, a little light
> Of love's bestowing—and so, good-night!
>
> A little fun, to match the sorrow
> Of each day's growing—and so, good-morrow!
>
> A little trust that when we die
> We reap our sowing! And so—good-bye!

A CATALOG OF SELECTED
DOVER BOOKS
IN ALL FIELDS OF INTEREST

A CATALOG OF SELECTED DOVER
BOOKS IN ALL FIELDS OF INTEREST

CONCERNING THE SPIRITUAL IN ART, Wassily Kandinsky. Pioneering work by father of abstract art. Thoughts on color theory, nature of art. Analysis of earlier masters. 12 illustrations. 80pp. of text. 5⅜ × 8½.   23411-8 Pa. $3.95

ANIMALS: 1,419 Copyright-Free Illustrations of Mammals, Birds, Fish, Insects, etc., Jim Harter (ed.). Clear wood engravings present, in extremely lifelike poses, over 1,000 species of animals. One of the most extensive pictorial sourcebooks of its kind. Captions. Index. 284pp. 9 × 12.   23766-4 Pa. $10.95

CELTIC ART: The Methods of Construction, George Bain. Simple geometric techniques for making Celtic interlacements, spirals, Kells-type initials, animals, humans, etc. Over 500 illustrations. 160pp. 9 × 12. (USO)   22923-8 Pa. $8.95

AN ATLAS OF ANATOMY FOR ARTISTS, Fritz Schider. Most thorough reference work on art anatomy in the world. Hundreds of illustrations, including selections from works by Vesalius, Leonardo, Goya, Ingres, Michelangelo, others. 593 illustrations. 192pp. 7⅛ × 10¼.   20241-0 Pa. $8.95

CELTIC HAND STROKE-BY-STROKE (Irish Half-Uncial from "The Book of Kells"): An Arthur Baker Calligraphy Manual, Arthur Baker. Complete guide to creating each letter of the alphabet in distinctive Celtic manner. Covers hand position, strokes, pens, inks, paper, more. Illustrated. 48pp. 8¼ × 11.

24336-2 Pa. $3.95

EASY ORIGAMI, John Montroll. Charming collection of 32 projects (hat, cup, pelican, piano, swan, many more) specially designed for the novice origami hobbyist. Clearly illustrated easy-to-follow instructions insure that even beginning papercrafters will achieve successful results. 48pp. 8¼ × 11.   27298-2 Pa. $2.95

THE COMPLETE BOOK OF BIRDHOUSE CONSTRUCTION FOR WOOD-WORKERS, Scott D. Campbell. Detailed instructions, illustrations, tables. Also data on bird habitat and instinct patterns. Bibliography. 3 tables. 63 illustrations in 15 figures. 48pp. 5¼ × 8½.   24407-5 Pa. $1.95

BLOOMINGDALE'S ILLUSTRATED 1886 CATALOG: Fashions, Dry Goods and Housewares, Bloomingdale Brothers. Famed merchants' extremely rare catalog depicting about 1,700 products: clothing, housewares, firearms, dry goods, jewelry, more. Invaluable for dating, identifying vintage items. Also, copyright-free graphics for artists, designers. Co-published with Henry Ford Museum & Greenfield Village. 160pp. 8¼ × 11.   25780-0 Pa. $8.95

HISTORIC COSTUME IN PICTURES, Braun & Schneider. Over 1,450 costumed figures in clearly detailed engravings—from dawn of civilization to end of 19th century. Captions. Many folk costumes. 256pp. 8⅜ × 11¾.   23150-X Pa. $10.95

FRANK LLOYD WRIGHT'S HOLLYHOCK HOUSE, Donald Hoffmann. Lavishly illustrated, carefully documented study of one of Wright's most controversial residential designs. Over 120 photographs, floor plans, elevations, etc. Detailed perceptive text by noted Wright scholar. Index. 128pp. 9¼ × 10¾.
27133-1 Pa. $10.95

THE MALE AND FEMALE FIGURE IN MOTION: 60 Classic Photographic Sequences, Eadweard Muybridge. 60 true-action photographs of men and women walking, running, climbing, bending, turning, etc., reproduced from rare 19th-century masterpiece. vi + 121pp. 9 × 12.
24745-7 Pa. $10.95

1001 QUESTIONS ANSWERED ABOUT THE SEASHORE, N. J. Berrill and Jacquelyn Berrill. Queries answered about dolphins, sea snails, sponges, starfish, fishes, shore birds, many others. Covers appearance, breeding, growth, feeding, much more. 305pp. 5¼ × 8¼.
23366-9 Pa. $7.95

GUIDE TO OWL WATCHING IN NORTH AMERICA, Donald S. Heintzelman. Superb guide offers complete data and descriptions of 19 species: barn owl, screech owl, snowy owl, many more. Expert coverage of owl-watching equipment, conservation, migrations and invasions, etc. Guide to observing sites. 84 illustrations. xiii + 193pp. 5⅜ × 8½.
27344-X Pa. $7.95

MEDICINAL AND OTHER USES OF NORTH AMERICAN PLANTS: A Historical Survey with Special Reference to the Eastern Indian Tribes, Charlotte Erichsen-Brown. Chronological historical citations document 500 years of usage of plants, trees, shrubs native to eastern Canada, northeastern U.S. Also complete identifying information. 343 illustrations. 544pp. 6½ × 9¼.
25951-X Pa. $12.95

STORYBOOK MAZES, Dave Phillips. 23 stories and mazes on two-page spreads: Wizard of Oz, Treasure Island, Robin Hood, etc. Solutions. 64pp. 8¼ × 11.
23628-5 Pa. $2.95

NEGRO FOLK MUSIC, U.S.A., Harold Courlander. Noted folklorist's scholarly yet readable analysis of rich and varied musical tradition. Includes authentic versions of over 40 folk songs. Valuable bibliography and discography. xi + 324pp. 5⅜ × 8½.
27350-4 Pa. $7.95

MOVIE-STAR PORTRAITS OF THE FORTIES, John Kobal (ed.). 163 glamor, studio photos of 106 stars of the 1940s: Rita Hayworth, Ava Gardner, Marlon Brando, Clark Gable, many more. 176pp. 8⅜ × 11¼.
23546-7 Pa. $10.95

BENCHLEY LOST AND FOUND, Robert Benchley. Finest humor from early 30s, about pet peeves, child psychologists, post office and others. Mostly unavailable elsewhere. 73 illustrations by Peter Arno and others. 183pp. 5⅜ × 8½.
22410-4 Pa. $4.95

YEKL and THE IMPORTED BRIDEGROOM AND OTHER STORIES OF YIDDISH NEW YORK, Abraham Cahan. Film Hester Street based on Yekl (1896). Novel, other stories among first about Jewish immigrants on N.Y.'s East Side. 240pp. 5⅜ × 8½.
22427-9 Pa. $5.95

SELECTED POEMS, Walt Whitman. Generous sampling from *Leaves of Grass*. Twenty-four poems include "I Hear America Singing," "Song of the Open Road," "I Sing the Body Electric," "When Lilacs Last in the Dooryard Bloom'd," "O Captain! My Captain!"—all reprinted from an authoritative edition. Lists of titles and first lines. 128pp. 5³⁄₁₆ × 8¼.
26878-0 Pa. $1.00

PIANO TUNING, J. Cree Fischer. Clearest, best book for beginner, amateur. Simple repairs, raising dropped notes, tuning by easy method of flattened fifths. No previous skills needed. 4 illustrations. 201pp. 5⅜ × 8½. 23267-0 Pa. $4.95

A SOURCE BOOK IN THEATRICAL HISTORY, A. M. Nagler. Contemporary observers on acting, directing, make-up, costuming, stage props, machinery, scene design, from Ancient Greece to Chekhov. 611pp. 5⅜ × 8½. 20515-0 Pa. $10.95

THE COMPLETE NONSENSE OF EDWARD LEAR, Edward Lear. All nonsense limericks, zany alphabets, Owl and Pussycat, songs, nonsense botany, etc., illustrated by Lear. Total of 320pp. 5⅜ × 8½. (USO) 20167-8 Pa. $5.95

VICTORIAN PARLOUR POETRY: An Annotated Anthology, Michael R. Turner. 117 gems by Longfellow, Tennyson, Browning, many lesser-known poets. "The Village Blacksmith," "Curfew Must Not Ring Tonight," "Only a Baby Small," dozens more, often difficult to find elsewhere. Index of poets, titles, first lines. xxiii + 325pp. 5⅜ × 8¼. 27044-0 Pa. $7.95

DUBLINERS, James Joyce. Fifteen stories offer vivid, tightly focused observations of the lives of Dublin's poorer classes. At least one, "The Dead," is considered a masterpiece. Reprinted complete and unabridged from standard edition. 160pp. 5³⁄₁₆ × 8¼. 26870-5 Pa. $1.00

THE HAUNTED MONASTERY and THE CHINESE MAZE MURDERS, Robert van Gulik. Two full novels by van Gulik, set in 7th-century China, continue adventures of Judge Dee and his companions. An evil Taoist monastery, seemingly supernatural events; overgrown topiary maze hides strange crimes. 27 illustrations. 328pp. 5⅜ × 8½. 23502-5 Pa. $7.95

THE BOOK OF THE SACRED MAGIC OF ABRAMELIN THE MAGE, translated by S. MacGregor Mathers. Medieval manuscript of ceremonial magic. Basic document in Aleister Crowley, Golden Dawn groups. 268pp. 5⅜ × 8½. 23211-5 Pa. $7.95

NEW RUSSIAN-ENGLISH AND ENGLISH-RUSSIAN DICTIONARY, M. A. O'Brien. This is a remarkably handy Russian dictionary, containing a surprising amount of information, including over 70,000 entries. 366pp. 4½ × 6⅜. 20208-9 Pa. $8.95

HISTORIC HOMES OF THE AMERICAN PRESIDENTS, Second, Revised Edition, Irvin Haas. A traveler's guide to American Presidential homes, most open to the public, depicting and describing homes occupied by every American President from George Washington to George Bush. With visiting hours, admission charges, travel routes. 175 photographs. Index. 160pp. 8¼ × 11. 26751-2 Pa. $10.95

NEW YORK IN THE FORTIES, Andreas Feininger. 162 brilliant photographs by the well-known photographer, formerly with *Life* magazine. Commuters, shoppers, Times Square at night, much else from city at its peak. Captions by John von Hartz. 181pp. 9¼ × 10¾. 23585-8 Pa. $12.95

INDIAN SIGN LANGUAGE, William Tomkins. Over 525 signs developed by Sioux and other tribes. Written instructions and diagrams. Also 290 pictographs. 111pp. 6⅛ × 9¼. 22029-X Pa. $3.50

THE INFLUENCE OF SEA POWER UPON HISTORY, 1660–1783, A. T. Mahan. Influential classic of naval history and tactics still used as text in war colleges. First paperback edition. 4 maps. 24 battle plans. 640pp. 5⅜ × 8½.
25509-3 Pa. $12.95

THE STORY OF THE TITANIC AS TOLD BY ITS SURVIVORS, Jack Winocour (ed.). What it was really like. Panic, despair, shocking inefficiency, and a little heroism. More thrilling than any fictional account. 26 illustrations. 320pp. 5⅜ × 8½.
20610-6 Pa. $7.95

FAIRY AND FOLK TALES OF THE IRISH PEASANTRY, William Butler Yeats (ed.). Treasury of 64 tales from the twilight world of Celtic myth and legend: "The Soul Cages," "The Kildare Pooka," "King O'Toole and his Goose," many more. Introduction and Notes by W. B. Yeats. 352pp. 5⅜ × 8½.
26941-8 Pa. $7.95

BUDDHIST MAHAYANA TEXTS, E. B. Cowell and Others (eds.). Superb, accurate translations of basic documents in Mahayana Buddhism, highly important in history of religions. The Buddha-karita of Asvaghosha, Larger Sukhavativyuha, more. 448pp. 5⅜ × 8½. ,
25552-2 Pa. $9.95

ONE TWO THREE . . . INFINITY: Facts and Speculations of Science, George Gamow. Great physicist's fascinating, readable overview of contemporary science: number theory, relativity, fourth dimension, entropy, genes, atomic structure, much more. 128 illustrations. Index. 352pp. 5⅜ × 8½.
25664-2 Pa. $7.95

ENGINEERING IN HISTORY, Richard Shelton Kirby, et al. Broad, nontechnical survey of history's major technological advances: birth of Greek science, industrial revolution, electricity and applied science, 20th-century automation, much more. 181 illustrations. ". . . excellent . . ."—Isis. Bibliography. vii + 530pp. 5⅜ × 8¼.
26412-2 Pa. $13.95